Machine Learning for Biometrics

Concepts, Algorithms, and Applications

Cognitive Data Science in Sustainable Computing

Machine Learning for Biometrics

Concepts, Algorithms, and Applications

Edited by

Partha Pratim Sarangi
Assistant Professor, Computer Science and Engineering, Seemanta Engineering College, Jharpokharia, Baripada, Odisha, India

Madhumita Panda
Assistant Professor, Master in Computer Applications, Seemanta Engineering College, Jharpokharia, Baripada, Odisha, India

Subhashree Mishra
Assistant Professor, School of Electronics Engineering, KIIT University, Bhubaneswar, Odisha, India

Bhabani Shankar Prasad Mishra
Associate Professor, School of Computer Engineering, KIIT University, Bhubaneswar, Odisha, India
Dean, School of Computer Engineering, KIIT University, Bhubaneswar, Odisha, India

Banshidhar Majhi
Director, IIITDM, Kancheepuram, Chennai, Tamil Nadu, India

Series Editor

Arun Kumar Sangaiah
School of Computing Science and Engineering, Vellore Institute of Technology (VIT), Vellore, India

ACADEMIC PRESS
An imprint of Elsevier

ELSEVIER

Academic Press is an imprint of Elsevier
125 London Wall, London EC2Y 5AS, United Kingdom
525 B Street, Suite 1650, San Diego, CA 92101, United States
50 Hampshire Street, 5th Floor, Cambridge, MA 02139, United States
The Boulevard, Langford Lane, Kidlington, Oxford OX5 1GB, United Kingdom

Library of Congress Cataloging-in-Publication Data
A catalog record for this book is available from the Library of Congress

British Library Cataloguing-in-Publication Data
A catalogue record for this book is available from the British Library

ISBN 978-0-323-85209-8

For information on all Academic Press publications
visit our website at https://www.elsevier.com/books-and-journals

Publisher: Mara Conner
Editorial Project Manager: Andrae Akeh
Production Project Manager: Swapna Srinivasan
Cover Designer: Christian J. Bilbow

Typeset by STRAIVE, India

Working together
to grow libraries in
developing countries
www.elsevier.com • www.bookaid.org

Contents

1. Machine learning approach for longitudinal face recognition of children

Vaishali H. Kamble and Manisha P. Dale

Contributors

Numbers in paraentheses indicate the pages on which the authors' contributions begin.

Sumitav Acharya (143), Department of Computer Science and Engineering, National Institute of Science and Technology, Berhampur, India

A. Anandh (105), Department of Computer Science and Engineering, Kamaraj College of Engineering and Technology, Madurai, India

Saurabh Bilgaiyan (155), School of Computer Engineering, KIIT Deemed to be University, Bhubaneswar, Odisha, India

P.V.S.S.R. Chandra Mouli (65), Department of Computer Science, Central University of Tamil Nadu, Thiruvarur, India

Manisha P. Dale (1), MES College of Engineering, Savitribai Phule Pune University, Pune, India

Rupam Das (155), School of Electronics Engineering, KIIT, Deemed to be University, Bhubaneswar, India

K. Devendran (87), Computer Science and Engineering, Kongu Engineering College, Erode, Tamil Nadu, India

Sachit Dhamija (155), School of Electronics Engineering, KIIT, Deemed to be University, Bhubaneswar, India

R. Jai Ganesh (129), K. Ramakrishnan College of Technology, Trichy, India

G.K. Kamalam (177), Department of Information Technology, Kongu Engineering College, Erode, Tamil Nadu, India

Vaishali H. Kamble (1), AISSMS IOIT, Savitribai Phule Pune University, Pune, India

M. Kavitha (129), K. Ramakrishnan College of Technology, Trichy, India

P. Keerthika (87,177), Department of Computer Science and Engineering, Kongu Engineering College, Erode, Tamil Nadu, India

Chirag Kyal (29), Department of Computer Science and Engineering, National Institute of Science and Technology, Berhampur, India

K. Logeswaran (177), Department of Information Technology, Kongu Engineering College, Erode, Tamil Nadu, India

V.M. Manikandan (201), Computer Science and Engineering, SRM University-AP, Amaravati, Andhra Pradesh, India

R. Manjula Devi (87,177), Department of Computer Science and Engineering, Kongu Engineering College, Erode, Tamil Nadu, India

Bhabani Shankar Prasad Mishra (47,155), School of Computer Engineering, KIIT Deemed to be University, Bhubaneswar, India

Subhashree Mishra (47), School of Computer Engineering, KIIT Deemed to be University, Bhubaneswar, Odisha, India

Samrat Mondal (217), Department of Computer Science and Engineering, Indian Institute of Technology Patna, Bihta, India

H. Muthukrishnan (177), Department of Information Technology, Kongu Engineering College, Erode, Tamil Nadu, India

K. Muthulakshmi (105), Department of Computer Science and Engineering, Kamaraj College of Engineering and Technology, Madurai, India

Madhumita Panda (47), Master of Computer Applications, Seemanta Engineering College, Jharpokharia, India

Suryakanta Panda (217), Department of Computer Science and Engineering, Indian Institute of Technology Patna, Bihta, India

Harsh Poddar (29), Department of Computer Science and Engineering, National Institute of Science and Technology, Berhampur, India

R. Ramya (105), Department of Computer Science and Engineering, Kamaraj College of Engineering and Technology, Madurai, India

Motahar Reza (29,143), Department of Mathematics, GITAM Deemed to be University, Hyderabad, India

C. Sagana (87), Computer Science and Engineering, Kongu Engineering College, Erode, Tamil Nadu, India

M. Sangeetha (87), Computer Science and Engineering, Kongu Engineering College, Erode, Tamil Nadu, India

Partha Pratim Sarangi (47,87), School of Computer Engineering, KIIT Deemed to be University, Bhubaneswar, India

Priyanshu Sarmah (155), School of Electronics Engineering, KIIT, Deemed to be University, Bhubaneswar, India

K. Sentamilselvan (177), Department of Information Technology, Kongu Engineering College, Erode, Tamil Nadu, India

P. Suresh (87,177), Department of Information Technology, Kongu Engineering College, Erode, Tamil Nadu, India

S. Venkatesh (105), Microland, Bengaluru, India

Dilip Kumar Yadav (65), Department of Computer Applications, National Institute of Technology, Jamshedpur, India

Gaurav Yadav (65), Department of Computer Applications, National Institute of Technology, Jamshedpur, India

Preface

The biometric systems automatically recognize the identity of a person by using his/her physiological and behavioral characteristics. The improvement in sensor technology attracts many researchers' attention to introduce a number of new biometric traits for providing privacy and security in various applications ranging from industrial to healthcare systems. In the last decades, with the aim of improving the recognition performance, a large number of machine learning algorithms have been presented in numerous biometric applications. The significance of machine learning algorithm is to determine the identity of individuals by associating biometric patterns with their respective enrolled users. However, in high-security applications, security and recognition accuracy are major concerns that can be addressed by designing multimodal biometric systems. As the name depicts, multimodal biometrics incorporates two or more different biometric characteristics (for example, fingerprint, iris, face, plamprint, etc.), which works in the similar way like unimodal biometrics except an extra module of information fusion. Due to the increasing number of biometric systems and their applications, a profound amount of research and developments are still required in this field of biometrics.

So far, a numerous biometric systems are exhibiting limited identification rate or accuracy in unconstrained scenarios due to the poor quality of image acquisition that includes poor contrast, varying illumination, and noncooperation by users. These challenges encourage many researchers to work in its diverse segments such as extracting discriminative features, employing efficient classifiers, and fusion of information at different stages of the multimodal biometric systems. Furthermore, another direction of research is to provide security to the biometric information system in case of online mode of identity recognition of individuals in many applications. This book covers the most recent research progresses in the field of biometrics to enhance recognition performance and security problems in several applications, such as online transaction, e-commence, access control, law enforcement, boarder security, healthcare, and so on.

In this book, we specifically address the current research progress in the field of biometrics and biometric-based applications with the objective of improving personal identity recognition performance. This book comprises 12 chapters, in which each chapter delivers the concepts and fundamentals of a recent topic on biometrics, presents reviews on up-to-date methodologies, reveals results, and compares with state-of-the-art, highlighting its effectiveness in the recognition and future directions. Furthermore, the contents of this book are organized according to the well-accepted biometric traits and a few novel ones along with biometric security and recent applications, so that each chapter can be read autonomously from the others. A concise and chapter-wise introduction of this book is described below.

Chapter "Machine Learning Approach for longitudinal face recognition of children" presents a novel application of identity recognition of children using the face biometric trait. Face recognition of children below 6 years of age helps to identify children for their healthcare services and investigation of missing children. In this chapter, the authors developed a new face database in which they collected face images of the individual over a period of time, especially at a gap of few months, and named it as longitudinal face database. Extensive experiments are performed using different machine learning classifiers such as support vector machine (SVM), K-nearest neighbor (KNN), logistic regression (LR), decision tree, Gaussian Naive Bayes, and convolutional neural networks (CNN). Comparison of experimental results demonstrates the effectiveness and superiority of the proposed method using CNN with improved accuracy. Finally, the authors suggest to increase the database size and improvement in the model as some possible research directions in future.

Chapter "TBFR: Thermal Biometric Face Recognition—A Noncontact Face Biometry" proposes a novel thermal face recognition method to diminish the effect of varying light intensity, poses, accessories, aging, etc. of the existing face biometric systems. In this chapter, the authors fused face geometry features with pretrained ResNet-50 features to improve recognition performance, and experimental results revealed the proposed method to be more robust in comparison with the existing methods.

Chapter "Multimodal Biometric Recognition using Human Ear and Profile Face: An Improved Approach" discusses an improved approach for ear biometrics based on fusion of ear and profile face-handcrafted features at the feature-level fusion and score-level fusion schemes. Recently, some convolutional neural network models have been proposed for ear biometrics, and their experiment results show competent performance compared to state-of-the-art methods. However, deep-learning-based biometrics applications need a large number of training images, huge memory for data processing, and enormous computational complexity at the cost of improving the identification rate. In this chapter, the authors focus on a multimodal approach based on ear and profile face, to enhance the recognition performance with less processing complexity. Several experiments with comparisons are performed to test the effectiveness and superiority of the proposed approach.

Chapter "Statistical Measures for Palmprint Image Enhancement" provides the overview of image enhancement methods and their quality measurements in palmprint images. In the palmprint image enhancement techniques, the most widely used databases are discussed with further details. However, the image enhancement plays an important role in the preprocessing step of biometric systems to provide a better recognition performance in terms of accuracy and identification rate.

In chapter "Retina Biometrics for Personal Authentication," an attempt is made to explore the retina biometrics using the ANFIS model. In this chapter, ANFIS-based Retina Biometric Authentication System (ARBAS) for person's authentication and its significance are discussed. Besides, this chapter provides readers with the required amount of knowledge to select suitable features' set and adequate techniques to develop robust research in this field.

Chapter "Gender Recognition from facial Images using Multi-Channel Deep Learning Framework" demonstrates Multi-Channel Deep Learning Framework based on an automated gender recognition approach. In this work, the authors try to extract discriminative features from raw facial images from GoogleNet. They fuse feature vectors obtained from two sources: first, feature vectors are obtained from featured images generated from LDP filters and second, feature vectors are directly obtained from raw facial images, and then both are separately applied as inputs to GoogleNet. Finally, the feature sets are combined together using CCA/DCA to provide input to SVM classifier for gender recognition of the given input image. A series of experiments are conducted, and a comprehensive explanation of experimental results is illustrated.

Chapter "Implementation of Cardiac Signal for Biometric Recognition from Facial Video" discusses the Heartbeat Signal from Facial Video (HSFV) as a biometric evidence for recognizing the identity of individuals. This chapter impacts researchers to get motivation and knowledge toward working in a novel direction in the field of biometrics.

Chapter "Real-Time Emotion Engagement Tracking of Students using Human Biometric Emotion Intensities" describes an automatic method to detect an absent-minded face present in a class using FAU (Facial Action Unit). Furthermore, this chapter covers multiple aspects of tracking, ranging from the student entering the classroom. Experimental results presented by the authors can achieve excellent results for emotion detection and recognition of students' face images.

Chapter "Facial Identification Expression Based Attendance Monitoring and Emotion Detection—A Deep CNN Approach" discusses the challenges of taking attendance and gauging emotions of the students in a new online classroom environment. In this chapter, with the help of advance machine learning approach, the authors introduce an automatic biometric-based attendance and facial expression recognition system.

Chapter "Contemporary Survey on Effectiveness of Machine and Deep Learning Techniques for Cyber Security" reviews the practicality of biometrics in cyber security based on efficient machine learning and deep learning techniques. The objective of this survey is to provide an impact on readers to acquire the fundamental concepts of biometric authentication and identification using different machine learning techniques for cyber security systems.

Chapter "A Secure Biometric Authentication System for Smart Environment using reversible Data Hiding through Encryption Scheme" introduces the notion of reversible data hiding (RDH) scheme to achieve a secure online biometric data communication. In a RDH-based encryption scheme, the biometric images are encrypted by hiding the important information in an image. In this chapter, the author presents a new model wherein the compressed fingerprint data is used as a secret message, and it will be embedded into the face image through a reversible data hiding-based encryption scheme. In order to maintain secure communication, encrypted image obtained after RDH scheme is transmitted to the cloud service provider in a secure manner.

Chapter "An Efficient and Untraceable Authentication Protocol for Cloud Based Healthcare System" provides Telecare Medical Information System (TMIS), which is very important in pandemic situations, for example, Covid-19. In this technique, the patient's mobile device has a major role for communicating with doctors. Furthermore, mutual authentication and key agreement scheme is required to protect vital information from any kind of mischief activities from adversaries in the insecure communication channel. In this chapter, the authors propose a biometric hashing technique to provide secure authentication and key agreement for communication between the patient and the doctor.

Finally, we hope that our readers including the graduate students, research scholars, young researchers, academicians, and industrial professionals find the contributed chapters in this book thought-provoking, and this piece of work will motivate future research breakthrough to progress further advances in the machine learning-based biometrics applications.

Partha Pratim Sarangi
Madhumita Panda
Subhashree Mishra
Bhabani Shankar Prasad Mishra
Banshidhar Majhi

Acknowledgments

The editors would like to gratefully acknowledge all of the contributors for continuous effort and timely submission of their chapters. This book would not have been feasible without the cooperation of the chapter authors. All the chapters have been reviewed for several rounds to facilitate the selection of final chapters in our book. Valuable suggestions and guidance from the reviewers helped the authors in refining individual chapters. Thanks also go to the reviewers in enhancing the quality of the chapters of this book.

The editors would like to extend gratitude to Sonnini Ruiz Yura from Elsevier for inspiration over the year. We would like to gratefully acknowledge Andrae Akeh and Judith Clarisse Punzalan (Elsevier) for their patience during the preparation of this book. In addition, we shall thank Swapna Srinivasan at Elsevier for her sincere help and patience during the final preparation of this book. Finally, we shall extend gratefulness to our family members and friends for all their support.

Chapter 1

Machine learning approach for longitudinal face recognition of children

Vaishali H. Kamble[a] and Manisha P. Dale[b]

[a]AISSMS IOIT, Savitribai Phule Pune University, Pune, India, [b]MES College of Engineering, Savitribai Phule Pune University, Pune, India

1 Introduction

Face of an individual is a popular and well-accepted biometric trait that can be used to perform identity recognition of adults as well as children. Children are the most valuable and jeopardy group in society; hence they should be under supervision continuously. Security and healthcare of children is an important aspect of all countries [1]. Automatic recognition of children using their face is a useful investigative tool to help identify missing children. Though the development of the face of a child starts in the mother's womb from 3 months, it is not proportional to the development of other parts of the body. Therefore, recognition of children below 6 years is still an open research problem. Children recognition using different modalities needs to be studied to solve the problems related to security and healthcare. As per the literature survey, still there is not even one commercial biometric system in use for recognition of toddlers. Various researchers have discussed about biometric recognition of adults; however, very few papers on toddlers are available. A meager amount of work has been traced in biometric identification of toddlers or children. It is most challenging to recognize a toddler from his own single photograph after a few months. But, in some instances, such as missing children, we have only the face image. So, the recognition of children from their face image is very important. Facial images can be acquired without users' active involvement using ordinary cameras from a distance. Also in survey, we noted that that most of the toddler's biometric recognition is in verification mode.

Sahar Siddique studied longitudinal face recognition using the Extended Newborn Database and Children Multimodal Biometric Database. Identification accuracy achieved using CNN is 62.7% and 85.1% on both the databases,

Machine Learning for Biometrics. https://doi.org/10.1016/B978-0-323-85209-8.00011-0

1

respectively [2]. Rowden et al. studied the longitudinal face recognition of children between 0 and 4 years of age. The same-session accuracy they achieved is 93% and cross-session accuracy 43% after 6 months [3]. Local Binary Pattern (LBP) is widely used texture-based method for recognition of face biometrics [4]. This method is also used for children face recognition [5,6].

This chapter is presenting a machine learning and deep learning approach for face recognition of children. As per the literature review, the study of children recognition with the help of their face modality started in 2010 in India [5,6]. Most of the papers studied same-session face recognition. The meager amount of work is carried out longitudinally, that is, images of the same subject taken over a period of time. There are very few readily available databases for newborns like FG-NET [7]. There are very few images of children below 5 years in these datasets. CMBD database of IIIT Delhi (India) [8] is one of the children longitudinal face recognition databases, but due to security reasons the face database is not publicly available [9]. Therefore, database collection is the major task in infants and toddler's recognition. For this study, the database of 81 subjects for the same session and 48 subjects for the cross session is collected. The span between the data acquisition sessions is 3–6 months. The major stages of the proposed work are preprocessing of face images, which include manually cropping of face images of size 120×120 and converting it into gray scale. Feature extraction is based on principal component analysis and linear discriminant analysis, and CNN is proposed. The classification of subjects is done using machine learning classifiers on the children database of the same session and cross session. Further, the work is extended using convolutional neural network (CNN) in which we have proposed our own optimized model with data augmentation used to compare the machine learning and deep learning classifiers on our database.

The major contributions of the proposed work are as follows.

1. Due to the nonavailability of reference databases for children below 6 years, the collection of longitudinal databases of children faces itself is a great challenge. In the proposed work, we have captured the face images of toddlers with the mobile camera of resolution 20 MP, with consent from their parents in two sessions. Time period between two sessions is 2 months to 1 year. In the same session, 730 images of 81 toddlers are taken. In the second session, 485 images of 48 toddlers are captured.

2. In this chapter, we are proposing feature extraction using PCA, LDA, and CNN approaches on the facial images and their comparative study. In PCA and LDA approaches, we have applied different machine learning techniques for classification of subjects, such as Support Vector Machine (SVM), Logistic Regression (LR), Gaussian Naive Bayes, K-Nearest Neighbors (KNN), Decision Tree, and Random Forest. In CNN, feature extraction is done by convolution layers and classification is done by dense layers.

3. In this work, we implemented CNN from basic level to optimized level. First, CNN is of three convolution layers for the same session and cross session. Further, the CNN is modified in terms of data augmentation, and six-layer convolution model is used with L2 kernel regularization and batch normalization for enhancing the accuracy.

4. We compare the effectiveness of different feature extraction and classification techniques in identification mode. Further, we optimize the CNN for our children database to increase the accuracy. We compare the recognition performance of the proposed CNN with the conventional PCA- and LDA-based method using classification technique.

2 Face modality for children face recognition

Human beings can be recognized using its inherent biological feature's analysis and measurement. Science of recognizing human beings with the help of its biological features is called biometrics.

Biometric recognition is based on two prominent characteristics of human beings:

(1) Physiological characteristics: face, fingerprint, iris, palmprint, footprint, palm vein, ear, DNA, etc.
(2) Behavioral characteristics: voice, gait, signature, etc.

Indian biometrics market survey graph about the usage of different biometric modalities for the year 2019 is shown in Fig. 1.

As per biometric market fingerprint is widely used for recognition of human beings. Children's fingerprints are tiny, and are not easy to capture. The second-largest used biometric modality is face. Face images are easy to capture and

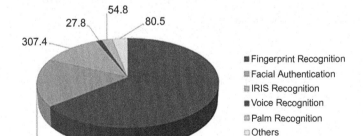

Indian Biometrics Market In US $ Million, 2019

- ■ Fingerprint Recognition
- ▦ Facial Authentication
- ▩ IRIS Recognition
- ■ Voice Recognition
- ▨ Palm Recognition
- ▢ Others

FIG. 1 Indian biometric market share in US million [10].

useful in the case of missing children. Therefore, we are using face biometrics for recognition of children. An example of different biometrics of children from our database is shown in Fig. 2.

Human face is a 3D model, we can recognize it by its features such as eyes, shape of face, and color. Automatic face recognition is based on 2D photographs of a person. In 1964 and 1965, Woody Bledsoe, along with Helen Chan and Charles Bisson, recognized human faces using computers for the first time. Nowadays adult face recognition achieves very high accuracy in the range of 99.63% [11]. Face recognition of children is still an open challenge. All face recognition algorithms evaluate on false negative identification rate (FNIR) which is dependent on age. The FNIR of children is higher as compared to adults or seniors. The comparison of FNIR and false positive identification rate (FPIR) is given in Table 1 for various stages of child age.

Child face development: Studies from the paper by Farkas discuss that in the first 2 years of a child face development, mouth width of child increases whereas mouth height decreases. Mouth shape alters from "rosebud-like" to a more adult type. Growth of facial features is very fast in the first year, less rapid in the second year. Subsequent changes were slow and irregular from the age of 3 to 9 years [12].

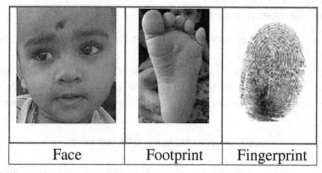

| Face | Footprint | Fingerprint |

FIG. 2 Different biometrics for recognition of children.

TABLE 1 Comparison of FNIR and FPIR of children for different age.

Subjects	FNIR	FPIR
Babies	0.7	0.2
Kids	0.4	In between 0.2 and 0.05
Pre-teen	0.29	0.05

There are other difficulties as well in recognition of children, such as they are generally in a playful mood, it leads to expression and pose variations. Though adult supervision and motivation helps in improved quality data capture, the attention span of young children is very limited. Only expression variation is allowed during the frontal face acquisition. If any other variations such as pose, illumination, or blurriness are observed by visual inspection of captured images, the image needs to be reacquired [5].

Therefore, calmness during data collection is highly recommendable. Time required for data collection is also more compared to adult data collection. Due to these hurdles publicly available databases of children are lean.

3 Children face databases

In this section, various databases for children of various modalities are discussed here. Mostly, all of the databases are of two or more sessions. But most of them are not available for study purposes due to security reasons.

3.1 Newborn face database

Newborn face database is the first longitudinal database collected by Bharadwaj et al. for newborn face identification [5,6]. It consists of 34 newborns with the age ranges from 0 to few weeks. Total images of newborns are 347. Now, this database is extended up to 450 newborns with total images of 1200. Each baby's 1–10 images are captured in it. It is IIIT Delhi's database. This database will be made available publicly soon.

3.2 Newborn, infants, and toddler's longitudinal face database (NITL)

Database collected by Best-Rowden et al. is of Indian children [3]. It is collected in four sessions. Time span between consecutive sessions is of 2–6 months. It consists of 314 subjects in the age range of 0–4 years. Altogether, 3144 images of children are in the database. This database is not publicly available.

3.3 Children multimodal biometric database (CMBD)

The database is of IIIT Delhi, collected by Basak et al. [8]. It comprises two-session databases. In the first session, they collected 2590 images of 141 subjects and in the second session 1410 images of 118 subjects. The age span of face image captured is 18 months to 4 years. As it is multimodal, it consists of face, fingerprint and iris images of children. Iris and fingerprint databases are publicly available. Face database is not publicly available due to security reasons.

3.4 Extended newborn face database

Siddiqui et al. collected this database from India [2]. It is a private database of 204 children. The age range of children is in between 0 and preschool. Total images taken are 1185. This database is an extension of Newborn Face Database.

Other databases such as CFA, CLF, UTKFace, and VADANA are private. Most of these are not focused on children face recognition study. CFA has an age range of 2 years to 20 years. CLF has an age range of 2–20 years, and VADANA has an age range of 0–18 years. UTKface has an age range of 0–32 years. Publicly available databases of face are ITWCC, ITWCC-D1, Adience, and FG-NET.

In publicly available databases, FG-NET has 82 subjects. Total face images are 1002 of age range 0–69 years. It consists of children's face images, but it has only one image of one particular age. We need multiple images of one particular age to train our model. Some of the images of the FG-NET database are shown in Fig. 3. This database has images collected from photographs of individual subjects.

Main hurdle of study of face recognition of children is unavailability of a public database. We collected our own database. We have collected most of the face images of children from preprimary schools and some from neighborhood. We have taken permission from preprimary schools for collection of images. Consent from parents was also obtained regarding use of biometric details of their children for research purposes. Children's images were captured with the help of mobile cameras of resolution greater than 20 Megapixels. Database is taken in two sessions. All images that are captured first time are called same-session database. All images that are captured second time are called cross-session database. Span of capturing images of the same person is from 2 to 8 months. The age range of children in the database is 2 months to 5 years. In each session, approximately six images are captured for each subject.

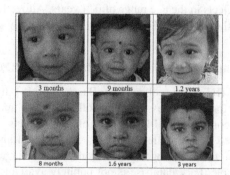

FIG. 3 Sample images of two children row wise after time span from FG-NET database.

To make the images of the same size, we have used 224 × 224 image size. Sample images of our database are shown in Fig. 4.

Face the same session 81 subject database is collected, age group 0–5 years.

\Face\same-session: Has 510 faces in .jpg format against 81 subjects (81 subjects * 6 (avg) face * 6, Total ≈ 486)

Face cross session 48 subject is collected, age group 0–5 years.

\Face\cross-session: Has 485 faces in. jpg format against 48 subjects (48 subjects * 10(avg) face * 10, Total ≈485)

Here, Fig. 5 shows the distribution of images of each subject for same session.

Here, Fig. 6 shows the distribution of images of each subject for cross session.

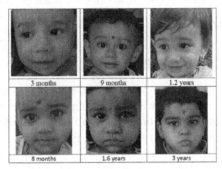

FIG. 4 Sample images of two children row wise after time span from own database.

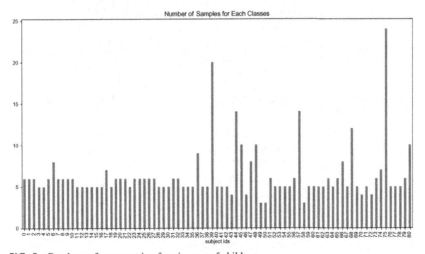

FIG. 5 Database of same-session face images of children.

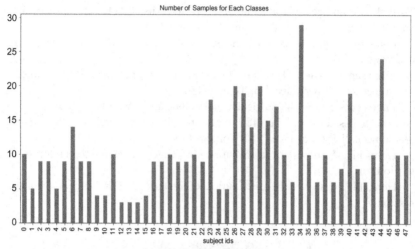

FIG. 6 Database of cross-session face images of children.

4 Face recognition of children

General face recognition system consists of face images as input. Further stages are preprocessing to make the face images suitable for different machine learning algorithms. Feature extraction is the significant step before classification. General face recognition system is shown in Fig. 7.

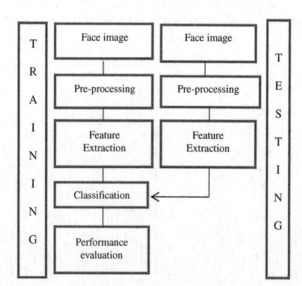

FIG. 7 Block diagram of face recognition of children.

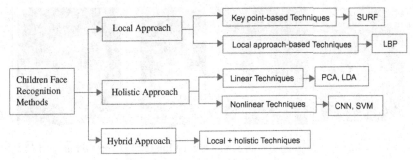

FIG. 8 Longitudinal face recognition methods' study.

In this study, we have compared face recognition accuracy of same-session and cross-session data collected. Two techniques of feature extraction PCA and LDA are studied in detail. For robustness of recognition algorithm, fivefold cross validation and leave-one-out validation are also used. Classification is done by different machine learning classifiers such as Support Vector Machine, Linear Discriminant Analysis, Gaussian Naive Bayes, K-Nearest Neighbors, Decision Tree, Logistic Regression, and Random Forest.

Various approaches used for children face recognition in this chapter are shown in Fig. 8.

4.1 Database preprocessing

As per the literature study of face recognition of children, preprocessing is done manually [2]. Siddique [13] detected faces from images using the Viola-Jones face detector and aligned using affine transformation with the intereye distance set as 100 pixels. Further, histogram normalization and 2D order-statistic filtering are also done for preprocessing.

Preprocessing steps normalize faces, make images of the same size, line up with respect to eyes, and normalize intensities. According to the need of feature extraction algorithm, face images are manually cropped to different sizes. Fig. 9 shows the sample of manually cropped images. In this study, gray scale conversion is done for PCA and LDA algorithms and RGB images are used for CNNs. Each subject's cropped images (5–10) are kept in a separate folder. Finally, all folders of subjects are kept in one database folder.

According to the study, it is observed that manually cropped images are giving good results. Therefore, we have cropped all images manually, making them of the same size. Conversion of RGB to gray color is done in PCA and LDA feature extraction algorithms. RGB images are used for CNN.

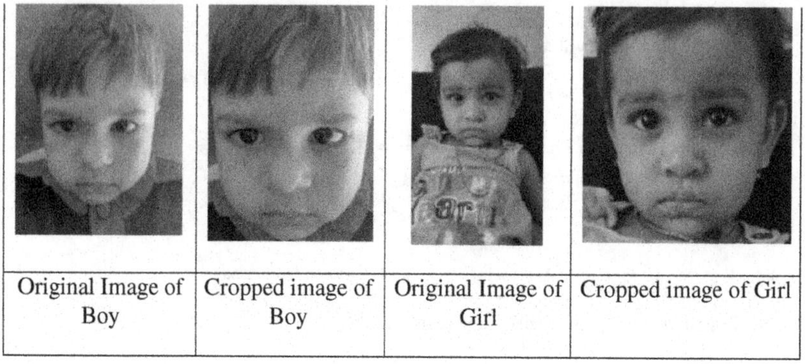

Original Image of Boy	Cropped image of Boy	Original Image of Girl	Cropped image of Girl

FIG. 9 Preprocessed images.

4.2 COTS—Commercial off-the-shelf face matchers

It is a complete solution inclusive of feature extraction. Most of the children's face recognition study is done using COTS matchers [3, 14–16]. These matchers are available in the market. They provide performance parameters such as receiver operating characteristic curve. But they meant for only adult face matching. To achieve good performance of such a system for children's faces, we need to upsample the children's face images.

5 Feature extraction techniques

Feature extraction is the process, in which the main goal is to reduce the number of features from the images of the database. From these features only, the system is able to recognize the face images of different persons. Features can be a line, distance between two eyes, a dot, and distance between lips and eyes. Also, it creates new features from the existing features. The new created features are less in number, which help in reducing the computational complexity. The feature extraction technique performance is depending upon how it is useful for recognizing the original image with the help of these reduced features. Here, we have summarized machine learning feature extraction algorithms used for children face recognition. The performance of these algorithms is totally relied on feature extraction.

5.1 PCA—Principal component analysis

PCA is the simple and extensively used appearance-based algorithm. It is an unsupervised learning algorithm that means PCA does not use class labels in its algorithm. In the preliminary study of face recognition of newborns, Bharadwaj et al. state that performance of PCA increases by decreasing the resolution of image [5,6]. PCA works well in well disseminative classes with small databases [17,18].

In PCA for face recognition, the face image database is prepared by preprocessing the images.

$$S = \{\Gamma_1, \Gamma_2, \Gamma_3, \dots \Gamma_M\} \tag{1}$$

Let each image be of size 224×224 pixels. Convert it in a vector of dimension $M \times N$. Now, the image vector is of size 50,176. Calculate the average face. The average face vector (Ψ) has to be calculated by using Eq. (2).

$$\Psi = \frac{1}{M} \sum_{n=1}^{M} \Gamma n \tag{2}$$

The average face image of the child is shown in Fig. 10.

The average face vector is subtracted from the original faces, and the result is stored in the variable,

$$\varphi_i = \Gamma_i - \Psi \tag{3}$$

Then, the covariance matrix C is obtained in the following manner,

$$C = \frac{1}{M} \sum_{n=1}^{M} \varphi_n \varphi_n^T \tag{4}$$

$$C = AA^T \quad N^2 \times N^2 \text{ matrix,}$$

Average Face

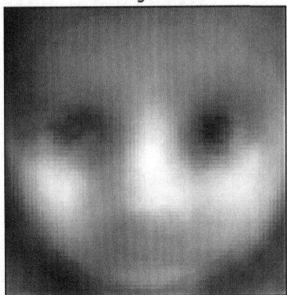

FIG. 10 Average face image of the child.

where $A = [\varphi_1,\ \varphi_2,\ \varphi_3,\ \varphi_4,\ \dots\ \varphi_M]$ $N^2 \times M$ matrix.

Further, the eigenvectors and eigenvalues of the covariance matrix are calculated. The covariance matrix C in Eq. (4) has a high dimensionality. For a 224×224, one must compute a $50{,}176 \times 50$, 176 matrix and calculate $50{,}176$ eigenfaces. Computationally, this is not very efficient as most of those eigenfaces are not useful for our task.

Therefore, we consider the matrix ($M \times M$ matrix).

$$\text{Now compute eigenvectors } v_i \text{ of } L = AA^T, \tag{5}$$

The M eigenvectors of L are used to find the M eigenvectors of C that form eigenface basis and 90 eigen faces of a child are shown in Fig. 11.

$$u_i = \sum\nolimits_{i=1}^{M} v_i\, \varphi_i \tag{6}$$

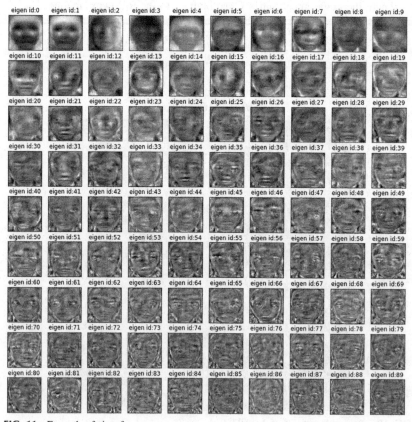

FIG. 11 Example of eigenfaces.

Keep only K eigenvectors (corresponding to the K largest eigenvalues), and other eigenfaces with low eigenvalues can be omitted, as they explain only a small part of characteristic features of the faces. Fig. 12 shows the PCA projection of the children faces.

Then, we plot the eigenvalue spectrum graph (Fig. 13) to decide the number of principal components. After analyzing the graph, we understand that after 90 components the variance is almost constant. Therefore, we used the first 90 principal components for our study.

PCA reduces the dimension of the data and gives better results for small databases. Since no class membership information (unsupervised learning) is used, examples of the same class and of different classes are treated the same way.

Confusion matrix can be used as a performance parameter. It shows the predicted accuracy versus actual accuracy. Same class PCA feature extraction and SVM classification give 76% of accuracy. Its confusion matrix is shown below in Fig. 14.

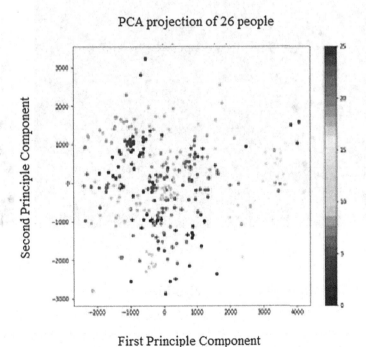

FIG. 12   PCA projection of the children.

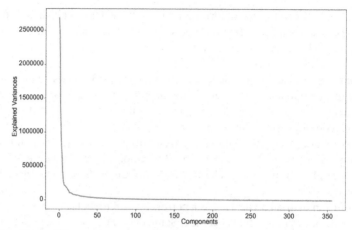

FIG. 13 Graph of eigenvalues versus principal components.

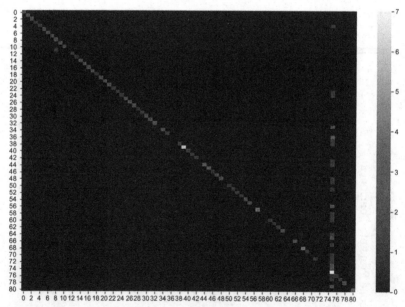

FIG. 14 Confusion matrix of same-session database.

5.2 LDA—Linear discriminant algorithm

LDA is a supervised learning algorithm that means it uses class labels. LDA is an enhancement to the PCA method. It is best suited for class separation. It uses within-class and between-class scatter matrices. Tiwari et al. used FLDA for face recognition of infants and achieved good accuracy for 10 classes with

l^2 – norm [17,18]. Also, Bharadwaj et al. proposed one shot similarities with LDA have given remarkable outputs for identification as well as verification of newborn faces.

Suppose we have C classes, μ_i be the mean vector of class i, $i = 1,2,3, ...,$ C. M_i be the number of samples within class i, $i = 1,2,3, ..., C$.

Let $M = \sum_{i=0}^{C} M_i$ be the total number of samples.

Now, scatter matrix is calculated as within-class matrix by between-class matrix.

$$S_w = \sum_{i=1}^{C} \sum_{j=1}^{M} (Xj - \mu_i)(Xj - \mu_i)^T \qquad (7)$$

$$S_b = \sum_{i=1}^{C} (\mu_i - \mu)(\mu_i - \mu)^T \qquad (8)$$

where $\mu = \frac{1}{C}\sum_{i=1}^{C} \mu_i$ mean of entire dataset.

Projection of the data is given in Eq. (9),

$$y = U^T x \qquad (9)$$

where U^T is projection matrix.

LDA computes the transformation that maximizes the between-class scatter and minimizes the within-class scatter

$$\max \frac{|U^T S_b U|}{|U^T S_w U|} = \max \frac{|\tilde{S}_b|}{|\tilde{S}_w|} \qquad \text{Products of eigenvalues} \qquad (10)$$

$\tilde{S}_b$, $\tilde{S}_w$: scatter matrices of projected data y.

LDA gives best results for larger databases. As it uses labels, it gives well between-class classifications. The results of LDA are not optimal for smaller databases.

LDA feature extraction and linear regression classifier are giving 84% of accuracy for the cross-session database. Confusion matrix of the same is given below in Fig. 15.

6 Machine learning classification methods

Machine learning classification refers to automatic classification or categorization of data. In this study, we are performing identification of children of multiple classes. Therefore, multiclass classification techniques are given in detail. Different classification techniques are given in Fig. 16.

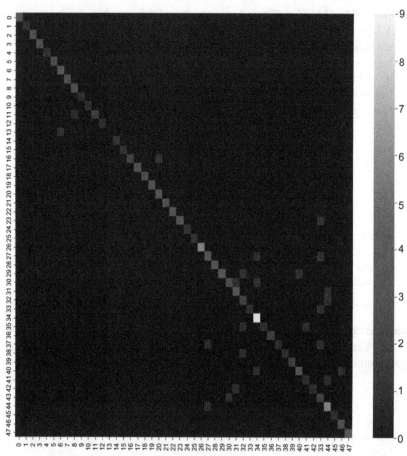

FIG. 15 Confusion matrix of cross-session database.

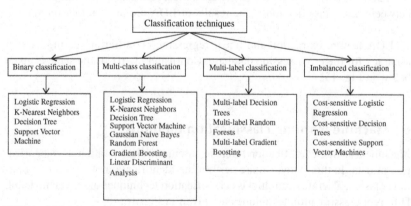

FIG. 16 Different classification techniques.

6.1 Logistic regression

Logistic regression is a statistical method mostly used for binary classification. It is derived from linear regression by using sigmoid function.

Linear regression equation.

$$y = \beta 0 + \beta 1 X1 + \beta 2 X2 + \dots + \beta n Xn \tag{11}$$

where y is dependent variable and $X1, X2, \dots Xn$ are independent variable.

Sigmoid function:

$$S(x) = \frac{1}{1 + e^{-x}} \tag{12}$$

We will get logistic regression equation by applying sigmoid function on linear regression.

$$S(x) = {}^{1}/_{1 + e^{-\beta 0 + \beta 1 X1 + \beta 2 X2 + \dots + \beta n Xn}} \tag{13}$$

The equation always gives us output between 0 and 1. Multinomial logistic regression can be used to classify multiple classes. It uses a softmax function to classify multiple classes.

$$\hat{y} = softmax\,(xW + b) \tag{14}$$

6.2 K-Nearest Neighbors

It is a supervised learning algorithm, which does not use probability for classification. Instead, it uses distance metrics for classification. KNN algorithm works on search for feature similarity. It believes similar features are always near each other. In KNN algorithm, K is the number of nearest neighbors. Selection of K is user dependent; it is an odd number. Mostly, the value of K is square root of n. Distance metrics used in KNN are Minkowski, Manhattan, and Euclidean distances.

Minkowski distance equation is generalized, and we can derive Manhattan and Euclidean distances from it.

$$d(x, y) = \left(\sum_{i=1}^{n} |x_i - y_i|^p \right)^{1/p} \tag{15}$$

$p = 1$, Manhattan Distance
$p = 2$, Euclidean Distance
$p = \infty$, Chebyshev Distance

6.3 Decision Tree

It is a supervised learning algorithm. In this algorithm, data are continuously split into smaller parts until it reaches its class. It uses the terminologies like nodes, edges, and leaf nodes. In the Decision Tree classifier, first we compute the entropy of our database. It tells us the amount of uncertainty of our database. The smaller the uncertainty value, the better is the classification results. Each feature's information gain is calculated. This then tells us how much uncertainty reduces after spitting the database. Finally, all the information gain is calculated for all features, and now, we split the database which has high information gain. The process repeats until all nodes are cleared. The basic diagram of Decision Tree classifier and its implementation is shown in Fig. 17.

6.4 Support Vector Machine

It is a supervised learning algorithm. We are using it for image classification. The aim of SVM is to find the correct hyperplane for the features of the database. Correct hyperplane is that which maximizes the margin between two and more data points. With the help of these hyperplanes, we will be able to classify between different data points. In Fig. 18, three hyperplanes A, B, and C are given which separates the data points. Hyperplane B has a maximum margin from both the data points. Therefore, B is the correct hyperplane for classifying these two classes. To classify more than two classes, multiclass SVM is used [19].

6.5 Gaussian Naive Bayes

Naive Bayes classifier is based on Bayes theorem. It provides strong independence between the features of images. They are from the background of probabilistic classifiers. These classifiers are simple to implement, and therefore,

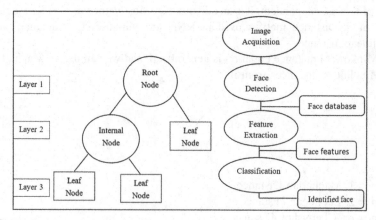

FIG. 17 Basic structure of Decision Tree and implementation.

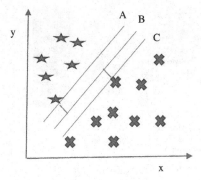

FIG. 18 Support Vector Machine classifier.

they are widely used in machine learning classification. The Bayes theorem is given in Eq. (16).

$$P(A|B) = \frac{P(B|A)(P(A)}{P(B)} \tag{16}$$

Gaussian Naive Bayes is one of the classification models of Naive Bayes. Continuous data have normal (Gaussian) distribution. Therefore, we use the Gaussian Naive Bayes to classify continuous data. It is easier to calculate mean and standard deviation from the training database with Gaussian mode.

7 Deep learning approach

Deep learning is the arm of machine learning which combines feature extraction and classification processes. It performs better than machine learning algorithms with big dataset. For face recognition of children, we are using the CNN. In the first layer of CNNs, it learns low-level features of face images like lines and edges. As layers of CNN go on increasing, it learns high-level features. Therefore, deep learning approach is a master in high-level features.

In this study, we implemented CNN from basic level to optimized level. First, CNN is of 3 convolution layers, and then, layers incremented to six for same-session and cross-session databases. Activation function used is Relu and at the dense layer softmax. Loss is sparse categorical cross entropy loss. Training is 70%, and test data is 30%. The CNN architecture is shown in Fig. 19.

8 Results

In Table 2, different machine learning classification techniques are tested for PCA and LDA features of face images of children. Here, the database is divided into 70% and 30%. That is, 70% of face images are used for training and 30% is used for testing. In same session, 357 images are for training and 153 images are

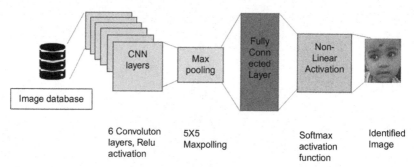

FIG. 19 Architecture of CNN optimized model.

TABLE 2 PCA and LDA feature extraction with machine learning classification techniques for same session.

Classifier	Same-session accuracy	
	PCA feature extraction	*LDA feature extraction*
Support Vector Machine	0.76	0.71
Linear Discriminant Analysis	0.43	0.77
Logistic Regression	0.92	0.83
Gaussian Naive Bayes	0.59	0.67
K-Nearest Neighbors	0.61	0.56
Decision Tree	0.54	0.42
Random Forest	0.90	0.77

for testing, and the total images are 510. In cross session, 339 images are for training and 146 images are for testing, and the total images are 485. Cross-session accuracy is shown in Table 3.

8.1 K-fold cross validation

K-fold cross validation is one of the validation methods for multiclass classification. We can validate our results by distributing our dataset randomly in different groups. In this, one set is used for validation and other K-1 set is used for training.

Now, we will validate our result with fivefold cross validation. Shuffle the dataset, divide it into five sets, and one set is taken for validation and other four for training. Repeat the process for all five sets. The results of the K-fold cross validation are given in Tables 4 and 5 for same session and cross session, respectively.

TABLE 3 PCA and LDA feature extraction with machine learning classification techniques for cross session.

Classifier	Cross-session accuracy	
	PCA feature extraction	LDA feature extraction
Support Vector Machine	0.81	0.41
Linear Discriminant Analysis	0.84	0.46
Logistic Regression	0.85	0.84
Gaussian Naive Bayes	0.67	0.16
K-Nearest Neighbors	0.85	0.46
Decision Tree	0.48	0.16
Random Forest	0.79	0.84

TABLE 4 Fivefold cross validation accuracy for same session.

Classifier	Same-session accuracy with fivefold cross validation	
	PCA feature extraction	LDA feature extraction
Support Vector Machine	0.51	0.64
Linear Discriminant Analysis	0.86	0.97
Logistic Regression	0.79	0.98
Gaussian Naive Bayes	0.27	0.55
K-Nearest Neighbors	0.47	0.76
Decision Tree	0.38	0.45
Random Forest	0.69	0.92

8.2   Leave-one-out cross validation

In this validation process, only one of the samples of a class is used for testing. Others are used for training. This procedure is repeated until each sample is used for testing. Recognition accuracy of this approach is shown in Tables 6 and 7 for same session and cross session.

The results of deep learning feature extraction and classification using basic three-layer CNN are given below. Here, 70% of data is used for training and 30% of data is used for testing. Model accuracy and loss for basic CNN for same

TABLE 5 Fivefold cross validation accuracy for cross session.

Classifier	Cross-session accuracy with fivefold cross validation	
	PCA feature extraction	LDA feature extraction
Support Vector Machine	0.59	0.93
Linear Discriminant Analysis	0.77	0.94
Logistic Regression	0.75	0.95
Gaussian Naive Bayes	0.59	0.66
K-Nearest Neighbors	0.43	0.91
Decision Tree	0.42	0.57
Random Forest	0.68	0.91

TABLE 6 Leave-one-out cross validation accuracy for same session.

Classifier	Same session with leave one out	
	PCA feature extraction	LDA feature extraction
Logistic Regression	0.84	0.84
Linear Discriminant Analysis	89	0.97

TABLE 7 Leave-one-out cross validation accuracy for cross session.

Classifier	Cross session with leave one out	
	PCA Feature extraction	LDA Feature extraction
Logistic Regression	0.74	0.96
Linear Discriminant Analysis	0.83	0.94

TABLE 8 Basic CNN accuracy for same session.

Feature extraction	Classifier	Validation accuracy
Three convolution layers, max pooling, and softmax activation function	Fully connected layer	0.81

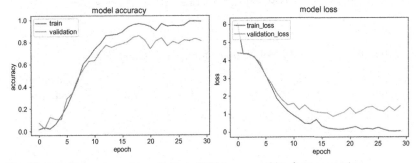

FIG. 20   Model accuracy and loss for basic CNN face recognition for same session.

TABLE 9 Basic CNN accuracy for cross session.

Feature extraction	Classifier	Validation accuracy
Three convolution layers, after that max pooling, and softmax activation function	Fully connected layer	0.76

session are shown in Table 8 and Fig. 20 and for cross session are shown in Table 9 and Fig. 21.

Further for enhancing the results, data augmentation is used. Data augmentation is the technique used to increase the diversity in the database without collecting new data. Cropping, padding, and flipping are the techniques used in data augmentation. More the number of training images, more will be the model accuracy. Six-layer convolution model is used with L2 kernel regularization and batch normalization. Validation accuracy of customized CNN for same session is given in Table 10 and shown in Fig. 22 and for cross session is given in Table 11 and Fig. 23, respectively.

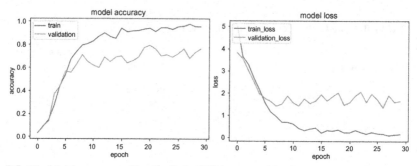

FIG. 21 Model accuracy and loss for basic CNN face recognition for cross session.

TABLE 10 Customized CNN accuracy for same session.

Feature extraction	Classifier	Validation accuracy
Six convolution layers, max pooling, and then softmax activation function	Fully connected layer	0.86

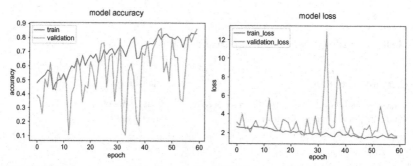

FIG. 22 Model accuracy and loss for customized CNN face recognition for same session.

TABLE 11 Customized CNN accuracy for cross session.

Feature extraction	Classifier	Validation accuracy
Six Convolution layers, max pooling, and then softmax activation function	Fully connected layer	0.94

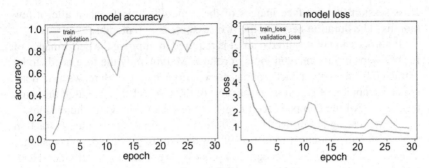

FIG. 23 Model accuracy and loss for customized CNN face recognition for cross session.

The advantages of the proposed approach are illustrated as follows:

1. Longitudinal database collected for around 81 subjects of same session and 48 subjects of cross session which is not readily available. Most of the databases are of the same session.
2. The algorithm is used in identification mode while most of the work in literature uses verification mode.
3. The maximum cross-session identification accuracy achieved in this work is 95% which is comparable with the literature.

9 Discussion and conclusion

Children's health and security is an important aspect for any country. Robust face recognition system for children is the need of an hour. Biometric recognition of children using face recognition can help in taking a child's health as well as investigation of missing children. Face recognition systems should be able to handle different variations that occur due to children's natural movement. Moreover, the algorithm should be strong enough to track the longitudinal changes in a child's face. In this chapter, we have presented a machine learning and deep learning approach for the face recognition of children.

Major hurdle in building the face recognition system is the database collection. As discussed in the chapter, many face image databases are available online but most of them have adult face images and few children face images. Also, the children's images are taken only a few and mostly in a single session. To have real time study of children's faces, we need a longitudinal dataset of children. It suggests that the dataset to be collected over a period (with a gap of a few months) to record the changes in the faces and tune the recognition system accordingly. Hence, we have collected our own longitudinal dataset. The dataset consists of 81 subjects from the same session and 48 subjects of cross session that are face images of the same 48 subjects taken after a few months. The duration between the two sessions is 3–6 months.

Preprocessing of acquired dataset is required to improve the performance of further steps in face recognition algorithms. Mainly, only the face needs to be extracted from all other backgrounds present in each image. Here, we have done manual cropping of face images, as most of the researchers have used the same technique. All the cropped face images are resized to the same dimensions.

Preprocessing is followed by the feature extraction step. Feature extraction deals with dimensionality reduction of raw data in such a way that it is manageable as well as makes the recognition process computationally efficient. Here, mainly we have used PCA- and LDA-based methods for feature extraction which are more commonly used for adult face recognition. After extracting the features, we have used multiclass classification techniques based on machine learning. Comparative study and evaluation of Support Vector Machine (SVM), K-Nearest Neighbors (KNN), Logistic Regression (LR), Decision Tree, and Gaussian Naive Bay are done in this study. Results obtained with LDA features and Logistic Regression are more promising. It is well known that LDA is an enhancement of PCA and best suited for class separation. Logistic Regression is a statistical method used for multiclass classification with the help of softmax function. At the machine learning-based classifier level, many algorithms are available to compare but for our database of children faces, LDA and LR are promising.

To improve the performance particularly for cross-session face image recognition, we implemented a deep learning approach. Deep learning is part of machine learning using the artificial neural network. CNN is one of the methods of deep learning. CNN is mainly used for image recognition and classification. CNN does not require complex preprocessing algorithms and detects distinctive features on its own. We first implemented the basic CNN and then optimized it so that it is suitable for children's face database. In an optimized CNN with a number of layers 6 and activation function Relu, the cross-session accuracy is improved from 86% to 94%.

Here, we have shown that machine learning and deep learning can be used to track the facial changes in childhood and they can give good recognition accuracy. The major highlights of the work presented here are cross-session facial images (database) collected, identification mode is used while most of the literature talks about verification mode, and the accuracy obtained with machine learning approach is comparable with that presented by other researchers. Further study is needed with larger database and augmented data to train the network and get better results.

References

[1] J.E. Gray, G. Suresh, R. Ursprung, W.H. Edwards, J. Nickerson, P.H. Shinno, Patient misidentification in the neonatal intensive care unit: quantification of risk, Pediatrics 117 (2006) e6–e47.

[2] S. Siddiqui, M. Vatsa, R. Singh, Face recognition for newborns, toddlers and pre-school children: a deep learning approach, in: International Conference on Pattern Recognition, 2018.

[3] L. Best-Rowden, Y. Hoole, A. Jain, Automatic face recognition of newborns, infants and toddlers: a longitudinal evaluation, in: Biometrics Special Interest Group (BIOSIG), 2016, International Conference, Darmstadt, Germany, 2016.

[4] T. Ahonen, A. Hadid, M. Pietikäinen, Face description with local binary patterns: application to face recognition, IEEE Trans. Pattern Anal. Mach. Intell. 28 (12) (2006) 2037–2041.

[5] S. Bharadwaj, H.S. Bhatt, R. Singh, M. Vatsa, S.K. Singh, Face recognition for newborns: a preliminary study, in: Biometrics: Theory Applications and System (BTAS), 2010 fourth IEEE international Conference, Washington, DC, USA, 2010.

[6] S. Bhardwaj, H.S. Bhatt, Domain specific learning for newborn face recognition, IEEE Trans. Inf. Forensics Secur. 11 (7) (2016) 1630–1641.

[7] F. Yanwei, T.M. Hospedales, T. Xiang, Y. Yao, S. Gong, Interestingness prediction by robust learning to rank, in: ECCV, 2014.

[8] P. Basak, S. De, M. Agarwal, A. Malhotra, M. Vatsa, R. Singh, Multimodal biometric recognition for toddlers and pre-school children, in: IEEE International Joint Conference on Biometrics (IJCB), Oct 2017, pp. 627–633.

[9] P. Basak, S. De, M. Agarwal, M. Vatsa, R. Signh, Multimodal biometric recognition for toddlers and pre-school children, IEEE International Conference: Biometrics (IJCB) 1st October, Denver, USA, 2017.

[10] https://yourstory.com/mystory/biometrics-boon-farmers. (Accessed 4 May 2020).

[11] https://www.thalesgroup.com/en/markets/digital identity and security/government/biometrics/facial-recognition. (Accessed 10 May 2020).

[12] L.G. Farkas, J.C. Posnick, T.M. Hreczko, G.E. Pron, Growth patterns of the nasolabial region: a morphometric study, Cleft Palate Craniofac. J. 29 (4) (1992) 318–324, https://doi.org/10.1597/1545-1569_1992_029_0318_gpotnr_2.3.co_2. 1643060.

[13] H. Bay, A. Ess, T. Tutelaars, L.V. Gool, Surf: speeded up robust features, Comput. Vis. Image Underst. 110 (3) (2008) 346–359.

[14] D. Deb, N. Nain, A.K. Jain, Longitudinal study of child face recognition, in: 2018 International Conference on Biometrics (ICB), Feb 2018, pp. 225–232.

[15] D. Michalski, The impact of age and threshold variation on facial recognition algorithm performance using images of children, in: International Conference on Biometrics, ICB 2018, Gold Coast, Australia, February 20-23, 2018, IEEE, 2018. ISBN 978-1-5386-4285-69.

[16] N. Srinivas, K. Ricanek, D. Michalski, D.S. Bolme, M. King, Face recognition algorithm bias: performance differences on images of children and adults, in: Conference on Computer Vision and Pattern Recognition Workshops, IEEE Explore, 2019.

[17] S. Tiwari, S. Kumar, S.K. Singh, A. Singh, in: Newborn Recognition Using Multimodal Biometric, IGI Global, 2015, pp. 4347–4357. https://www.igi-global.com/viewtitlesample.aspx?id=112877&ptid=76156&t=Newborn%20Recognition%20Using%20Multimodal%20Biometric&isxn=9781466658882.

[18] S. Tiwari, A. Singh, S.K. Singh, Multimodal database of newborns for biometric recognition, Int. J. Bio-Sci. Bio-Technol. 5 (2) (2013) 89–100.

[19] P.S. Chandran, N.B. Byju, R.U. Deepak, K.N. Nishakumari, P. Devanand, P.M. Sasi, Missing child identification system using deep learning and multiclass SVM, in: 2018 IEEE Recent Advances in Intelligent Computational Systems (RAICS), Trivandrum, December 6–8, 2018.

Chapter 2

Thermal biometric face recognition (TBFR): A noncontact face biometry

Chirag Kyal[a], Harsh Poddar[a], and Motahar Reza[b]
[a]*Department of Computer Science and Engineering, National Institute of Science and Technology, Berhampur, India,* [b]*Department of Mathematics, GITAM Deemed to be University, Hyderabad, India*

1 Introduction

At present, people are very much alert when it comes to the matter of their protection and safety. Conventional methods of verification, such as passwords and personal identification numbers (PINs) are generally less secure and unreliable. Besides this, biometric features are free from such drawbacks and are now being recognized in several development activities associated with security and authentication systems. Moreover, humans possess various physiological properties such as circumvention, permanence, uniqueness, and acceptability [1], which can be used by various biometric systems to successfully identify a candidate. In addition to these, significant amount of works have been done in the past, which involves the usage of infrared (IR) images for the extraction of various biometric features [1–6]. Prevalence and appropriateness of such a system may be affected by various factors such as operability under different lighting conditions, successful identification of human, highest throughput, and so on. Until today, it is not an astonishing fact that none verification techniques based on biometric exists, which possess the capability to account for all these requirements [7].

1.1 Outline of aim and objective of problem

The main contributions of the chapter are as follows:

- We proposed a novel face recognition algorithm for thermal IR images. We named it as thermal biometric face recognition (TBFR). In order to have an algorithm capable of solving this problem, thermal IR face has been detected

Machine Learning for Biometrics. https://doi.org/10.1016/B978-0-323-85209-8.00012-2

29

and then aligned based on canonical coordinates. This has been achieved with the help of 73 fiducial landmark points over the thermal face.

- Using these annotated images, a deep learning-based model has been trained to specialize the task to annotation. Annotated images are then used to extract additional information related to the person's face geometry, which is later fused with the feature vector obtained from a ResNet-50 layer. The fusion of these information gives an upper hand in accurately classifying a person and thus giving a state-of-the-art algorithm.
- Our proposed method attains better recognition performance compared to other methods. Experiments of face recognition using thermal imaging are validated against several publicly existing databases to prove the efficacy of the algorithms, proposed for feature extraction, feature fusion, and identification of a person.

1.2 Chapter organization

The rest of this chapter has been divided into following sections: Section 2 discusses the existing approaches for face recognition. In Section 3, the proposed TBFR method is explained in detail. Section 4 presents experimental results and comparison with other methods. The conclusion is discussed in Section 5.

2 Existing approaches

Face recognition using RGB images is highly affected due to ambient light illumination and hence reducing the biometric security. Many researchers, scientists who are actively working on biometrics, have accepted this issue of deidentification of human data. In most of the state-of-the-art algorithms on face biometric, machine learning and deep learning have proven a significant performance, particularly convolution neural networks (CNN) have given excellent results for image learning. In [8], de Freitas Pereira et al. extracted image features using a deep CNN. They particularly notified that advanced or high-level image features cannot exist in the same dimension as the original image. In their work, Batchuluun et al. [9] combined CNN and LSTM to create a compound neural network. This network can extract image features and temporal features simultaneously using CNN and LSTM, respectively. Combining spatial and temporal features can increase face recognition biometric efficiency and accuracy but cannot improve biological security.

In their work, Jian et al. [10] proposed a face recognition algorithm by acquiring the temperature emitted from a thermal IR facial image. In [11], Vigneau et al. represented the problem of using thermal IR images in face recognition with changes of time. They analyzed the impact of nontime-varying local binary pattern for facial images. Kaur and Khanna [12] used cancelable biometrics and template protection method to recognize thermal facial images. In [13, 14], researchers have shown the importance of fiducial points over thermal face images. Sun and Zheng [15] proposed an face alignment method without relying on eye-center positioning. In their work, Li et al. [16] developed a framework to predict thermal comfort level by collecting skin temperature from facial images. In [17], the authors have used physiological information and Bayesian framework to recognize human faces. They have further extracted thermal grids from the face images and used linear SVM for the classification task. In [18], the authors have proposed IR face recognition method using automatic feature extraction from CNN by incorporating five convolutional layers along with five max-pooling layers.

Some scientists have also identified facial recognition improvement by clubbing thermal images and RGB images. Cao et al. [19] and Hermosilla et al. [20] proposed a novel face recognition method by fusing visible and thermal feature descriptors. Peng et al. [21] implemented CRSM that can calculate the similarity between graphical representations for face recognition. In [22], Wang et al. described a new face recognition method by incorporating the features of both thermal and visible images and applying SVMs on top of it as a classifier.

3 Proposed work

In this chapter, we have proposed a novel face recognition algorithm that works efficiently with images obtained in the IR range of light. In this system, we have clubbed the benefits of deep learning with the techniques of shallow learning models to give an algorithm having state-of-the-art features.

The image of the person is sent into the system that outputs a label associated with the identity of the person. The input image is first sent into an algorithm capable of detecting human faces in thermal images. Later, it is annotated using an existing trained deep learning-based model, presented in our previous work [14]. Later, we have used this annotated image to calculate the facial geometry features related to a person, which is considered as unique. These features are distances between their eyes, distance of eyes from mouth, length and width of the person's face, etc. The ResNet-50 model is used to obtain a feature vector of 2048 size for the input image. We have combined the feature vector obtained from ResNet-50 with the above calculated vector containing geometrical information about the person's face. This combination has made our system more robust toward issues related to images of people with similar heat signatures. Finally, deep subspace clustering is used to group all these feature vector according to their individual subject label representing different biometric identification for every human being. The entire algorithmic flow of our proposed work is represented in Fig. 1.

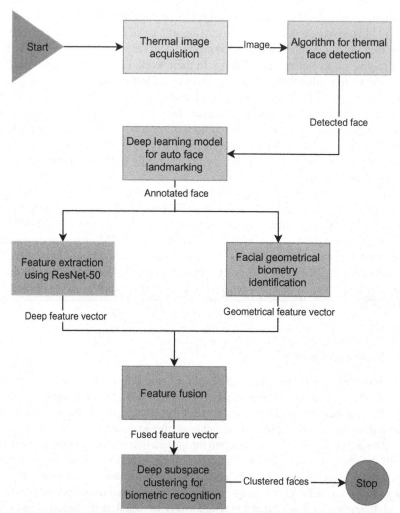

FIG. 1 Schematic representation of the proposed algorithm.

3.1 Thermal face detection

Various issues have been tackled by detecting faces in visual domain of light. It is not a perfect solution and, thus, fails to solve certain problems such as:
1. detecting faces at less illuminated places;
2. capability to differentiate between a real face and a printed image [23]; and
3. identifying various types of stress and emotions in images [24].

Unlike visual imagery, the thermal cameras possess the capability to detect heat radiation emitted by the objects. Fig. 2 depicts the detailed implementation of thermal face detection, presented in our previous work [25].

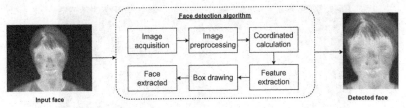

FIG. 2 Workflow of thermal face detection [25].

In this process, the input thermal image is preprocessed with operations like thresholding, opening, and closing to get the object boundary of the face. Four coordinate points, that is, head point, left ear point, right ear point, and neck point, are detected by feature point calculation and histogram plot. At the end, the human face is detected by creating a rectangular box over the image.

3.2   Face landmarking

Various problems related to facial images captured in thermal domain can be addressed with the aid of modern deep learning-based approaches. Several types of convolutional neural networks are currently dominating the area of research.

For the task of facial landmark localization, three datasets, namely USTC-NVIE [26], UCH-TTF [11], and PUCV-TTF [27], have been harnessed to train a learning model [14]. The frames selected for these databases were manually annotated with 73 fiducial landmark points. Fig. 3 presents the exact location of these points on an image. Although the model annotates an image with 73 fiducial points, in this work, we have used only 10 points out of them. Anyone wishing to develop a model to annotate these 10 points can actually refer to our previous work [14] in detail on the methodology of doing so with less number of points. These landmarks provide the dataset with reusable property, making it suitable for various other types of problem statements.

3.3   Feature extraction

Feature extraction is a key process of extracting valuable information from the images and then using this information to get our work done. It is also a part of the dimensionality reduction process. An important characteristic of larger datasets is that they have a large number of variables, because of which they require a lot of computing resources to process them. So, feature extraction is basically a key process of extracting valuable information from these datasets and then using this information to accomplish the work.

Image processing is one of the domains in which we apply feature extraction processes to scale down our input images and extract valuable information from them, thus reducing the high need of storage and computing power of the system. There are several methods or algorithms defined to perform the task of

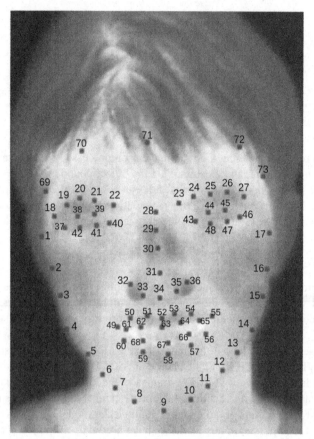

FIG. 3 Seventy-three landmark points with their coordinate in the face.

feature extraction. One of those methods involves the usage of pretrained models like VGG-16 [28], ResNet [29], and AlexNet [30] to extract these information from the image. Here, we are going to use the pretrained ResNet-50 model with its last layer removed to extract the 2048 dense activations from it.

Residual Networks or ResNet is a conventional neural network, which along with being a winner of the ImageNet Challenge (2015), is widely used for tackling various tasks related to computer vision. The biggest benefit of using it is the capability to train extremely deep neural networks without any constraint. Prior to this, achieving the same task was a cumbersome process because of the existence of vanishing gradients. ResNet is able to do so by introducing the concept of "skip connection," as depicted in Fig. 4. It has convolutional layers stacked at the top of each other with skip connections, shown by curved arrows, between them. These skip connections (Fig. 5) allow weights to pass directly to the other layers in the forward propagation and updates to pass to these deep

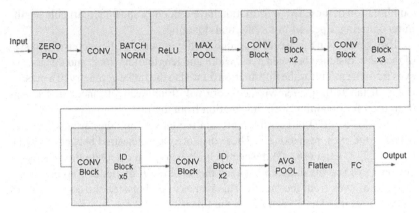

FIG. 4 Architecture of ResNet-50.

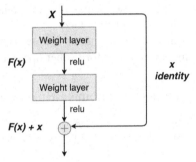

FIG. 5 Pictorial representation of skip connection in ResNet-50 where x-identity branch is our skip connection.

layers in the backward propagation. 50 in ResNet-50 refers to the number of layers that have weights.

Apart from ResNet [29], there are also other deep learning algorithms like VGG-16 [28], AlexNet [30], DenseNet [31], etc., which can be used for feature extraction purposes. However, the reason for which ResNet-50 is preferred over the others is because of its faster convergence compared to other counter parts of it. Also, the results obtained from ResNet are far better compared to the ones obtained from other models.

3.4 Facial geometrical biometry identification and feature fusion

ResNet-50 outputs a feature vector of 2048 vector size. This vector could be a useful feature vector for solving problems in the visual domain of light. However, in thermal domain, merely using this vector directly as an input to our biometric system would not be enough. Thus, we could be clubbing the feature vector with the information about the facial geometry of the person.

Combination of these two information have evidently shown remarkable results in recognizing a person in the thermal domain.

Every person in this world is unique. Believing this, we have considered size of the eyes, distance between eyes, width and length of the face, and distance of eyes from the mouth as the information related to the facial geometry of a person. Euler distance (https://en.wikipedia.org/wiki/Euclidean_distance) metric has been used for obtaining such information from the face.

Line *AB* and *CD* in Fig. 6A represent the closest and the farthest distance between the eyes, respectively. These distances are measured between fiducial points (22, 23) and (18, 27), respectively. It is used to calculate the size of the person's eye and the distance between them. Line *EF* in Fig. 6A represents the distance of eyes from the mouth. This is measured between the coordinates of the points marked as 28 and 63 on the image.

In Fig. 6B, line *AB* represents distance between the fiducial points 9 and 71, which further represents the length of a person's face. Line *CD* on the same image represents the distance between the fiducial points 1 and 17, which further represents the width of a person's face.

These five distances are combined with the feature vector acquired from the ResNet-50 to make it more prominent for further operations.

3.5 Deep subspace clustering for biometric recognition

In order to carry out the final biometric recognition step, we have used subspace clustering method by using deep neural network architecture [32]. Subspace

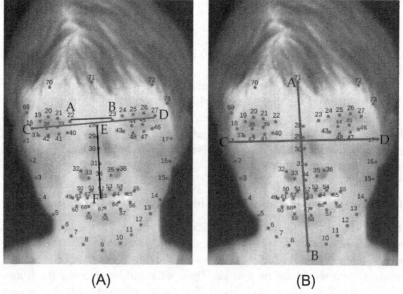

(A)   (B)

FIG. 6 Annotated image with facial geometry shown as *lines*.

clustering is used to classify images of various subjects based on their corresponding tags. The architecture of deep subspace clustering networks is based upon encoders, self-expressive layer, and decoders, which are stacked together and can nonlinearly clusters the feature vectors in a latent space through a standard back-propagation method. Fig. 7 represents the overall idea of deep subspace clustering. Several pretraining and fine-tuning techniques are used to make the proposed model more robust. We have modified the structure so that it can be used with 1D feature vectors. To this extent, each cluster is unique and can be labeled as individual biometric code. Every biometric code is mapped to a particular human and hence can be easily distinguished.

In the convolutional layers, rectified linear unit (ReLU) [30] is used for nonlinear activation and both horizontal and vertical kernels with stride 2 are operated for all the data points. In order to cluster N feature vectors, they all have been passed in a single batch. Each input vector has been transformed to a latent vector using encoder layers. Next, all the nodes in the self-expressive layer are fully connected by nonlinear activations and nonbiased weights. Finally, decoder layers are used to map the latent vectors back to original vector space. With the help of this method, we are able to cluster all the facial feature vectors in different clusters, denoting biometric difference among all the subject thermal faces.

3.6   Final biometrically clustered faces

To consider the challenges and difficulties of the face recognition, which admit changes in facial expression, variations in illumination, rotation through different angles, change in scale, etc., subspace clustering technique based on deep neural network architecture has been applied over UCH-TTF, PUCV-TTF, and USTC-NVIE datasets. A good agreement has been done with high accuracy, as shown in Fig. 8.

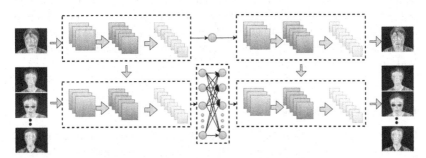

FIG. 7   Schematic diagram of deep subspace clustering networks [32].

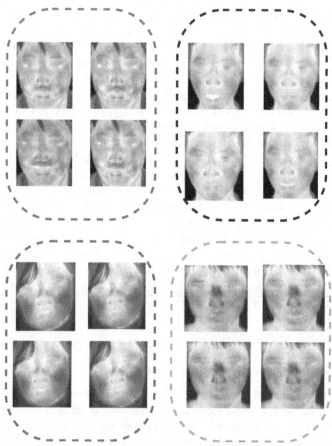

FIG. 8 Clustered thermal faces for each subject, different color of the box representing different face cluster.

4 Experimental results

This section elaborates the detailed implementation analysis of the proposed method. The experiments were implemented on a Windows PC infrastructure with 3.2 GHz, 32 GB RAM, and 2 GB NVIDIA GeForce 940MX Graphics. Python with Tensorflow-1.13.0 was chosen as the base programming framework to implement the work.

4.1 Choice of database

The choice of thermal face database plays a significant role in the evaluation of training and testing the model of TBFR. Datasets differ from each other because of various reasons, such as recording distances, quality of thermal camera, IR band, facial expression, recording environment, and pose. We carry out our proposed biometry on three standard thermal datasets. The samples of all the three datasets are presented in Fig. 9. We present the details of the datasets in the following section:

- *UCH Thermal Temporal Face (UCH-TTF) database [11]:* The database includes a total of 350 facial images captured in thermal domain with each image cropped and aligned in a particular dimensions of 150 × 81 pixels and 125 × 225 pixels. Fifty different images per 7 different subjects were obtained over a period of 69 days. FLIR TAU 320 camera (http://www.flir.com/cores/display/?id=60983) was used to acquire images with subjects located approximately at 1.1 m away from it.
- *PUCV Thermal Temporal Face (PUCV-TTF) database [27]:* In order to validate the results obtained from the UCH-TTF database, PUCV-TTF database was developed in 2015. The database contains 130 facial images with neutral expression and no accessories (like glasses, cap, or scarf). Ten acquisition sessions were set up to capture images from 13 different subjects, which were later cropped and aligned into 150 × 81 pixels and 125 × 225 pixels. For the capturing purpose, the FLIR Tau 2 (http://www.flir.com/cvs/cores/view/?id=54717) camera was located at a height of 115 cm using a tripod and was set at a distance of 91.5 cm away from the subjects. A white concrete wall has been used as the background to avoid the effect of thermal or visual changes during the process of image acquisition.
- *USTC-NVIE database [26]:* The USTC-NVIE database was created to identify various human emotions in thermal domain. It consists of two

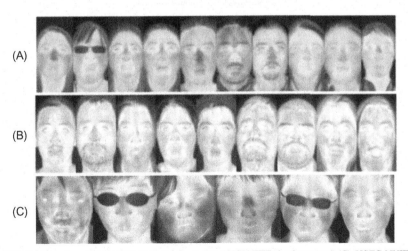

(A)

(B)

(C)

FIG. 9 Samples of (A) UCH-TTF database, (B) PUCV-TTF database, and (C) USTC-NVIE database.

subdatabases: first, a spontaneous database that includes image sequences from onset to apex and second, a posed database, that consists only of apex images. Each of these databases is enriched with image sequences taken simultaneously in both domains of light, visual and thermal, and under the influence of three distinct lightning conditions.

4.2   Results and discussion

This analysis involves examining the performance on subspace clustering method based on deep neural network architecture against the issue of temporal variations that can appear while capturing thermal images in various situations. Best performance of each dataset has been identified and are compared between the databases by this novel subspace clustering method. The results obtained for accuracy and converging time of subspace clustering method on the UCH-TTF, PUCV-TTF, and USTC-NVIE databases are presented in Figs. 10 and 11.

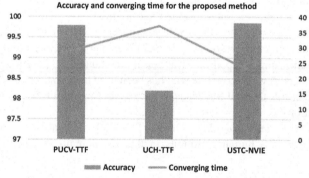

FIG. 10   Comparison results obtained for subspace clustering method on UCH-TTF, PUCV-TTF, and USTC-NVIE databases.

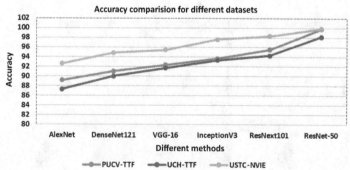

FIG. 11   Average accuracy comparisons obtained from different deep learning methods on UCH-TTF, PUCV-TTF, and USTC-NVIE databases.

4.2.1 Deep learning-based feature extractors compared

In the phase of feature extraction, we use several deep learning-based feature extractors such as AlexNet [30], DenseNet121 [31], VGG-16 [28], InceptionV3 [33], ResNext101 [34], and ResNet-50 [29], and we experimentally chose ResNet-50 in the proposed method due to its high accuracy and less error percentage for all the three datasets. We have tabulated the comparison results for all the feature extractors in Table 1 and have diagrammatically depicted in Figs. 12–17.

4.2.2 Methods compared

We compare the performance of our proposed algorithmic framework with other state-of-the-art approaches like DrunkSpace Classifier [27], GHFR [21], PSO-TFRS [20], and TFR-PI [17]. From Table 2, it can be figured out that our proposed method has outperformed other existing methods.

Since recognizing human faces from thermal images requires intensive amount of training data, we encourage researchers to test this method with other datasets and real life scenarios. This research is limited to PUCV-TTF, UCH-TTF, and USTC-NVIE datasets and only considers normal frontal thermal faces to train the model. It still has room for face images with immense background noise, obliqueness, and occlusion.

TABLE 1 The detailed comparison of accuracy percentage and error rate for different deep learning methods in PUCV-TTF, UCH-TTF, and USTC-NVIE datasets.

	PUCV-TTF		UCH-TTF		USTC-NVIE	
Methods	Accuracy (%)	Error (%)	Accuracy (%)	Error (%)	Accuracy (%)	Error (%)
AlexNet [30]	89.19	1.26	87.32	1.88	92.63	1.11
DenseNet121 [31]	91.01	1.08	90.01	1.36	94.84	0.98
VGG-16 [28]	92.32	0.87	91.72	0.92	95.42	0.75
InceptionV3 [33]	93.67	0.74	93.33	0.84	97.65	0.62
ResNext101 [34]	95.53	0.41	94.28	0.53	98.32	0.31
ResNet-50 [29]	99.79	0.35	98.19	0.49	99.85	0.22

It can be noticed that ResNet-50 is having the highest accuracy and lowest error rate for all the three datasets.

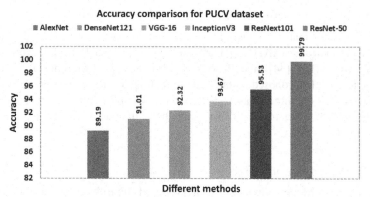

FIG. 12 Accuracy comparison for PUCV-TTF dataset with different deep learning methods.

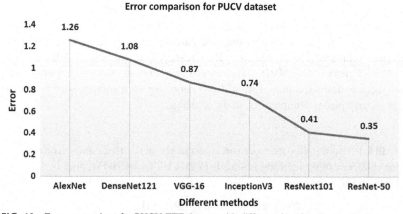

FIG. 13 Error comparison for PUCV-TTF dataset with different deep learning methods.

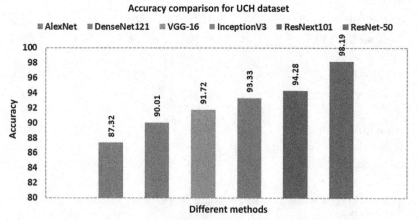

FIG. 14 Accuracy comparison for UCH-TTF dataset with different deep learning methods.

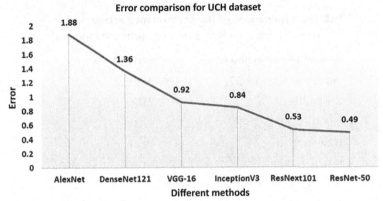

FIG. 15 Error comparison for UCH-TTF dataset with different deep learning methods.

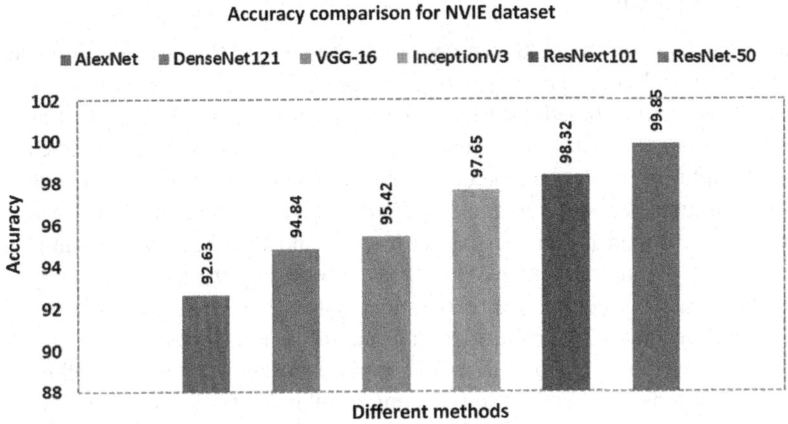

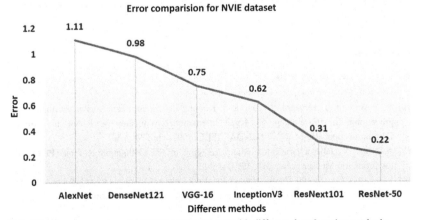

FIG. 16 Accuracy comparison for USTC-NVIE dataset with different deep learning methods.

FIG. 17 Error comparison for USTC-NVIE dataset with different deep learning methods.

TABLE 2 Comparison of the performance accuracy of different existing approaches and our proposed method.

State-of-the-art methods	Accuracy (%)
DrunkSpace Classifier [27]	86.96
GHFR [21]	95.38
PSO-TFRS [20]	99.34
TFR-PI [17]	99.71
TBFR (proposed)	99.85

5 Conclusion

The robustness of thermal sensors to illuminations changes has attracted researchers and commercial groups from around the globe as an alternative to visual spectrum-based security systems. They are capable of operating in dark environments. Also, the research has witnessed that IR cameras are capable of capturing new anatomical and physiological face information such as facial vascular networks, thermal signatures, and structure of blood vessels. These features can be unique to each person and thus have the potential to be used as biometric features for them. Following the same ideology, a thermal-based biometric face recognition system has been proposed in this chapter. Concepts of deep learning and feature fusion have been extensively used to provide more robustness to the proposed system. In order to tackle situations such as different persons having similar heat signatures, additional information related to a person's facial geometry was fused with the feature vector obtained from a ResNet-50 model. Results obtained from experimentation are quite satisfactory and are thus performing better than the existing state-of-the-art algorithms.

References

[1] A.K. Jain, R. Bolle, S. Pankanti, Biometrics: Personal Identification in Networked Society, vol. 479, Springer Science & Business Media, 2006.
[2] Y. Yoshitomi, T. Miyaura, S. Tomita, S. Kimura, Face identification using thermal image processing, in: Proceedings 6th IEEE International Workshop on Robot and Human Communication. RO-MAN'97 SENDAI, IEEE, 1997, pp. 374–379.
[3] A.J. Rice, A quality approach to biometric imaging, in: IEE Colloquium on Image Processing for Biometric Measurement, IET, 1994. p. 4-1.
[4] J.M. Cross, C.L. Smith, Thermographic imaging of the subcutaneous vascular network of the back of the hand for biometric identification, in: Proceedings the Institute of Electrical and

Electronics Engineers. 29th Annual 1995 International Carnahan Conference on Security Technology, IEEE, 1995, pp. 20–35.

[5] U. Saeed, Facial micro-expressions as a soft biometric for person recognition, Pattern Recogn. Lett. 143 (2021) 95–103.

[6] V. Wati, K. Kusrini, H.A. Fatta, N. Kapoor, Security of facial biometric authentication for attendance system, Multimed. Tools Appl. (2021), https://doi.org/10.1007/s11042-020-10246-4.

[7] C.-L. Lin, K.-C. Fan, Biometric verification using thermal images of palm-dorsa vein patterns, IEEE Trans. Circuits Syst. Video Technol. 14 (2) (2004) 199–213.

[8] T. de Freitas Pereira, A. Anjos, S. Marcel, Heterogeneous face recognition using domain specific units, IEEE Trans. Inf. Forensics Secur. 14 (7) (2018) 1803–1816.

[9] G. Batchuluun, H.S. Yoon, J.K. Kang, K.R. Park, Gait-based human identification by combining shallow convolutional neural network-stacked long short-term memory and deep convolutional neural network, IEEE Access 6 (2018) 63164–63186.

[10] B.-L. Jian, C.-L. Chen, M.-W. Huang, H.-T. Yau, Emotion-specific facial activation maps based on infrared thermal image sequences, IEEE Access 7 (2019) 48046–48052.

[11] G.H. Vigneau, J.L. Verdugo, G.F. Castro, F. Pizarro, E. Vera, Thermal face recognition under temporal variation conditions, IEEE Access 5 (2017) 9663–9672.

[12] H. Kaur, P. Khanna, Random distance method for generating unimodal and multimodal cancelable biometric features, IEEE Trans. Inf. Forensics Secur. 14 (3) (2018) 709–719.

[13] P.M. Prendergast, Facial proportions, in: Advanced Surgical Facial Rejuvenation, Springer, 2012, pp. 15–22.

[14] C.K. Kyal, H. Poddar, M. Reza, Human emotion recognition from spontaneous thermal image sequence using GPU accelerated emotion landmark localization and parallel deep emotion net, in: D. Gupta, A. Khanna, S. Bhattacharyya, A.E. Hassanien, S. Anand, A. Jaiswal (Eds.), International Conference on Innovative Computing and Communications, Springer, Singapore, 2021, pp. 931–943.

[15] L. Sun, Z. Zheng, Thermal-to-visible face alignment on edge map, IEEE Access 5 (2017) 11215–11227.

[16] D. Li, C.C. Menassa, V.R. Kamat, Non-intrusive interpretation of human thermal comfort through analysis of facial infrared thermography, Energy Build. 176 (2018) 246–261.

[17] S.D. Lin, K. Chen, W. Chen, Thermal face recognition based on physiological information, in: 2019 IEEE International Conference on Image Processing (ICIP), IEEE, 2019, pp. 3497–3501.

[18] B. Abd El-Rahiem, A. Sedik, G.M. El Banby, H.M. Ibrahim, M. Amin, O.-Y. Song, A.A.M. Khalaf, F.E. Abd El-Samie, An efficient deep learning model for classification of thermal face image, J. Enterp. Inf. Manag. (2020), https://doi.org/10.1108/JEIM-07-2019-0201.

[19] B. Cao, N. Wang, J. Li, X. Gao, Data augmentation-based joint learning for heterogeneous face recognition, IEEE Trans. Neural Netw. Learn. Syst. 30 (6) (2018) 1731–1743.

[20] G. Hermosilla, M. Rojas, J. Mendoza, G. Farias, F.T. Pizarro, C. San Martin, E. Vera, Particle swarm optimization for the fusion of thermal and visible descriptors in face recognition systems, IEEE Access 6 (2018) 42800–42811.

[21] C. Peng, X. Gao, N. Wang, J. Li, Graphical representation for heterogeneous face recognition, IEEE Trans. Pattern Anal. Mach. Intell. 39 (2) (2016) 301–312.

[22] S. Wang, B. Pan, H. Chen, Q. Ji, Thermal augmented expression recognition, IEEE Trans. Cybern. 48 (7) (2018) 2203–2214.

[23] M.-Y. Cho, Y.-S. Jeong, Face recognition performance comparison of fake faces with real faces in relation to lighting, J. Internet Serv. Inf. Secur. 4 (4) (2014) 82–90.

[24] Y.S. Salas, D.V. Bermudez, A.M.L. Peña, D.G. Gomez, T. Gevers, Improving hog with image segmentation: application to human detection, in: International Conference on Advanced Concepts for Intelligent Vision Systems, Springer, 2012, pp. 178–189.

[25] C.K. Kyal, H. Poddar, M. Reza, Detection of human face by thermal infrared camera using MPI model and feature extraction method, in: 2018 4th International Conference on Computing Communication and Automation (ICCCA), 2018, pp. 1–5.

[26] S. Wang, Z. Liu, S. Lv, Y. Lv, G. Wu, P. Peng, F. Chen, X. Wang, A natural visible and infrared facial expression database for expression recognition and emotion inference, IEEE Trans. Multimed. 12 (7) (2010) 682–691.

[27] G. Hermosilla, J.L. Verdugo, G. Farias, E. Vera, F. Pizarro, M. Machuca, Face recognition and drunk classification using infrared face images, J. Sens. 2018 (2018) 1–8, https://doi.org/10.1155/2018/5813514.

[28] K. Simonyan, A. Zisserman, Very deep convolutional networks for large-scale image recognition, CoRR abs/1409.1556 (2015).

[29] K. He, X. Zhang, S. Ren, J. Sun, Deep residual learning for image recognition, in: Proceedings of the IEEE Conference on Computer Vision and Pattern Recognition, 2016, pp. 770–778.

[30] A. Krizhevsky, I. Sutskever, G.E. Hinton, Imagenet classification with deep convolutional neural networks, in: Advances in Neural Information Processing Systems, 2012, pp. 1097–1105.

[31] G. Huang, Z. Liu, L. Van Der Maaten, K.Q. Weinberger, Densely connected convolutional networks, in: Proceedings of the IEEE Conference on Computer Vision and Pattern Recognition, 2017, pp. 4700–4708.

[32] P. Ji, T. Zhang, H. Li, M. Salzmann, I. Reid, Deep subspace clustering networks, in: Advances in Neural Information Processing Systems, 2017, pp. 24–33.

[33] C. Szegedy, V. Vanhoucke, S. Ioffe, J. Shlens, Z. Wojna, Rethinking the inception architecture for computer vision, in: Proceedings of the IEEE Conference on Computer Vision and Pattern Recognition, 2016, pp. 2818–2826.

[34] S. Xie, R. Girshick, P. Dollár, Z. Tu, K. He, Aggregated residual transformations for deep neural networks, in: Proceedings of the IEEE Conference on Computer Vision and Pattern Recognition, 2017, pp. 1492–1500.

Chapter 3

Multimodal biometric recognition using human ear and profile face: An improved approach

Partha Pratim Sarangi[a], Madhumita Panda[b], Subhashree Mishra[a], and Bhabani Shankar Prasad Mishra[a]

[a]*School of Computer Engineering, KIIT Deemed to be University, Bhubaneswar, India,* [b]*Master of Computer Applications, Seemanta Engineering College, Jharpokharia, India*

1 Introduction

In recent years, biometrics has emerged as an alternative procedure for human identity recognition in various security and forensic applications. Biometric modalities, such as fingerprint, face, iris, palmprint, ear, finger vein patterns, voice, signature, and gait, are the most popularly and widely used biometric modalities for individual identity recognition and privacy protection [1–6]. In recent years, ear biometric has gained more attention by the researchers due to its several intrinsic merits, such as the high uniqueness even in case of twins, stable and consistent shape and appearance over long duration, nonintrusive and passive feature providing flexibility, less chance of spoof attacks, and increased recognition performance [7, 8]. Due to the nonintrusive and noncooperation in ear image acquisition, ear biometrics encounters several challenges in uncontrolled environment such as noisy data, poor contrast, illumination variation, pose changes, and partial occlusion. These factors drastically affect the recognition performance and find limited use in commercial applications. To overcome the above-mentioned challenges and improving performance, in recent years, many research works have been published in the field of multimodal biometrics in association with ear modality, namely, Kumar et al. [9], Toygar et al. [10], Hezil and Boukrouche [11], Huang et al. [12], and Rathore et al. [13], which have become a recent trend of research in the field of human recognition using biometrics. In spite of the potential advantages of multimodal biometrics, they suffer from a number of essential problems, including incompatibility of features of different modalities, additional sensor cost, requirement of more storage space, extra acquisition time, and increased computational cost. This motivated us to use ear and profile face-based multi-modal biometrics, in which both modalities can be captured using a single sensor and have inherent correlation among them. Except a limited number of research works [10, 13–16], this multimodal biometrics is still an understudied problem and have open challenges for new research in this direction.

To increase discrimination capability of the proposed approach, in this chapter, we use steerable pyramid transform (SPT) filter bank on ear and profile face images. These SPT filters decompose both the images to into a predefined number of subbands of different scales and orientations. Subsequently, all subbands are divided into a number of nonoverlapping blocks, and the local features (e.g., local binary patterns (LDP), local phase quantization (LPQ), and binarized statistical image features (BSIF)) are extracted separately on each block to generate histograms. These histograms are normalized and concatenated to represent the image. Then, both feature- and score-level fusions have been explored with chi-square similarity measure to improve recognition performance. Major contributions of the proposed approach are outlined as follows:

(i) We proposed a multimodal biometric recognition system that takes both ear and profile face images as input and obtained improved recognition results compared to unimodal ear biometrics.

(ii) The SPT has been applied to decompose ear and profile face images separately into a set of subbands along different scales and orientations. Each subband is further divided into a number of blocks, and the local texture descriptors are computed for each block to unitedly represent the feature vector.

(iii) We explored the effectiveness of three histogram-based local texture descriptors, LDP, LPQ, and BSIF, to extract more distinctive orientation information and derived the best among them. To achieve better recognition performance, we also investigated the feature- and score-level fusion schemes.

(iv) An extensive set of experiments have been carried out on two benchmark datasets, UND-E and UND-J2, to evaluate effectiveness of the proposed method. The results obtained using score-level fusion are superior compared to ear-based unimodal and state-of-the-art multimodal biometrics.

The rest of this chapter is organized as follows: Section 2 describes related work. Section 3 briefly describes SPT and three local texture descriptors used for feature extraction. A detailed description of the proposed multimodal recognition method is given in Section 4. Experiments and results are discussed in Section 5, and finally, conclusion is derived in Section 6.

2 Related work

The most recent well-structured and comprehensive survey on ear biometrics was published by Refs. [17–20]. Despite several research findings, until now the performance of identity recognition is not promising under uncontrolled scenarios. Along with degrading identification accuracy, unimodal biometric suffers from various inherent issues, such as missing data, intraclass variations, interclass similarity, nonuniversality, and spoof attacks. Hence, many researchers are motivated to explore multimodal biometrics. Recently, many multimodal biometrics [9, 11, 12, 21–26] in association with ear as one of the modalities have been proposed to overcome the limitations of ear biometrics. However, ear and profile face-based multimodal biometric systems have not given much more importance, and only limited research papers have been published till date instead of several advantages.

Yuan et al. [27] combine the face profile with the ear to represent a multimodal image. They used Full Space Linear Discriminant Analysis (FSLDA) for feature extraction and recognition. Experiments were conducted using USTB multimodal image database. USTB database contains 79 subjects, for each subject three face profile images with variations of the head position and slightly facial expressions are selected for training and one image for testing.

Xu and Mu [28] proposed a multimodal system based on ear and profile face biometrics. Both ear and profile face images are classified using FSLDA. In case of the multimodal system, recognition of individuals are carried out using fusion of ear and profile face based on the combination methods of Product, Sum, and Median rules. In the experiments, the authors used USTB database, which contains 294 images and 42 persons. Each subject has seven profile face images with changes in head position at different angles (-10, $+10$, -20, $+20$, -30, and $+30$ degrees) and slightly facial expressions. Out of seven images of each person, five images are selected for training and the remaining two are used for testing. The experimental results indicate that the ear and face profile multimodal biometrics achieved higher recognition result than both unimodal biometrics.

Xu and Mu [29] studied ear and profile face-based multimodal approach in which both modalities used kernel canonical correlation analysis (KCCA) to extract nonlinear discriminative features. Its performance achieved a better identification rate than the canonical correlation analysis (CCA)-based approach.

Xu et al. [30] used kernel Fisher discriminant analysis (KFDA) to fuse profile face and ear images. The results showed that the weighted-sum rule-based feature-level fusion technique considerably increased identification rates in comparison to the ear and profile face alone.

Pan et al. [31] presented a novel feature-level fusion algorithm based on KFDA to combine nonlinear features of ear and profile face. They used three different feature-level fusion schemes, product rule, average rule, and weighted-sum rule, to generate fused nonlinear feature vectors. Experiments were performed using USTB dataset, and the results revealed that weighted-sum rule-based fusion of ear and profile face obtained promising results.

Rathore et al. [13] proposed a multimodal biometrics approach using ear and profile face. The authors applied three enhancement schemes separately for both modalities and shape and rotation invariant local features extracted using SURF descriptors. In this work, both feature- and score-level fusion of ear and profile face images verified. They used three databases, IITk, UND collection E, and collection J2, for experiments and found the score-level fusion performs better than the feature-level fusion.

Youssef et al. [32] presented the fusion of face profile and ear multimodal biometrics. The authors employed block-based local binary pattern (LBP) for feature extraction in ear and face profile images. Finally, score-level fusion based on simple mean rule is used to combine feature distributions of both modalities. Experiments were conducted on the University of Notre Dame (UND) collection E database, which contains 464 side face images from 114 individuals. Experimental results show that the accuracy of multimodal biometrics outperforms over unimodal ear and profile face biometrics.

Sarangi et al. [33] explored combined feature vector, that is, concatenation of LDP and LPQ local features, to represent the ear and profile face modalities. Combined feature vector increases the dimensionality of each modality. Combined feature vector representation of ear and profile face increases discriminative power at the cost of large feature dimension. In order to reduce dimension of each modality, the authors employed linear subspace projection using PCA. Then, the nonlinear feature-level fusion of both modalities performed using KDCV. Experimental results based on two databases, namely, UND-E and UND-J2, illustrated significantly better identification rate compared to existing methods.

Sarangi and Panda [16] proposed an efficient multimodal technique using ear and profile face. The feature vectors for ear and profile face images are separately extracted using Gabor wavelets to minimize the effect of illumination variation and image degradation. The authors employed KCCA for feature-level fusion, which is compared with CCA. Extensive experiments were conducted using UND-E and UND-J2, and the results showed that KCCA-based feature-level fusion outperforms in generating discriminant feature vector and obtained increased identification rate compared to existing methods.

The recognition accuracy achieved by the earlier approaches still needs potential improvements. The proposed multimodal framework using ear and profile face significantly improves the recognition performance.

3 Background

In this work, we localized ear part from the side face image using Sarangi et al. [34, 35] method to extract the ear part from the side face images. Then, the side

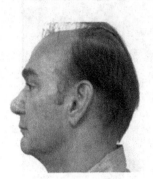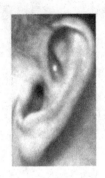

FIG. 1   A sample side face image with extracted ear and profile face images from UND-J2 dataset.

face portion is manually cropped from the remaining part of the profile face images. The ear and profile face images are the parts of a side face image, as shown in Fig. 1.

3.1   Steerable pyramid transform

SPT [36] is a linear transformation in which a signal is represented as multiscale and multiorientation subbands. SPT is a filter bank that contains series of basis filters. It decomposes signal into a number of subbands of different scales and orientations using basis filters. In this work, SPT is used to represent ear and profile face image as a set of images of different scales and orientations. In decomposition process, in the first scale (S_1), SPT applied high-pass filter and low-pass filter on the image to generate two subbands H_0 and L_0. In the second scale (S_2), the subband L_0 is decomposed into p-oriented $\left(\frac{2\pi}{p}\right)$ subbands using directional band-pass filters B_k and a low-pass subband L_1. In the third scale (S_3), L_1 is down-sampled by a factor 2 and it is decomposed into p-oriented subbands and a low-pass subband L_2. Next levels of decomposition process recursively continue until a given scale was encountered. Fig. 2 shows decomposition of ear image using SPT with three scales and four orientations. In this process, an ear image is represented by total numbers of 14 subbands (1 residual of high-pass subband, 12 band-pass subbands of different scales and orientations, and 1 residual of low-pass subband).

3.2   Local texture descriptors

After SPT-based decomposition of ear and profile face images, local texture descriptors are more robust to extract discriminative information from subbands in uncontrolled conditions. In the literature [7, 8, 37–42], it is found that local directional features are efficient in extracting discriminative features from ear

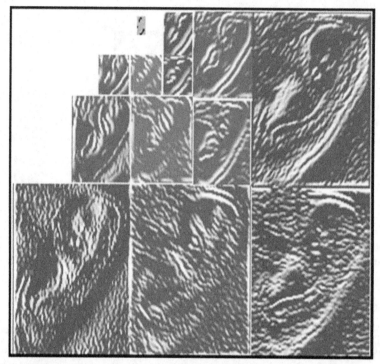

FIG. 2 Decomposition of an ear image using SPT with three scales and four orientations.

images. The best performing local texture descriptors for ear biometrics are LDP [43], LPQ [37, 44, 45], and BSIF [33, 37].

4 Proposed multimodal biometric recognition

The proposed method consists of five stages: preprocessing, local feature extraction, multimodal fusion, and person recognition are explained in Algorithm 1 and the proposed pipeline is shown in Fig. 3.

4.1 Preprocessing

To smooth the noises present in the input side face images, Gaussian low-pass filter is employed. The convolution operation is performed between Gaussian kernel (G) and side face image (I) to obtain smoothed input image (I') as follows:

$$I' = I * G(u,v,\sigma),$$
$$G(u,v,\sigma) = \frac{1}{\sqrt{2\pi}\sigma} \exp\left(-\frac{u^2 - v^2}{2\sigma^2}\right), \tag{1}$$

where σ is the standard deviation of Gaussian kernel.

Algorithm 1 The proposed multimodal biometric recognition.

Input: Given training and test sets of segmented ear and profile face images
Output: Recognized identity

1: Apply the Gaussian filter to smooth each ear and profile face images using Eq. (1).
2: Employ steerable pyramid filter bank to generate multiscale and orientation subbands of training and test samples.
3: Apply block-based local texture descriptor to each subbands of training and test images.
4: Concatenate block-wise histograms to acquire training and test feature vector sets.
5: **for** each ear test feature vector **do**
6:    Compute matching scores using chi-square measure between test feature vector and all training feature vectors by Eq. (2).
7:    Determine recognized identity of ear test sample based on matching scores using kNN classifier.
8: **end for**
9: **for** each profile face test feature vector **do**
10:    Compute matching scores using chi-square measure between test feature vector and all training feature vectors by Eq. (2).
11:    Determine recognized identity of profile face test sample based on matching scores using kNN classifier.
12: **end for**
13: Calculate Accuracy and EER for ear and profile face biometrics modalities.
14: **for** each ear and profile face matching score **do**
15:    Compute fused matching scores using weighted sum rule of score-level fusion using Eq. (5).
16:    Determine recognized identity of each sample based on fused matching scores using kNN classifier
17: **end for**
18: Evaluate overall Accuracy (%) and EER (%) of the proposed recognition method.

4.2   Feature extraction using block-based SPT-BSIF descriptor

In this work, we employ three-scale and six-orientation steerable pyramid filter bank on ear and profile images, which decompose an image into 18 subbands of different scales and orientations. Then, all subbands are divided into a number of nonoverlapping blocks and being applied BSIF feature extractor to all blocks. The normalized histogram texture descriptors of all blocks are concatenated to form a (SPT-BSIF) feature vector. Finally, we obtained two normalized feature vectors F_{Ear} and F_{PF} for ear and profile face, respectively.

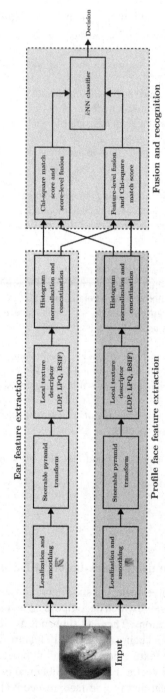

FIG. 3 Pipeline of the proposed method.

4.3   Matching and classification

Before performing classification, the matching scores of all probe samples are computed in two steps: (1) compare each probe image with all gallery images to generate a set of matching scores using chi-square measure as given in Eq. (2), and (2) kNN classifier has used to obtain single matching score for each probe sample.

$$\chi(F_1, F_2) = \sum_{k=1}^{N} \frac{(f_{1,k} - f_{2,k})^2}{(f_{1,k} + f_{2,k})}. \tag{2}$$

In this chapter, we used the proposed method in a verification mode. In this case, the probe image is matched with the gallery images to verify the individual's claimed identity. Finally, matching scores of probe samples are used to compute false acceptance rate (FAR) and false rejection rate (FRR) to evaluate the recognition accuracy in (%) of the proposed method using Eq. (3). Another recognized performance measure is equal error rate (EER), which is the rate at which FAR and FRR are equal [46].

$$Accuracy = 100 - \frac{(FAR + FRR)}{2}. \tag{3}$$

4.4   Multimodal fusion

In this work, both feature-level and score-level fusions have been examined to determine higher recognition performance of the proposed method.

4.5   Feature-level fusion

In feature-level fusion, ear feature F_{Ear} and profile face feature F_{PF} are consolidated into a single feature vector F_{Fused} as follows:

$$F_{Fused} = F_{Ear} \cup F_{PF}. \tag{4}$$

4.6   Score-level fusion

In score-level fusion, the matching score of ear S_{Ear} and profile face S_{PF} are individually calculated using chi-square distance measure and are fused based on Eq. (5) to obtain a fused score for recognizing individual using kNN classifier.

$$S_{Fused} = \frac{A_{Ear} \times S_{Ear} + A_{PF} \times S_{PF}}{A_{Ear} + A_{PF}}, \tag{5}$$

where A_{Ear} and A_{PF} are the recognition accuracy of ear and profile face modalities, respectively.

5 Experiments and results

In this section, we present various experiments to demonstrate the effectiveness of the proposed method. First, we discuss UND-E and UND-J2 datasets used in the experiments and experimental setup to tune the different parameters of steerable pyramid filter bank and local feature extractors, namely, LDP, LPQ, and BSIF. Second, we perform experiments for feature-level fusion and score-level fusion of ear and profile face feature sets. Third, we compare the recognition accuracy of the proposed method with existing methods, which have been implemented on UND-E and UND-J2 datasets.

5.1 Datasets

UND-E [47] dataset comprises 464 color side face images from 114 subjects. Each subject has samples between three and nine. All the images were captured at a distance at different viewing angles, varying illumination conditions, and at different days.

UND-J2 [47] dataset contains 2430 color side face images from 415 subjects. Variation from 2 to 22 samples captures under poor contrast lighting conditions with different viewing angles. In our experiments, we have considered 273 subjects with a minimum of three samples. Fig. 4 illustrates sample ear and profile face samples from different subjects of the UND-E and UND-J2 databases, respectively.

5.2 Experimental setup

In all experiments, three samples were selected from each subject in the UND-E and UND-J2 datasets. Both the datasets use all-to-all test strategy, in which three possible combinations of training-test sets were formed, that is, every time one is selected for test sample and remaining two samples are used for training.

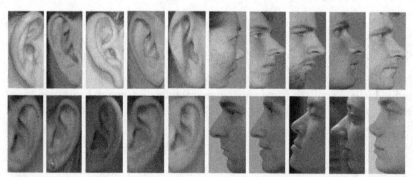

FIG. 4 Dataset sample images of some subjects' ear and profile face from UND-E (*first row*) and UND-J2 (*second row*).

In all experiments, three-scale and six-orientation SPTs are used for better results. In the experiments, three different combinations of SPT are explored with feature descriptor, namely, SPT-LDP, STP-LPQ, and SPT-BSIF. Finally, fusion at feature level or score level is performed to improve the recognition performance.

5.3 Results

The recognition performance of the proposed method is evaluated for unimodal biometrics using ear and profile face and for multimodal biometrics based on fusion at feature level and score level. In these experiments, SPT-LDP, SPT-LPQ, and SPT-BSIF feature extractors are used to generate discriminative feature vectors. In these experiments, matching of the probe feature vector with gallery feature vectors is obtained by the chi-square measure for personal recognition using kNN classifier. The recognition performance is measured in terms of Accuracy and EER in percentage. The performance results of unimodal (ear and profile face) and multimodal (feature-level and score-level) biometrics on UND-E and UND-J2 datasets are shown in Table 1.

TABLE 1 Average recognition results of the proposed method on UND-E and UND-J2 datasets for different local texture descriptors.

Dataset	Descriptor	Results	Ear	Profile face	Feature fusion	Score fusion
UND-E	SPT-LDP	Accuracy (%)	93.87	91.17	96.47	99.95
		EER (%)	6.12	8.82	3.52	0.04
	SPT-LPQ	Accuracy (%)	97.36	93.86	98.42	99.97
		EER (%)	2.63	7.02	1.75	0.02
	SPT-BSIF	Accuracy (%)	**97.73**	**94.73**	**98.47**	**99.98**
		EER (%)	**1.67**	**5.26**	**1.59**	**0.01**
UND-J2	SPT-LDP	Accuracy (%)	94.13	90.2	97.79	99.92
		EER (%)	5.86	9.79	2.20	0.07
	SPT-LPQ	Accuracy (%)	97.06	91.66	97.86	99.95
		EER (%)	93	8.33	2.13	0.05
	SPT-BSIF	Accuracy (%)	**97.54**	**90.35**	**98.24**	**99.97**
		EER (%)	**2.45**	**9.64**	**1.75**	**0.04**

Bold values indicate the best performance.

The proposed method is executed using either ear and profile face alone for unimodal identity recognition, and both modalities are combined using feature-level fusion and score-level fusion for multimodal identity recognition. The highlighted values in Table 1 indicate the best results in terms of Accuracy and EER in the experiments. Experimental results in ear biometrics obtained accuracy (97.73% and 97.54%) with EER (1.67% and 2.45%) on both UND-E and UND-J2 datasets, respectively. In our experiments, an encouraging recognition performance can be achieved when the ear modality is combined with profile face using feature-level fusion and score-level fusion than each single modality. In addition, it is also observed that the proposed method using score-level fusion provides significantly higher accuracy (99.98% and 99.97%) with EER (0.01% and 0.04%) than feature-level fusion accuracy (98.47% and 98.24%) with (1.59% and 1.75%) on UND-E and UND-J2 datasets, respectively. Furthermore, out of three different combination of feature extractors, the histogram descriptors SPT-LPQ and SPT-BSIF are offering better performance results that STP-LDP, and the SPT-BSIF feature descriptor-based proposed method outperforms all other feature descriptors. ROC curves of the proposed recognition methods on UND-E and UND-J2 datasets are shown in Fig. 5A and B, respectively.

5.4 Comparison with state-of-the-art methods

Table 2 provides a detailed comparison of the proposed methods with the existing techniques, which have been implemented on UND-E and UND-J2 datasets. Reasons behind the selection of these two datasets are (i) both have a number of side face images of many persons compared to USTB. (ii) Due to multiple subjects, thorough evaluation of the proposed method is possible. (iii) UND-E images with a large illumination variation and UND-J2 images with poor resolution are challenging to recognize the individuals. The experimental results indicate the recognition accuracy based on score-level fusion obtained higher than feature-level fusion of ear and profile face biometrics. In all experiments, we have used two gallery (training) images and one probe (testing) image. In practice, it has shown that more gallery images per subject improve the recognition accuracy. Based on recognition accuracy in Table 2, it is proved that the proposed method is performing significantly better than the mentioned existing methods.

5.5 Discussion

The main objective of our work is to fuse ear and profile face modalities for improved recognition performance. The rationale behind this are as follows: (1) many multimodal approaches using ear modality have been studied while ear and profile face-based multimodal biometrics is understudied. (2) Ear

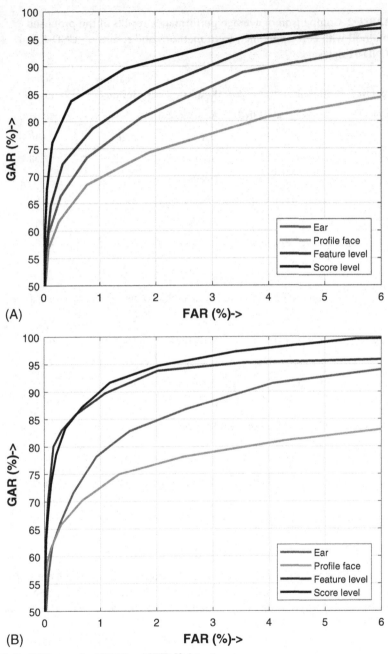

FIG. 5   ROC curve for UND-E and UND-J2 datasets.

TABLE 2 Comparison of average performance results of the proposed method with corresponding recent methods and results on UND-E and UND-J2 datasets.

Dataset	Author	Results	Feature fusion	Score fusion
UND-J2	Rathore et al. [13]	Accuracy (%)	97.54	98.02
		EER (%)	4.28	2.83
	Youssef et al. [32]	Accuracy (%)	–	97.98
		EER (%)	–	–
	Sarangi et al. [33]	Accuracy (%)	97.73	99.53
		EER (%)	2.27	0.46
	Sarangi and Panda [16]	Accuracy (%)	98.26	–
		EER (%)	1.73	–
	Proposed method	Accuracy (%)	**98.47**	**99.98**
		EER (%)	**1.59**	**0.01**
UND-J2	Rathore et al. [13]	Accuracy (%)	95.71	96.02
		EER (%)	5.09	4.39
	Sarangi et al. [33]	Accuracy (%)	97.06	99.58
		EER (%)	2.93	0.42
	Sarangi and Panda [16]	Accuracy (%)	97.95	–
		EER (%)	2.04	–
	Proposed method	Accuracy (%)	**98.24**	**99.95**
		EER (%)	**1.75**	**0.046**

Bold values indicate the best performance.

and profile face modalities have compatible feature vectors, which are suitable for feature-level and score-level fusion. (3) Biometric modalities are captured simultaneously by using single sensor that reduces sensor cost and enrollment time.

6 Conclusion

In this chapter, we presented an improved multimodal ear and profile face biometrics for identity recognition using SPT and local texture descriptors.

Comparison of effectiveness of three local descriptors, LDP, LPQ, and BSIF, are performed. Finally, feature vectors of ear and profile face are integrated using two separate fusion techniques: feature-level and score-level fusion. Experimental results demonstrated that the proposed multimodal recognition method achieved better performance than the individual ear and profile face biometrics in an uncontrolled environment. The proposed method with BSIF feature descriptor obtained promising recognition accuracy compared to state-of-the-art multimodal biometrics. In future, a more efficient multimodal biometric system could be designed by exploring various nonhandcrafted features along with other effective fusion schemes.

References

[1] D.D. Zhang, Introduction to biometrics, in: Automated Biometrics, Springer, 2000, pp. 1–21.

[2] J. Wayman, A. Jain, D. Maltoni, D. Maio, An Introduction to Biometric Authentication Systems, Springer, 2005.

[3] R.S. Reillo, Biometric recognition: an overview, Mathware Soft Comput. 18 (1) (2011) 44–50.

[4] A.K. Jain, A. Kumar, Biometric recognition: an overview, in: Second Generation Biometrics: The Ethical, Legal and Social Context, Springer, 2012, pp. 49–79.

[5] A.K. Jain, K. Nandakumar, A. Ross, 50 Years of biometric research: accomplishments, challenges, and opportunities, Pattern Recogn. Lett. 79 (2016) 80–105.

[6] S. Dargan, M. Kumar, A comprehensive survey on the biometric recognition systems based on physiological and behavioral modalities, Expert Syst. Appl. 143 (2020) 113114.

[7] M. Hassaballah, H.A. Alshazly, A.A. Ali, Ear recognition using local binary patterns: a comparative experimental study, Expert Syst. Appl. 118 (2019) 182–200.

[8] M. Hassaballah, H.A. Alshazly, A.A. Ali, Robust local oriented patterns for ear recognition, Multimed. Tools Appl. 79 (41) (2020) 31183–31204.

[9] A.M. Kumar, A. Chandralekha, Y. Himaja, S.M. Sai, Local binary pattern based multimodal biometric recognition using ear and FKP with feature level fusion, in: 2019 IEEE International Conference on Intelligent Techniques in Control, Optimization and Signal Processing (INCOS), IEEE, 2019, pp. 1–5.

[10] Ö. Toygar, E. Alqaralleh, A. Afaneh, Symmetric ear and profile face fusion for identical twins and non-twins recognition, Signal Image Video Process. 12 (6) (2018) 1157–1164.

[11] N. Hezil, A. Boukrouche, Multimodal biometric recognition using human ear and palmprint, IET Biom. 6 (5) (2017) 351–359.

[12] Z. Huang, Y. Liu, X. Li, J. Li, An adaptive bimodal recognition framework using sparse coding for face and ear, Pattern Recogn. Lett. 53 (2015) 69–76.

[13] R. Rathore, S. Prakash, P. Gupta, Efficient human recognition system using ear and profile face, in: 6th IEEE International Conference on Biometrics: Theory, Applications and Systems (BTAS), IEEE, 2013, pp. 1–6.

[14] D. Yaman, F.I. Eyiokur, H.K. Ekenel, Multimodal age and gender classification using ear and profile face images, in: Proceedings of the IEEE Conference on Computer Vision and Pattern Recognition Workshops, 2019.

[15] D. Yaman, F.I. Eyiokur, H.K. Ekenel, Multimodal soft biometrics: combining ear and face biometrics for age and gender classification, Multimed. Tools Appl. (2021) 1–19, https://doi.org/10.1007/s11042-021-10630-8. In press.

[16] P.P. Sarangi, M. Panda, Combining human ear and profile face biometrics for identity recognition, in: Security and Privacy: Select Proceedings of ICSP 2020, vol. 744, 2021, p. 13.

[17] A. Pflug, C. Busch, Ear biometrics: a survey of detection, feature extraction and recognition methods, Biometrics IET 1 (2) (2012) 114–129.

[18] A. Abaza, A. Ross, C. Hebert, M.A.F. Harrison, M.S. Nixon, A survey on ear biometrics, ACM Comput. Surv. 45 (2) (2013) 22.

[19] Ž. Emeršič, V. Štruc, P. Peer, Ear recognition: more than a survey, Neurocomputing 255 (2017) 26–39.

[20] Z. Wang, J. Yang, Y. Zhu, Review of ear biometrics, Arch. Comput. Meth. Eng. 28 (1) (2019) 149–180.

[21] B. Victor, K. Bowyer, S. Sarka, An evaluation of face and ear biometrics, in: 16th International Conference on Pattern Recognition (ICPR), vol. 1, IEEE, 2002, pp. 429–432.

[22] K. Chang, K.W. Bowyer, S. Sarkar, B. Victor, Comparison and combination of ear and face images in appearance-based biometrics, IEEE Trans. Pattern Anal. Mach. Intell. 25 (9) (2003) 1160–1165.

[23] A.P. Yazdanpanah, K. Faez, R. Amirfattahi, Multimodal biometric system using face, ear and gait biometrics, in: 10th IEEE International Conference on Information Sciences Signal Processing and Their Applications (ISSPA), IEEE, 2010, pp. 251–254.

[24] P. Gnanasivam, S. Muttan, Ear and fingerprint biometrics for personal identification, in: International Conference on Signal Processing, Communication, Computing and Networking Technologies (ICSCCN), IEEE, 2011, pp. 347–352.

[25] Z. Huang, Y. Liu, C. Li, M. Yang, L. Chen, A robust face and ear based multimodal biometric system using sparse representation, Pattern Recogn. 46 (8) (2013) 2156–2168.

[26] M. Regouid, M. Touahria, M. Benouis, N. Costen, Multimodal biometric system for ECG, ear and iris recognition based on local descriptors, Multimed. Tools Appl. 78 (16) (2019) 22509–22535.

[27] L. Yuan, Z. Mu, Y. Liu, Multimodal recognition using face profile and ear, in: 2006 1st International Symposium on Systems and Control in Aerospace and Astronautics, IEEE, 2006, p. 5 pp.

[28] X. Xu, Z. Mu, Multimodal recognition based on fusion of ear and profile face, in: Fourth International Conference on Image and Graphics (ICIG 2007), IEEE, 2007, pp. 598–603.

[29] X. Xu, Z. Mu, Feature fusion method based on KCCA for ear and profile face based multimodal recognition, in: IEEE International Conference on Automation and Logistics, IEEE, 2007, pp. 620–623.

[30] X.-N. Xu, Z.-C. Mu, L. Yuan, Feature-level fusion method based on KFDA for multimodal recognition fusing ear and profile face, in: International Conference on Wavelet Analysis and Pattern Recognition (ICWAPR), vol. 3, IEEE, 2007, pp. 1306–1310.

[31] X. Pan, Y. Cao, X. Xu, Y. Lu, Y. Zhao, Ear and face based multimodal recognition based on KFDA, in: International Conference on Audio, Language and Image Processing (ICALIP), IEEE, 2008, pp. 965–969.

[32] I.S. Youssef, A.A. Abaza, M.E. Rasmy, A.M. Badawi, Multimodal biometrics system based on face profile and ear, in: Biometric and Surveillance Technology for Human and Activity Identification XI, vol. 9075, International Society for Optics and Photonics, 2014, p. 907506.

[33] P.P. Sarangi, B.S.P. Mishra, S. Dehuri, Multimodal biometric recognition using human ear and profile face, in: 4th International Conference on Recent Advances in Information Technology (RAIT), IEEE, 2018, pp. 1–6.

[34] P.P. Sarangi, M. Panda, B.S.P. Mishra, S. Dehuri, An automated ear localization technique based on modified Hausdorff distance, in: International Conference on Computer Vision and Image Processing, Springer, 2016, pp. 229–240.

[35] P.P. Sarangi, A. Sahu, M. Panda, B.S.P. Mishra, Automatic ear localization using entropy-based Binary Jaya algorithm and weighted Hausdorff distance, Int. J. Swarm Intell. Res. 12 (1) (2021) 50–76.

[36] W.T. Freeman, E.H. Adelson, et al., The design and use of steerable filters, IEEE Trans. Pattern Anal. Mach. Intell. 13 (9) (1991) 891–906.

[37] A. Benzaoui, A. Hadid, A. Boukrouche, Ear biometric recognition using local texture descriptors, J. Electron. Imaging 23 (5) (2014) 053008.

[38] P.P. Sarangi, B.S.P. Mishra, S. Dehuri, Ear recognition using pyramid histogram of orientation gradients, in: 4th IEEE International Conference on Signal Processing and Integrated Networks (SPIN), IEEE, 2017, pp. 590–595.

[39] P.P. Sarangi, B.S.P. Mishra, S. Dehuri, Pyramid histogram of oriented gradients based human ear identification, Int. J. Control Theory Appl. 10 (15) (2017) 125–133.

[40] I. Omara, M. Emam, M. Hammad, W. Zuo, Ear verification based on a novel local feature extraction, in: International Conference on Biometrics Engineering and Application, ACM, 2017, pp. 28–32.

[41] I. Omara, X. Li, G. Xiao, K. Adil, W. Zuo, Discriminative local feature fusion for ear recognition problem, in: International Conference on Bioscience, Biochemistry and Bioinformatics, ACM, 2018, pp. 139–145.

[42] Z. Youbi, L. Boubchir, A. Boukrouche, Human ear recognition based on local multi-scale LBP features with city-block distance, Multimed. Tools Appl. 78 (11) (2018) 14425–14441.

[43] P.P. Sarangi, B.S.P. Mishra, S. Dehuri, Fusion of PHOG and LDP local descriptors for kernel-based ear biometric recognition, Multimed. Tools Appl. 78 (2018) 9595–9623.

[44] V. Ojansivu, J. Heikkilä, Blur insensitive texture classification using local phase quantization, in: International Conference on Image and Signal Processing, Springer, 2008, pp. 236–243.

[45] A. Pflug, P.N. Paul, C. Busch, A comparative study on texture and surface descriptors for ear biometrics, in: International Carnahan Conference on Security Technology (ICCST), IEEE, 2014, pp. 1–6.

[46] R.M. Bolle, S. Pankanti, N.K. Ratha, Evaluation techniques for biometrics-based authentication systems (FRR), in: 15th International Conference on Pattern Recognition, vol. 2, IEEE, 2000, pp. 831–837.

[47] P. Yan, K.W. Bowyer, Biometric recognition using 3D ear shape, IEEE Trans. Pattern Anal. Mach. Intell. 29 (8) (2007) 1297–1308.

Chapter 4

Statistical measures for Palmprint image enhancement

Gaurav Yadav[a], Dilip Kumar Yadav[a], and P.V.S.S.R. Chandra Mouli[b]
[a]*Department of Computer Applications, National Institute of Technology, Jamshedpur, India,*
[b]*Department of Computer Science, Central University of Tamil Nadu, Thiruvarur, India*

1 Introduction

In essence, visual improvement of an image increases the analysis and interpretability of images for users. In digital image processing, it plays an integral role. In everyday life, precise recognition and authentication of artifacts are always required, with high accuracy, and here, image enhancement becomes significant. The image enhancement aims to change an image's characteristics so that it can fulfill desire specific purpose for a particular observer [1]. The enhancement of images can be broadly divided into the following two categories: first, spatial domain-based and second, frequency domain-based techniques. Although the orthogonal transformation of an image is exploited instead of the image itself during the frequency domain process [2]. In the last few decades, we have witnessed new technologies such as recorded images, scanned fingerprints, bar code schemes, and authentication ID, for a long period with different biometric techniques. Biometrics is also one of the imaging technologies for images. For user identification, biometrics refers to systems that quantify and interpret attributes of human body. The scheme for biometric-based authentication depends on the following two modes: registration and identification. The biometric image data are collected from the sensor in the enrolment mode and kept in a database together with the identity of the individual for identification. Biometric-based data are obtained from the sensor in the identification mode to do comparison with stored data to ascertain the identity of the user. Uniqueness and permanence are the foundation of biometric identification. The distinctiveness suggests that there are none feature resemblance between the two distinct data from biometrics. For starters, even though they are twins, but they have different fingerprint feature. And it is called permanence because the properties of biometrics do not vary

Machine Learning for Biometrics. https://doi.org/10.1016/B978-0-323-85209-8.00010-9

65

with course of life or aging. Biometrics may have features of physiology or behavior. The physiological features of the physical portion of the body are as follows: iris, palmprint, fingerprint, face, retina, DNA, and hand geometry. Behavioral features depend on the action performed using an entity, such as keystroke-based scan, voice recognition, and signature scans.

Palm is used to tell the fortune of the person around three thousand years ago, but [3] the palmprints are used as a personal identification in 1998, and this became primary kind of physical biometrics. Geometry-based principle lines (head, life, and heart), delta point, minutiae, and wrinkles [4–6] are the features of palmprint which are discovered by Wei and David [3]. No two palms are the same for humans. Palmprint enhancement is a preprocessing step of palmprint authentication and recognition [7]. The efficiency and precision of the device can be improved by incorporating effective palmprint enhancement techniques. A little work on palmprint [8] improvement has been finished so far. No consideration is paid to incorporating optimization methods into the palmprint authentication method in order to achieve performance enhancement. By either fusing palmprint features or using separate matching algorithms [9], many of the works are aimed at increasing performance [10]. This study presents a few efficient improvement approaches that have increased performance and accuracy. The palm space is larger in comparison with fingerprint space, so there was additional information in the palm as compared to a fingerprint. Palmprint contains pattern of valleys and ridges similar to fingerprints. But it also contains primary lines and wrinkles. A lower resolution sensor can capture the main lines and wrinkles. Ridges and valleys of the palm are captured through high resolution. The ridges in the palmprint are presented as lines of dark shade, and the valleys between them are represented with lines of white intensity. The minutiae are the points where, like bifurcation and endpoint, the ridges have changed [11, 12]. The region of the palmprint is greater than the region of the fingerprint, and the number of minutiae in the palmprint is approximately 10 times that of the minutiae in the fingerprint [13–16]. It is possible to capture the palm from normal scanners. The human palm applies to the interior region between the wrist and the fingertips. Compared to fingerprints, the palmprint area is much larger. Palmprint consists of more features [17–21] than a fingerprint. The palmprint is very similar in valleys and ridges to the fingerprint. But the palm also has wrinkles and main lines that become observable with a lower resolution scanner. For reference, the readers are advised to check Figs. 1, 2 and 4 in [22].

Termination—The place in which a ridge ends.

Bifurcation—The position of a mountain where it is broken into two different ridges.

Binarization—Converting a grayscale image to a binary image.

Thinning—The method to grow each ridge's width by a single pixel.

Termination Angle—Angle that exists between the ridge's horizontal angle and its path.

Bifurcation Angle—Angle formed in-between the direction and horizontal of bifurcations terminating in valley.

Matching Score—It is determined between given input and prototype data are determined.

False Nonmatching ratio—The possibility is that the device would refuse entry to an authenticated person.

There is frequent need to correctly identify and verify individuals in everyday life; obviously, high precision during identification is required [23,24]. In literature, the work on hyperspectral palmprint recognition is very minimal. Hyperspectral imaging provides new possibilities for identification of palmprint, hyperspectral images are rich in details, and many difficult tasks are presented by processing the hyperspectral data. Because of its high dimensionality, hyperspectral imaging can be useful for increasing precision. Different image enhancement techniques discussed in this chapter are based on spatial domain enhancement, frequency domain enhancement, and image reconstruction techniques. First, spatial domain enhancement techniques discussed are power law transformation, negative image, and log transform. Second, frequency domain-based enhancement methods such as Gaussian low-pass filter (GLPF), Butterworth low-pass filter (BLPF), Butterworth high-pass filter (BHPF), and Gaussian high-pass filter (GHPF). The third is the image reconstruction-based methods namely 2D order statistics, modified image adaptive filter (MIAF), median filter (MF), decorrelation stretch (DS), and "contrast limited adaptive histogram equalization" (CLAHE). This chapter's organization is mentioned as follows: Section 2 illustrates the description of a number of biometric palmprint image enhancement–based techniques; in next Section 3, discussion and reviews based on the image quality measures are presented; in Section 4, discussion and analysis is presented; and Section 5 contains the conclusion of the chapter.

2 Palmprint image enhancement

In digital image processing [22], palmprint image enhancement plays a significant role [25–27]. As any image is taken by a computer, lighting, temperature, sensor limitations, and various lighting conditions can influence the clarity of the image. This may add to the lack of image data or low quality. Image enhancement's primary goal is to get extra erudition about an object concealed in an image and illuminate the valuable information. Low-quality images are transferred in this process, and high-quality images are used for particular device output. A significant parameter for picture perception is the spatial variance of a scene. This is likely to highlight such features to get improved interpretability by modifying the spatial-based scattering of the radiance values belonging to an image. For images which are distorted and involve noise, enhancement is ultimately necessary. Spatial filtering approaches are therefore commonly used to improve images by reducing noise [1]. Spatial filtering [28] amends the values of individual pixel on the basis of neighboring pixel values. This also reduces noise of the signal.

The reasons for performing image enhancement are mainly for highlighting interesting features in the images, eliminating existing noise [24] and rendering images for more visual appealing [29–32]. Therefore, finding the right image enhancement technique for hyperspectral palmprint images [33] is based on image quality measurement. The Gaussian smoothing for the initial palmprint image was given by Kin et al. [17] and then converted into binary image. A boundary detection algorithm was used to locate the boundaries; then, the tangent between the two finger differences was calculated to get the Y-axis; and a subimage of a fixed scale dependent on the coordinate system was eventually collected. However, the field of fingers was clipped in Ref. [18] to bring down the time taken for tangent computation and increase the region of interest to expand the gray level to 256 for making the lines for feature extraction. After translating the image into binary images [34], they are applied to obtain palmprint scanner images, using the boundary locating algorithm, and then found respective five finger tips and four finger roots. By using the ROI and wavelet-based segmentation, coordinate is established from the points of ring finger. Chuang et al. [19] studied and implemented the opening morphology-based operation to eliminate the noise existing in the palmprint's binary conversion. The next step is to segment the palmprint region from the image. The lower and upper bound must be lesser than the pixels of white intensity. The left and right bound must be lesser than the pixels of white intensity. To detect the boundary, Sobel edge detection is used. Three points between fingers can be located by double derivation of the palm boundary. By joining the two points as mentioned in the lower curve and upper curve, a line forms and this line is used to coordinate the palmprint biometric image differential. Multiple works on the palmprint feature authentication and recognition are also studied in [13,23,35–39].

An extreme enhancement of contrast can be obtained by the traditional histogram equalization (HE) method. This provides an artificial look to the processed image and causes visual artifacts [7, 40]. Better contrast enhancement is offered by the Local Contrast Palmprint Enhancement (LCPE) solution suggested in this work. The input image histogram is split into two depending on the mean value by bi-histogram equalization with threshold (BHEWT). It is achieved so that the overall light remains constant. Then, after thresholding, the sub-histograms are equalized. This phase increases the contrast and retains the brightness as well. The RHE algorithm recursively breaks down histogram of an input image into two or more respective sub-histograms which depends on its mean. It adjusts the sub-histograms through a weighting-based mechanism on the basis of normalized power law function and then separately equalizes the weighted sub-histograms. This approach maintains the mean brightness of a given image, increases the contrast, and creates more images that appear more realistic than the other methods of equalization of the histogram.

Using the genetic algorithm (GA) and HE process, Entropy Optimized Palmprint Enhancement (EOPE) uses the genetic algorithm to refine the enhancement algorithm parameters to achieve maximal entropy value. In the input image, curvelet transform–based enhancement reduces noise. Therefore, the presence of noise in the input image would not affect the palm's characteristics. This makes the average performance of the automated systems higher [3, 41, 42]. Using curvelet and recursive histogram equalization (RHE), advanced palmprint recognition overcomes the limitations of existing systems and makes palmprint recognition easier and more precise. The palmprint recognition method utilizes the palmprint characteristics of symbolic aggregate approximation. The curvelet transform is used in the input image to eliminate noise, while RHE is used to enhance image contrast. When both curvelet and RHE approaches are used for palmprint enhancement, the identification rate is optimal. Recognition of palmprint using multiple palmprint features with enhanced palmprint image integrates the technique of image enhancement in the system's preprocessing stage to improve throughput. As an enhancement tool, it uses curvelet and RHE.

Traits of the images in palmprint:

It includes ridge patterns and valleys. Features include main lines, wrinkles, and points of datum. It is easy to obtain through a low-resolution scanner.

Some concerns such as noisy data, universality, differences in class, and attacks (spoof) can be studied. In contrast to the digit, the palm area is much wider. More distinctive, it is. The Separate image enhancement technique is not required for offline palmprinting images.

2.1   Spatial domain-based enhancement

The method of direct processing of an image's pixels for enhancement is termed as spatial domain-based enhancement. The spatial domain-based enhancement is achieved by manipulating directly the pixels of an image.

$$g(m, n) = T[F(m, n)] \tag{1}$$

Spatial domain image enhancement techniques are as follows:

2.1.1   Power law transform

In power law transformation [43], small range of low intensity pixel values are mapped to higher range and vice versa. Two types of power law transformation are nth power and nth root transformation.

$$s = c^\gamma \tag{2}$$

where c is positive constants, s is the output respectively, and γ is positive constant.

2.1.2 Negative image

The negative image [44] method is useful when white or gray detail needs to be enhanced in dark regions of an input image. A normal image refers to a positive image whereas a negative image is its inverse, in which dark areas appear light and vice versa. Color-reversed is also referred as negative color image. As green color appears as magenta, red color appears as cyan and blue appear as yellow, and vice versa. Every value present in the input biometric image is reduced. The resultant values are then mapped onto the output image.

$$s = L - 1 \tag{3}$$

2.1.3 Log transform

To map a limited range of low input gray level values to a broader range values, logarithmic or log transform is employed [45]. Logarithmic transform is helpful in showing the frequency-based contents of the input image. It takes a small span of low gray level intensity values of the image and maps to a broader range of output values. To enlarge the values of low intensity pixels of image during compression, transformation is applied to higher-level values. The logarithmic transfer function possesses an important attribute that it compresses the dynamic range with large change of intensity values [46]. The opposite transformation can be performed by the inverse logarithmic transformation. Log transforms find their applicability in bringing out the details from an image.

$$s = c \log(r + 1) \tag{4}$$

where c is constant; s is output image; and r is pixel values, respectively. So 1 is applied to each of the input image's pixels. Since, if input image has a pixel strength of 0, then log (0) = infinity. Low contrast histogram components are obtained for negative and log transforms. The image quality appears to be poor because the component of the histogram is oriented toward the middle of the gray scale. The transformation of power law gives a dark image.

2.2 Frequency domain-based enhancement

The manipulation based on an image's orthogonal transform is termed as frequency domain techniques [47, 48], and image enhancement in this technique is simple. First, we calculate the Fourier transform of the image to be enhanced. Then, the outcome obtained is multiplied by a filter. Then, taking inverse transform produces enhanced image. Blurring or sharpening of image is done by dropping or enhancing its high-frequency components. This is intuitively simple to recognize. In the spatial domain, it is much efficient to implement these convolutions by small spatial filters, and this is also suitable computationally. The frequency domain concepts are important. Frequency domain enhancement techniques are important as they are not as limited as the spatial domain.

So, there is no direct manipulation in the image. The basic model for this is as follows:

$$G(m, n) = H(m, n)\,F(m, n) \tag{5}$$

Four types of frequency domain image enhancement approaches are known as follows.

2.2.1   Gaussian low-pass filter (GLPF)

The common use of Gaussian low-pass filter is to eliminate noise and smooth images. In Gaussian low-pass filter, the frequency coefficients are not cut abruptly, but smoother cutoff process is used instead [49]. The below given equation represents the transfer function of GLPF. It is defined as:

$$H(m, n) = e^{-D^2(m,\,n)/2D_0^2} \tag{6}$$

2.2.2   Gaussian high-pass filter (GHPF)

The below given equation represents the transfer function of GHPF. It is defined as:

$$H(m, n) = 1 - e^{-D^2(m,\,n)/2D_0^2} \tag{7}$$

2.2.3   Butterworth low-pass filter (BLPF)

BLPF is implemented for image smoothing in the frequency domain. It removes high-frequency noise from a digital image and preserves low-frequency components. Butterworth filter is a type of filter whose frequency response is flat over the pass band region. The transfer function of BLPF is given in Eq. (8). It is defined as:

$$H(m, n) = \frac{1}{1 + [D(m, n)/D_0]^{2r}} \tag{8}$$

where r represents the order and D_0 is the distance from the origin with cutoff frequency.

2.2.4   Butterworth high-pass filter (BHPF)

To sharpen the image in the frequency domain, BHPF is used. Enhancing the fine details and highlighting of the edges in a digital image are done using the sharpening technique. This method preserves the high-frequency components and removes the low-frequency components of an input image. The BLPF is the reverse operation of the BHPF. The transfer function of BHPF is given in Eq. (9). It is defined as:

$$H(m, n) = \frac{1}{1 + [D_0/D(m, n)]^{2r}} \tag{9}$$

2.3 Image restoration

It deals with changing an image's appearance by reducing noise and gaining lost resolution that helps to better visualize an image using distinct image correction methods [50]. These methods can be carried out in both frequency domain and spatial domain. Deconvolution is the simplest and common method for image restoration. This is carried out in the frequency domain, and after calculation of Fourier transform point spread function (PSF) of both images, the blurring factors cause reverse of resolution loss. This deconvolution produces faulty deblurred image. Its direct inversion of the PSF which contains poor matrix condition number increases the noise. Hence, more sophisticated techniques, like regularized deblurring, that offer robust recovery under different types of noises and blurring functions have been developed. It mainly deals with the quality improvement of an image.

2.3.1 Median filter (MF)

The MF is known as a nonlinear digital filtering method. MF is implemented to remove noise from an input image or signal. In MF, a particular pixel is replaced by the median value of its neighborhood pixels [51]. The MF's noise reduction ability from the images is excellent. It retains the edges and removes the noise after filtering.

2.3.2 Contrast limited adaptive histogram equalization (CLAHE)

CLAHE is the generalization of adaptive histogram equalization [40]. CLAHE is used to avoid the issues of noise. The hidden features of the image become more visible by using this method. This is done by limiting the amplification.

2.3.3 Decorrelation stretch (DS)

DS has a pixel-wise and linear functioning. Also, the specific factors of pixel-wise process depend on the corresponding values of the real and the objective image data. Vector a belongs to A. a represents the given pixel value in every band of A. Here, A is an input image. Then, it is transformed into the pixel b, where b corresponds to the value in output image B.

$$b = T^*(a - m) + m\_target \tag{10}$$

2.3.4 2D adaptive filter

The adaptive filter [52] implements spatial process to identify the pixels affected by impulse noise. Generally, adaptive filters are used to restore image pixels by removing noise without suggestively blurring the existing structures in the image. By contrasting every pixels present in the image and its surrounding neighbor pixels, the adaptive filter characterizes those pixels as noise. The neighborhood size is adaptable. Very dissimilar pixels from the majority among its neighbors are labeled as impulse noise, as it is not adjusted to those pixels in the comparable image. The middle pixel estimation of the pixels is replaced with the noise pixels within the neighborhood which qualifies the test for noise labeling. Grounded on the statistical estimation from a local region of every pixel is done in adaptive Wiener method. The objective is to obtain an estimate $\hat{f}$. $\hat{f}$ is obtained based on the uncorrupted image f. The MSE that exists between f and $\hat{f}$ is minimized. Also, this error measure is represented by

$$e2 = E\{(f - \hat{f})2\} \tag{11}$$

2.3.5   2D order statistic filter

An order statistic filter (OSF) estimates the mean value of the data which uses a linear combination of order statistics. For a long time, statisticians have recognized order statistic filters as estimators, but were renamed and applied in the analysis of image processing problems by Bovik et al. [53]. For large domain matrices containing no zero-valued elements, 2D order statistic filters are used. Order statistic filters are basically nonlinear spatial filters. Pixel rankings which exist in the image are the basis of their response. The central pixel value is replaced with the value obtained using the ranking-based result.

2.3.6   Adjusted image

Image adjustment maps the image intensity values. Brightness adjustment is considered basic image processing operation. Desired changes are added in brightness to each of color components. Mapped values are such that 1% of the value is saturated at high and low input image intensities. The contrast of the output image is increased through this process.

3   Statistical measure

For most image processing applications, image feature calculation is important, a feature of an image that tests the perceived deterioration of the image relative to an ideal or perfect image. The assessment of the content of enhanced images and statistical quality measures are required. Either qualitative or quantitative may be the indicators. Due to the limitations of human vision, qualitative tests are normally used to increase the interpretability of the images visually.

In statistical modeling, however, objective measures are more desirable. Many image quality measures were developed to illustrate the necessity for quality assessment of the images that are enhanced. The quality of the picture is measured by subjective quality measures using histograms based on the human observations. The measurement using quantitative quality measures depends on the mathematical criteria. The quantitative assessment of image quality is much more preferable because of subjective content assessment. However, it is more time consuming, cumbersome, costly, and also differs from one person to the other.

The quality of multiple image enhancing techniques is assessed by implementation of the "Image Quality Measures." Image quality assessments are of two types: objective image quality measurement and subjective image quality measurement. The quality of the image is measured in subjective quality measurement using the histogram depends on human observance. The quality (objective) parameters are based on statistical quality measures. The subjective content calculation is a time-consuming procedure, cumbersome and costly, sluggish for practical usages, and differs from individual to individual. So it becomes necessary to use objective measurement of image quality. Seven kinds of quality relevant metrics are used to calculate objective image quality [2, 45, 51, 54] as given in Table 1.

In this work, we discussed good measures for palmprint image quality assessment using the spatial and frequency domain enhancement techniques with the least errors. This makes it more appropriate for a specified task. Multiple quantitative image quality metrics [4,55–57] (Table 2) such as Contrast Measure (CM), Mean Absolute Deviation (MAD), Entropy, Peak Signal-to-Noise Ratio (PSNR), Correlation Coefficient (CC), Normalized Least Square Error (NLSE), Mean Absolute Percentage Error (MAPE) and Standard Deviation (SD) respectively were used to test the image quality.

TABLE 1 Different set of parameter of image quality.

Sl. no.	Image quality measure	Quality of image
1	Mean Square Error (MSE)	Lower values represents Lower Quality
2	Peak Signal-to-Noise Ratio (PSNR)	Higher values represents Higher Quality
3	Average Difference (AD)	Higher values represents Lower Quality
4	Normalized Cross Correlation (NCC)	Score value in the range of one represents Higher Quality
5	Structural Content (SC)	Lower values represents Higher Quality
6	Normalized Absolute Error (NAE)	Large values represents Lower Quality
7	Maximum Difference (MD)	Higher values represents Higher Quality

TABLE 2 Statistical measure for image quality.

Sl. no.	Quality measure	Mathematical equation	Explanation/optimum value
1.	Contrast Measure	$CM = \frac{1}{N}\sum_{j=1}^{N}\frac{Var_j(processed)}{Var_j(original)}$	Where Var_j represents the variance of the intensity values of a patch size of 16×16. $Var_j(original)$ is variance computed on the original image, and $Var_j(processed)$ represents the variance computed on processed images. N represents the number of patches.
2	Peak Signal-to-Noise Ratio (PSNR)	$PSNR = 20\log_{10}\left(\frac{L^2}{\frac{1}{MN}\sum_{i=1}^{m}\sum_{j=1}^{n}(I_m(i,j) - I_g(i,j))^2}\right)$ Where L represents the number of gray levels present in the image.	PSNR is used for quantitative relationship between a signal's maximum power and the noise interrupting power that influences the reliability of its representation. The optimum values for PSNR corresponds to higher refer better.
3	Mean Absolute Deviation (MAD)	$MAD = \frac{\sum_{i=1}^{n}|A_i - F_i|}{n}$ Where A_i and F_i represent the values of pixel from the original image and the enhanced image, and n represents total observation.	MAD is evaluated to measure the standard error present in the enhanced version of the image. The optimal value corresponds to lower the value refers to better quality.
4	Correlation Coefficient (CC)	$C_c = \frac{\sum_{i=1}^{n}(x_i - \bar{x})(y_i - \bar{y})}{\sqrt{\sum_{i=1}^{n}(x_i - \bar{x})^2}\sqrt{\sum_{i=1}^{n}(y_i - \bar{y})^2}}$ Where x_i, y_i represents the homologous pixel's gray values.	Correlation coefficient is evaluated to measure the relationship between enhanced and original images, respectively. $C_c = 1$, this represents that the corresponding images are absolutely similar and it is the best value. $C_c = 0$, represents that the two images are completely uncorrelated. $C_c = -1$, this represents that the two images are completely anticorrelated.

Continued

TABLE 2 Statistical measure for image quality—cont'd

Sl. no.	Quality measure	Mathematical equation	Explanation/optimum value
5	Entropy	$Entropy = \sum_{i=0}^{255} p_i \log(p_i)$ Notation, p_i, represents the pixels having intensity i in-between the number of different intensity values (256 for 8-bit images).	Extreme value of the entropy that can be obtained for a specified image depends on the total number of existing gray scales.
6	Normalized Least Square Error (NLSE)	$NLSE = \sqrt{\dfrac{\sum_{x=1}^{M}\sum_{y=1}^{N}(f(xy)-r(xy))^2}{\sum_{x=1}^{M}\sum_{y=1}^{N}(r(xy))^2}}$	NLSE is evaluated to indicate the normalized difference between the enhanced version of the image and the original image. The lesser value of NLSE represents that quality is better.
7	Standard Deviation (SD)	$\sigma = \sqrt{\dfrac{1}{N}\sum_{i=1}^{n}(x_i - \overline{x})^2}$ Notation, x_i, represents the vector of data; the mean value is represented by x.	SD is evaluated for representing the contrast in the enhanced version of the image. A good quality images have less value of SD.
8	Mean Absolute Percentage Error (MAPE)	$MAPE = \dfrac{\sum_{t=1}^{n}\left|\dfrac{A_t - F_t}{A_t}\right|}{n} * 100$ n: total observations	A good quality images have smaller value of MAPE.

3.1 Subjective image quality assessment

Subjective image quality assessment is the product of human expert offering their view regarding the nature of the image. But the outcome may differ from person to person. In arbitrary calculations using histogram, the accuracy of the image is determined. Histograms are easy to measure and often lend themselves as economic hardware-based implementations so it can be effectively used for image enhancement purposes. This makes histogram a common method for processing images in real time. The histogram is a schematic representation of the image in the form of graph as gray-level values in the range of 0–255 versus the frequency. Histogram is divided into four essential characteristics of the gray level: light, dark, high contrast [34,58], and low contrast.

For dark images, the components of histogram are centered on the lower side (i.e., nearer to 0 value) of the existing gray scale. In similar manner, the elements of the bright image histogram are skewed against the gray scale's high edge. A wide spectrum of the gray scale is protected by the histogram in the high-contrast image. The pixel distribution is not very far from. Good quality is observed mostly for high-contrast images.

3.2 Objective image quality assessment

For mathematical algorithms, objective calculations are carried out. It is possible to group the objective image measure (IQM) metric into the corresponding three types as (i) full-reference (FR), (ii) reduced-reference, and (iii) no-reference [59]. The FR parameters often provide a function of the original image (called the "reference image") that is considered to be free from distortions. A fractional understanding of the reference image which is also known as "reduced reference" is required. Finally, the parameters do not provide any reference image details. Mean squared error (MSE) is the easiest and most commonly used full-reference output metric. Table 2 shows the PSNR measured between the blurred and reference image. In the case of optimization, they can be easily calculated, have straightforward physical definitions, and are mathematically simple and all these things make them appealing.

4 Discussion and analysis

Several existing methods and statistical measures are discussed for palmprint enhancement. A decent number of palmprint datasets have been proposed in recent years. Table 3 contains some recent contributions in the dataset repositories of palmprint images. 11K Hands, CASIA, Bosphorus, IITD, and GPDS150 hand datasets along with their quantity and side-based information are mentioned in Table 3. Fig. 2 shows the palmprint images from the IITD dataset [60] and palm as well as dorsal images from the 11K Hands dataset, which clearly indicates the difference in the capturing mechanism and

TABLE 3 Different palmprint image databases.

Dataset name	Total images	Hand side	Left-right hand	Size (pixels)
11K Hands [61]	11,076	Palm—dorsal	Both	1600 × 1200
CASIA [62]	5502	Palm	Both	640 × 480
Bosphorus [64,65]	4846	Palm	Both (left)	382 × 525
IITD [60]	2601	Palm	Both	1600 × 1200
GPDS150 hand [66]	1500	Palm	Right	NA

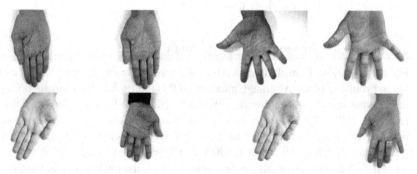

FIG. 1 Sample palmprint images from the 11K Hands dataset proposed by Afifi [56].

environment of both palmprint image databases. Fig. 1 shows a set of palmprint images taken from 11K Hands dataset proposed by Afifi [61]. Palmprint image examples from CASIA [62] Palmprint Database can be referred in [63]. The original palmprint image and the resized palmprint image [63] for processing are shown in Fig. 2. 11K Hands [61] dataset contains 11,076 number of hand images. This includes both palm and dorsal. The dataset contains both left and right hand images of size 1600 × 1200. CASIA contains a total number of 5502 images, only palm dataset. The dataset contains both left and right hand images of size 640 × 480. IITD [60] palmprint dataset contains a total number of 2601 images. This includes only palm dataset. The dataset contains both left and right hand images of size 1600 × 1200. Bosphorus [64,65] palmprint dataset contains a total number of 4846 images. This includes only palm dataset. The dataset contains both left and right hand images of size 382 × 525. GPDS150 hand

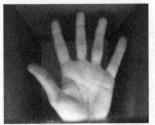

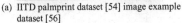

(a) IITD palmprint dataset [54] image example dataset [56]   (b) Image from the 11K Hands

FIG. 2   (A) and (B) represent the original palmprint image and the resized palmprint image. *(From M.M. El-Seddek, M.S. Morsy, F.W. Zaki, Processing and classification of palmprint images, in: 2014 31st National Radio Science Conference (NRSC), IEEE, 2014 Apr 28, pp. 150–156.)*

[66] palmprint dataset contains a total number of 1500 images. This includes only palm dataset. The dataset contains both left and right hand images.

In many cases, the image of hyperspectral palmprints is of high resolution. Table 4 contains the comparison between different palmprint image enhancement techniques, and parameters of image quality are presented based on the observations obtained on PolyU database by Khandizod and Deshmukh [8]. They have implemented 54 spectral bands (520–1050) for experiment, as the appropriate data are present in the spectral band. Therefore, to obtain enhanced image quality of palmprint multiple types of image enhancement techniques can be implemented. Also, the image quality statistical measures are useful to evaluate the quality of the enhanced image. Table 5 shows the summary related to the performance of different enhancement techniques employed in multiple palmprint recognition systems. The enhancement in the performances of different palmprint recognition system can be observed, although it is one of the supporting factors. But the enhancement plays a very fundamental role in preprocessing step of palmprint recognition systems to deliver a better performance in terms of accuracy.

5   Conclusion

The palmprint image contains very large number of features and information associated with it. Various techniques of palmprint image enhancement methods are implemented to improve the quality of the palmprint images are discussed in this chapter. Image quality statistical measures determine the quality of the palmprint image. Image adjustment and decorrelation extend the corresponding histogram portion. It depends on human perception that whether an image is of low contrast or good contrast, because human observation-based enhancement assessment is subjective measurement. Objective quality measurement is done to evaluate the best palmprint image enhancement technique. Different techniques for image enhancement were discussed. To enhance the

TABLE 4 Comparison of some different image enhancement techniques.

Sl. no.	Technique used	MSE	PSNR	NK	AD	SC	MD	NAE
1	Median Filter	14.67723	36.79143	0.998148	0.144341	0.258116	173.9074	0.018386
2	CLAHE	427.1094	21.88987	1.086433	−11.0797	0.83706	48.40741	0.131588
3	Butterworth Low pass	3878.773	12.24386	0.525608	62.24485	3.5422	64	0.486288
4	Butterworth High pass	6813.176	9.810128	0.557271	55.20869	2.219829	126.9074	0.568169
5	Gaussian Low pass	16,528.97	5.948344	1.94471	−127	1.002839	68.92593	0.992187
6	Gaussian High pass	11,539.28	7.521595	1.48391	−66.4453	0.379608	166.4074	0.767809
7	Logarithmic Transformation	651.5633	19.99125	0.804218	24.62499	1.544981	46.44444	0.192383
8	Power law Transformation	16,239.4	6.025113	0.01651	126.16	1883.501	164.7778	0.985625

Based on the observations from A.G. Khandizod, R.R. Deshmukh, Comparative analysis of image enhancement technique for hyperspectral palmprint images, Int. J. Comput. Appl. 121(23) (2015) 30–35.

TABLE 5 Summary of performance of different enhancement techniques implemented and palmprint recognition systems.

Reference	Enhancement technique used	Matching	Implemented database	Results (accuracy)
Xu et al. [67]	Gaussian smoothing, histogram equalization	Euclidean distance	Database with 500 palm * 12 sample	98.13%
Wu et al. [68]	Smoothing	Euclidean distance	PolyU 600 image (100 subject * 6 sample)	98%
Wu et al. [69]	Smoothing	Euclidean distance	The database, 3200 (320*10) image, 384*284	97.92% 97.5%
Li et al. [70]	Smoothing	Hamming distance	PolyU 384*284 pixel, 96 dpi, 386 subject each 20 samples	EER = 0.139
Chen and Moon [71]	Palm coordinate system-based correction	Point-wise matching	PolyU Version-II	EER = 0.6

quality of palmprint image and to assess the image quality, popularly available statistical metrics are presented and discussed in this chapter. It is difficult to rely on subjective analysis since it differs from individual to individual and depends on the basis of their interpretation of the image. This often becomes a time-consuming and biased process.

References

[1] R. Maini, H. Aggarwal, A comprehensive review of image enhancement techniques, J. Comput. 2 (3) (2010) 8–13.

[2] A.G. Khandizod, R. Deshnukh, R. Manza, Wavelet-based image fusion and quality assessment of multispectral palmprint recognition, in: 2nd National Conference on Computer Communication and Information Technology. Sinhgad Institute of Computer Science, Pandharpur, NC2IT, 2013.

[3] N.K. Ratha, K. Karu, S. Chen, A.K. Jain, A real-time matching system for large fingerprint databases, IEEE Trans. Pattern Anal. Mach. Intell. 18 (8) (1996) 799–813.

[4] Y. Chen, A.K. Jain, Beyond minutiae: a fingerprint individuality model with pattern, ridge and pore features, in: International Conference on Biometrics, Springer, Berlin, Heidelberg, 2009 Jun 2, pp. 523–533.

[5] Y. Terai, T. Goto, S. Hirano, M. Sakurai, Color image contrast enhancement by retinex model, in: 2009 IEEE 13th International Symposium on Consumer Electronics, IEEE, 2009 May 25, pp. 392–393.

[6] F. Zhao, X. Tang, Preprocessing and postprocessing for skeleton-based fingerprint minutiae extraction, Pattern Recogn. 40 (4) (2007) 1270–1281.

[7] Z. Guo, D. Zhang, L. Zhang, W. Liu, Feature band selection for online multispectral palmprint recognition, IEEE Trans. Inf. Forensics Secur. 7 (3) (2012) 1094–1099.

[8] A.G. Khandizod, R.R. Deshmukh, Comparative analysis of image enhancement technique for hyperspectral palmprint images, Int. J. Comput. Appl. 121 (23) (2015) 30–35.

[9] A.S. Deshpande, S.M. Patil, R. Lathi, I. HOD, K. BVCOE, A multimodal biometric recognition system based on fusion of palmprint, fingerprint and face, Int. J. Electron. Comput. Sci. Eng. 16 (2015) 1315–1320.

[10] T. Huang, G.J. Yang, G. Tang, A fast two-dimensional median filtering algorithm, IEEE Trans. Acoust. Speech Signal Process. 27 (1) (1979) 13–18.

[11] E.K. Yun, S.B. Cho, Adaptive fingerprint image enhancement with fingerprint image quality analysis, Image Vis. Comput. 24 (1) (2006) 101–110.

[12] F. Chen, X. Huang, J. Zhou, Hierarchical minutiae matching for fingerprint and palmprint identification, IEEE Trans. Image Process. 22 (12) (2013) 4964–4971.

[13] A.K. Jain, S. Prabhakar, L. Hong, A multichannel approach to fingerprint classification, IEEE Trans. Pattern Anal. Mach. Intell. 21 (4) (1999) 348–359.

[14] J. Ruili, F. Jing, VC5509A based fingerprint identification preprocessing system, in: 2008 9th International Conference on Signal Processing, IEEE, 2008 Oct 26, pp. 2859–2863.

[15] A. Makandar, B. Halalli, Image enhancement techniques using highpass and lowpass filters, Int. J. Comput. Appl. 109 (14) (2015) 12–15.

[16] W. Shu, D. Zhang, Automated personal identification by palmprint, Opt. Eng. 37 (1998) 2359–2362.

[17] J.K. Kin, S.H. Chae, S.J. Lim, S.B. Pan, A study on the performance analysis of hybrid fingerprint matching methods, Int. J. Futur. Gener. Commun. Netw. 1 (1) (2008) 23–28.

[18] K. Zebbiche, F. Khelifi, Region-based watermarking of biometric images: case study in fingerprint images, Int. J. Digit. Multimed. Broadcast. (2008) 1–13.

[19] K.W. Chuang, C.C. Liu, S.W. Zheng, A region-of-interest segmentation algorithm for palmprint images, in: Proceedings of the 29th Workshop on Combinatorial Mathematics and Computation Theory, 2012 Apr, pp. 96–102.

[20] A. Jain, L. Hong, R. Bolle, On-line fingerprint verification, IEEE Trans. Pattern Anal. Mach. Intell. 19 (4) (1997) 302–314.

[21] Y. Fu, Z. Ma, M. Qi, J. Li, X. Li, Y. Lu, A novel user-specific face and palmprint feature level fusion, in: 2008 Second International Symposium on Intelligent Information Technology Application, vol. 3, IEEE, 2008 Dec 20, pp. 296–300.

[22] M.M. Ali, A.T. Gaikwad, Multimodal biometrics enhancement recognition system based on fusion of fingerprint and palmprint: a review, Glob. J. Comp. Sci. Technol. 16 (2016) 13–26.

[23] G.R. Sinha, S. Patil, Biometrics: Concepts and Applications, Wiley, 2013.

[24] P. Amirtharani, R.A. Jothi, V. Palanisamy, Palmprint image denoising and enhancement using spatial domain filter, Int. J. Res. Anal. Rev. 6 (2019) 906–909.

[25] D. Zang, W. Shu, Two novel characteristics in palmprint verification: datum point invariance and line feature matching, Pattern Recogn. 32 (4) (1999) 691–702.

[26] D. Zhang, W.K. Kong, J. You, M. Wong, Online palmprint identification, IEEE Trans. Pattern Anal. Mach. Intell. 25 (9) (2003) 1041–1050.

[27] Z. Guo, D. Zhang, L. Zhang, W. Zuo, Palmprint verification using binary orientation co-occurrence vector, Pattern Recogn. Lett. 30 (13) (2009) 1219–1227.

[28] R.A. Jothi, V. Palanisamy, Performance enhancement of minutiae extraction using frequency and spatial domain filters, Int. J. Pure Appl. Math. 118 (7) (2018) 647–654.

[29] A. Kumar, D. Zhang, Combining fingerprint, palmprint and hand-shape for user authentication, in: 18th International Conference on Pattern Recognition (ICPR'06), vol. 4, IEEE, 2006 Aug 20, pp. 549–552.

[30] P.P. Sarangi, B.S. Mishra, B. Majhi, S. Dehuri, Gray-level image enhancement using differential evolution optimization algorithm, in: 2014 International Conference on Signal Processing and Integrated Networks (SPIN), IEEE, 2014 Feb 20, pp. 95–100.

[31] Z. Wang, A.C. Bovik, Modern image quality assessment, Synth. Lect. Image Video Multimed. Process. 2 (1) (2006) 1–56.

[32] X.Y. Jing, D. Zhang, A face and palmprint recognition approach based on discriminant DCT feature extraction, IEEE Trans. Syst. Man Cybern. B Cybern. 34 (6) (2004) 2405–2415.

[33] D. Zhang, Z. Guo, G. Lu, L. Zhang, W. Zuo, An online system of multispectral palmprint verification, IEEE Trans. Instrum. Meas. 59 (2) (2009) 480–490.

[34] C.C. Han, H.L. Cheng, C.L. Lin, K.C. Fan, Personal authentication using palm-print features, Pattern Recogn. 36 (2) (2003) 371–381.

[35] A.K. Jain, A.A. Ross, K. Nandakumar, Introduction to Biometrics, Springer Science & Business Media, 2011.

[36] A. Ross, A. Jain, J. Reisman, A hybrid fingerprint matcher, Pattern Recogn. 36 (2003) 1661–1673.

[37] J.Y. Gan, D.P. Zhou, A novel method for palmprint recognition based on wavelet transform, in: 2006 8th International Conference on Signal Processing, vol. 3, IEEE, 2006 Nov 16.

[38] J. You, W. Li, D. Zhang, Hierarchical palmprint identification via multiple feature extraction, Pattern Recogn. 35 (4) (2002) 847–859.

[39] J. You, W.K. Kong, D. Zhang, K.H. Cheung, On hierarchical palmprint coding with multiple features for personal identification in large databases, IEEE Trans. Circuits Syst. Video Technol. 14 (2) (2004) 234–243.

[40] K. Zuiderveld, Contrast limited adaptive histogram equalization, in: Graphics Gems IV, Academic Press Professional, Inc., USA, 1994, pp. 474–485.

[41] S. Saruchi, Adaptive sigmoid function to enhance low contrast images, Int. J. Comput. Appl. 55 (4) (2012) 45–49.

[42] S.S. Somvanshi, P. Kunwar, S. Tomar, M. Singh, Comparative statistical analysis of the quality of image enhancement techniques, Int. J. Image Data Fusion 9 (2) (2018) 131–151.

[43] S. Yelmanov, O. Hranovska, Y. Romanyshyn, Image enhancement technique based on power-law transformation of cumulative distribution function, in: 2019 3rd International Conference on Advanced Information and Communications Technologies (AICT), IEEE, 2019 Jul 2, pp. 120–124.

[44] Z.M. Win, M.M. Sein, Fingerprint recognition system for low quality images, in: SICE Annual Conference 2011, IEEE, 2011 Sep 13, pp. 1133–1137.

[45] A.G. Khandizod, R.R. Deshmukh, Analysis and feature extraction using wavelet-based image fusion for multispectral palmprint recognition, Int. J. Enhanc. Res. Manag. Comput. Appl. 3 (3) (2014) 57–64.

[46] F. Hossain, M.R. Alsharif, Image enhancement based on logarithmic transform coefficient and adaptive histogram equalization, in: 2007 International Conference on Convergence Information Technology (ICCIT 2007), IEEE, 2007 Nov 21, pp. 1439–1444.

[47] H. Ackar, A. Abd Almisreb, M.A. Saleh, A review on image enhancement techniques, Southeast Eur. J. Soft Comput. 8 (1) (2019).

[48] B.N. Chatterji, L. Dash, Image enhancement with emphasis on adaptive enhancement and deenhancement, J. Frankl. Inst. 331 (5) (1994) 479–494.

[49] R.A. Haddad, A.N. Akansu, A class of fast Gaussian binomial filters for speech and image processing, IEEE Trans. Signal Process. 39 (3) (1991) 723–727.

[50] M.R. Banham, A.K. Katsaggelos, Digital image restoration, IEEE Signal Process. Mag. 14 (2) (1997) 24–41.

[51] A.G. Khandizod, R.R. Deshmukh, Multispectral palm print image fusion—a review, Int. J. Eng. Res. Technol. 3 (2) (2014) 2054–2058.

[52] C.F. Westin, H. Knutsson, R. Kikinis, Adaptive image filtering, in: Handbook of Medical Imaging Processing and Analysis, Academic Press, 2000, pp. 3208–3212.

[53] A. Bovik, T.S. Huang, D. Munson, A generalization of median filtering using linear combinations of order statistics, IEEE Trans. Acoust. Speech Signal Process. 31 (6) (1983) 1342–1350.

[54] K. Karu, A.K. Jain, Fingerprint classification, Pattern Recogn. 29 (3) (1996) 389–404.

[55] M. Zahedi, O.R. Ghadi, Combining Gabor filter and FFT for fingerprint enhancement based on a regional adaption method and automatic segmentation, SIViP 9 (2) (2015) 267–275.

[56] G. Yadav, D.K. Yadav, P.V.S.S.R.C. Mouli, Enhancement of region of interest from a single backlit image with multiple features, in: S.K. Singh, P. Roy, B. Raman, P. Nagabhushan (Eds.), Computer Vision and Image Processing. CVIP 2020, Communications in Computer and Information Science, vol. 1377, Springer, Singapore, 2021.

[57] R. Soundrapandiyan, P.V.S.S.R. Chandra Mouli, Perceptual visualization enhancement of infrared images using fuzzy sets, Transactions on Computational Science XXV, Springer, Berlin, Heidelberg, 2015, pp. 3–19.

[58] G.R. Sinha, B.C. Patel, Medical Image Processing, PHI Learning Pvt. Ltd, 2014.

[59] M.M. Ali, V.H. Mahale, P.L. Yannawar, A.T. Gaikwad, A review: palmprint recognition process and techniques, Int. J. Appl. Eng. Res. 13 (10) (2018) 7499–7507.

[60] A. Kumar, Incorporating cohort information for reliable palmprint authentication, in: 2008 Sixth Indian Conference on Computer Vision, Graphics & Image Processing, IEEE, 2008 Dec 16, pp. 583–590.

[61] M. Afifi, 11K Hands: gender recognition and biometric identification using a large dataset of hand images, Multimed. Tools Appl. 78 (15) (2019) 20835–20854.

[62] Z. Sun, T. Tan, Y. Wang, S.Z. Li, Ordinal palmprint represention for personal identification [representation read representation], in: 2005 IEEE Computer Society Conference on Computer Vision and Pattern Recognition (CVPR'05), vol. 1, IEEE, 2005 Jun 20, pp. 279–284.

[63] M.M. El-Seddek, M.S. Morsy, F.W. Zaki, Processing and classification of palmprint images, in: 2014 31st National Radio Science Conference (NRSC), IEEE, 2014 Apr 28, pp. 150–156.

[64] E. Yoruk, E. Konukoglu, B. Sankur, J. Darbon, Shape-based hand recognition, IEEE Trans. Image Process. 15 (7) (2006) 1803–1815.

[65] E. Yörük, H. Dutağaci, B. Sankur, Hand biometrics, Image Vis. Comput. 24 (5) (2006) 483–497.

[66] M.A. Ferrer, A. Morales, C.M. Travieso, J.B. Alonso, Low cost multimodal biometric identification system based on hand geometry, palm and finger print texture, in: 2007 41st Annual IEEE International Carnahan Conference on Security Technology, IEEE, 2007 Oct 8, pp. 52–58.

[67] X. Xu, Z. Guo, Multispectral palmprint recognition using quaternion principal component analysis, in: 2010 International Workshop on Emerging Techniques and Challenges for Hand-Based Biometrics, IEEE, 2010 Aug 22, pp. 1–5.

[68] X.Q. Wu, K.Q. Wang, Palmprint recognition using valley features, in: 2005 International Conference on Machine Learning and Cybernetics, vol. 8, IEEE, 2005 Aug 18, pp. 4881–4885.

[69] X. Wu, K. Wang, D. Zhang, Palmprint recognition using directional line energy feature, in: Proceedings of the 17th International Conference on Pattern Recognition, 2004. ICPR 2004, vol. 4, IEEE, 2004 Aug 26, pp. 475–478.

[70] X. Li, X. Wu, K. Wang, Directional gaussian derivative filter based palmprint authentication, in: 2008 International Conference on Computational Intelligence and Security, vol. 2, IEEE, 2008 Dec 13, pp. 467–471.

[71] J. Chen, Y.S. Moon, Using SIFT Features in palmprint authentication, in: 2008 19th International Conference on Pattern Recognition, IEEE, 2008 Dec 8, pp. 1–4.

Chapter 5

Retina biometrics for personal authentication

R. Manjula Devi[a], P. Keerthika[a], P. Suresh[b], Partha Pratim Sarangi[c], M. Sangeetha[a], C. Sagana[a], and K. Devendran[a]

[a]Department of Computer Science and Engineering, Kongu Engineering College, Erode, Tamil Nadu, India, [b]Department of Information Technology, Kongu Engineering College, Erode, Tamil Nadu, India, [c]School of Computer Engineering, KIIT Deemed to be University, Bhubaneswar, India

1 Introduction

Nowadays, the Internet has become vital and unavoidable in our everyday life all around the world which exposed to more threats and insecurities. Increase in the usage of the Internet along with the computer/mobile integration in our everyday life depends on individual requirements and goals. With the increased integration of computers and Internet into our everyday life, lots and lots of sensitive and personal data have been shared digitally through Internet. At the same time, the need for mounting the security level and authentication system for identifying the person has increased constantly and delivered more interest in many medical and financial fields such as purchasing, confidential private data supervision, electronic payment, obtaining stock, banking, and entering corporate buildings. So, it is necessary to protect sensitive and personal data/system from accessing by unauthorized people.

In order to keep the data safe online from unauthorized people access, a secure authentication system is very essential. The main purpose of the system is to validate the right of the user to access the authentication system as well as to defend against identity fraud and theft. Traditionally, the authentication system for identifying the individual's rights is done using password, out-of-band, knowledge, answering secret questions, etc. However, these conventional methods have undergone many protests due to loss of information, fraudulent, inability to remember or reproduce consistently, etc. In order to overcome from these protests and also biometric identifiers are unique to individuals as well as more reliable in verifying identity, biometric authentication system has been recommended as a solution for the above mentioned traditional system used for authentication.

The word biometrics is derived from two terms: "Bio" and "Metrics." Bio means life and metrics means Measurements. The definition of biometric is the metric used for calibrating the human's characteristics for identifying or authenticating the person in a very unique manner. Based on the characteristics, biometric is broadly classified into physiological characteristics and behavioral characteristics. Physiological characteristic is the characteristic that is derived from the individual's physical characteristics such as ear, iris, face, palmprint, fingerprint, retina, and veins. Behavioral characteristic is the characteristic that is derived from the individual's behavior of the person such as voice, signature, keystroke dynamics, and gaits.

Biometric authentication is the process of authenticating the each and every individual identification based on biometric measures. The categories of biometric are shown in Fig. 1. Biometric authentication furnishes the following characteristics such as high security, uniqueness, convenient, easy to use, spoof-proof, and speed compared to other conventional authentication methods.

Biometric authentication system can also be applied by acquiring the biometric identifiers by screening through the following biometrics: fingerprint

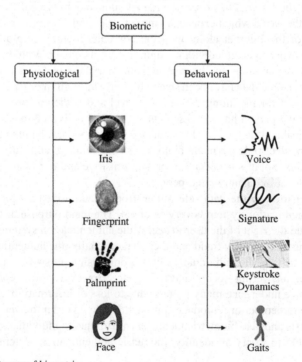

FIG. 1   Category of biometric.

[1], iris [2, 3], ear [2, 4], voice [4–6], face [7], palmprint [8, 9], signature [10, 11], keystroke dynamics [12, 13], and gait analysis [14, 15].

In recent years, many authentication systems based on various biometrics have now been developed, such as iris, finger, palmprint, face, and ear. Among the different biometrics, the retina is one of the biometrics considered in this paper for the individual's authentication since it is unique as well as stable. As it is unforgeable and lies behind the eye, the retina is considered to be very safe and stable source for recognizing the individual. By extracting the network of retina's blood vessels for individual recognition in the authentication method, the pattern matching is achieved. There is no full genetic determination of the network of blood vessels in the retina, because similar pattern does not exist for indistinguishable twins. Even among genetically indistinguishable twins, the characteristics extracted from the retina effectively distinguish individuals, because retinal patterns have highly unique traits. For each person, the blood vessels which are available at the back side the eye have a specific pattern. Using various image processing techniques, the network of blood vessels are segmented, and then, the segmented components are used for recognition of retina images.

2   Framework of authentication system using biometrics

The working process of authentication system using biometrics undergoes two phases: Enrollment Phase and Authentication Phase. In Enrollment Phase depicted in Fig. 2, the acquisition of biometric data from various individuals is preprocessed to extract the features. The template is generated from the extracted features and accumulated the extracted features in the database for authentication purpose for further processing in future.

In Authentication Phase depicted in Fig. 3, the biometric data have been extracted from the individual; the biometric pattern has been extracted from it using image processing technique and correlated the extracted pattern with the pattern stored in the database. If the biometric pattern matches with the template accumulated in the database, then the user is considered to be authenticated user. If the biometric pattern does not match with the template stored in the database, then the user is considered to be unauthenticated user.

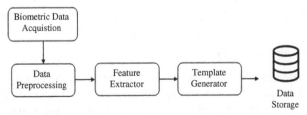

FIG. 2   Enrollment Phase.

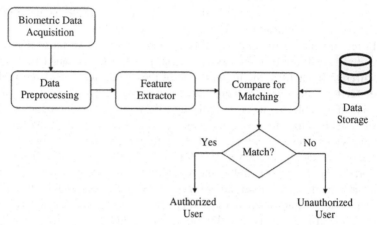

FIG. 3 Authentication Phase.

3 Related work

The standard process of biometric pattern recognition problem involves the following sequence of different stages: acquisition, image quality assessment, preprocessing, region of interest (RoI) determination (templates), and extracting the feature and biometric analogy.

In the literature, the various forms of biometric authentication system can be found that includes fingerprint recognition, eye-retina-iris recognition, ear recognition, odor identification, vein recognition, face recognition, gait recognition, typing recognition, voice-speaker authentication, hand geometry recognition, signature recognition, and so on.

3.1 Face authentication

Face authentication system captures a face's image of a person and extract the facial features from it which will be employed for authentication process. Using fuzzy-based SVM classifier with combined feature descriptors, a face authentication method specifically for an object has been suggested for liveness detection, allowing specific area to be selected from the whole object and extracting features that are extracted from specific object area brings reduction in time used for processing as well as complexity in extracting the feature [7].

3.2 Iris authentication

Iris authentication system captures the iris image from the human eyes using the iris scanner and extracts the unique pattern of the iris based on the edge of the iris, location of the pupil, and its edge. NeuroBiometric is a highly efficient biometric authentication system based on eye blink using an event-based neuromorphic vision sensor. This vision sensor has been introduced based on transient eye blink signals using the constructed biometric features from the eye blinks data such as energy features, speed features, duration features, frequency features, and ratio features. NeuroBiometric has been proved to be robust and secure with a very low false-positive rate [16]. A secure and verifiable classification-based iris authentication system (SvaS) has been developed in performing training and classification using privacy-preserving (PP). In order to execute training and classification using privacy-preserving, private multiclass perceptron (PMCP) and private nearest neighbor (PNN) algorithms are used and applied on the benchmark iris databases which is publicly available such as IITD, SDUMLA-HMT, CASIA-V 1.0, and CASIA-V3-Interval [3].

3.3   Palmprint authentication

Palmprint authentication is done based on the distinctive features such as principal lines, valleys, wrinkles, and ridges on the surface of the palm. The generalized net model of a biometric authentication system has been constructed by combining the palm vein authentication and palm geometry recognition methods based on palm geometry and palm vein matching using intuitionistic fuzzy evaluations [9]. Next, a framework has been developed for secured biometric confirmation enormously using palmprint that utilizes morphological ROI (Region of Interest) extraction and UDBW (Undecimated Biorthogonal Wavelet) transform has been presented for security application [8].

3.4   Fingerprint authentication

Fingerprint recognition systems work by examining a finger pressed against a smooth surface. The finger's ridges and valleys are scanned, and a series of distinct points, where ridges and valleys end or meet, are called minutiae. These minutiae are the points the fingerprint recognition system uses for comparison. In order to identify an individual, the valleys (minutiae) and ridges are used which are found on the surface tips of a human finger.

Due to the rapid advancement in sensor technology, a new biometric authentication system has been developed for handheld electronic devices which is robust. It has been implemented by fusing the movements of finger in 3D with cerebral activities in an intelligent manner to verify the signatures using the next-generation sensor consumer electronic (CE) devices and the classifiers such as Random Forest (RF) and Hidden Markov Model (HMM) [17]. A novel authentication system using biometric based on FPGA has been proposed by utilizing TRSG (True Random and Timestamp Generator) for implementing fast and secure fingerprint authentication with more accuracy [1].

3.5 Ear

The pinna's ear shape and tissue structure are special to every individual. The ear recognition approaches are focused on matching the distance of the pinna's prominent points from a landmark position on the ear. Fusion Based Multimodal Biometric Authentication System has been proposed with the images of fingerprint and ear by preprocessing and enhancing the images using the feature extraction techniques such as Binary Robust Invariant Scalable Keypoints (BRISK) and Speed Up Robust Features (SURF) [16]. In order to authenticate the smart home with the user's smartphone in a convenient manner, an ear biometric authentication system has been proposed [4].

3.6 Voice

Voice is also a physiological feature since each individual has a different pitch, but voice recognition is generally classified as behavioral biometric, largely focused on the study of how a person talks. An authentication system which is application-oriented has been developed using the voice verification of the speaker in two stages such as training stage and recognition stage [18]. Vocal-Print has been proposed which explores a secure and resilient system for voice authentication that captures the vocal vibrations of a user via mmWave biometric interrogation and analyzes it directly for user authentication [6]. In order to provide secure and usable authentication for smart home users which are controlled by voice, a voice-based biometric authentication system has been proposed [5].

3.7 Signature

Signature authentication checks the manner in which a user signs their signature. Other than the characteristics of signature's static shape, other signing characteristics are also considered for verification such as velocity, pressure, and speed. A novel secured authentication technique based on blockchain to enhance the protection of medical data, which is very sensitive, is transferred between hospitals and patients. In order to accomplish the safe transmission of sensitive medical data in cloud server-based environment with medical IoT network, the Lamport Merkle Digital Signature (LMDS) has been used to execute the creation and authentication of signature [10]. Alternative to the standard payment and currency system, an E-cash scheme in an online mode with a cryptosystem for authentication using digital signature has been proposed that tends to supplant the fiat currency that are used traditionally with the usage of Bitcoin [11].

3.8 Keystroke dynamics

Keystroke dynamics is a biometric feature used to verify the identity of person through their typing rhythm, which can also deal with professional typists and the novice two-finger typist. It is hard to mimic personal keystroke operation and can be used for identity authentication. Also, without disrupting the comfort of the user, the study of keystroke dynamics has desperately increased the degree of security in using the computer system, contributing to the selection of skills by classifiers, which significantly enhances user recognition [13]. Using deep learning approach, CNN-Detect which is a classifier has been proposed for user authentication based on the characteristics of keystroke dynamics which is considered for user authentication as a behavioral biometric using traditional PC keyboards on the CMU dataset [12].

3.9 Gaits

The basic way a person walks is gait biometric and is an intricate spatiotemporal biometric. Gait, however, is not meant to be very distinctive, but is favorable for verification in certain low-security applications. The classifier's model using recurrent, feedforward and hybrid neural network architectures is built for users' authentication based on monitoring of walking manner (gait) which perform gait verification using accelerometer and gyroscope data and also to investigate how the period of time, which we monitor users' gait, affects the accuracy of the predictions [14]. In order to verify and recognize the owner by pattern unlocking, Gaussian gray wolf boosting (RGGWB) model has been employed for attaining gait pattern authentication scheme [15].

4 Anatomy of retina

In this chapter, one of the most linguistic and safest modalities such as retina has been suggested for the biometric authentication system since it is very much protected inside the human eye [19]. Moreover, the retinal vascular network that can be extracted from the individual retina is unique in nature and does not change throughout the life of those particular individuals. In addition to that, the features such as high level of recognition, its difficulty to falsify, and its invariability over time are offered by the retina which is more suitable for high security applications. Fig. 4 shows the structure of retina when it is viewed by an ophthalmologist using an ophthalmoscope.

The retina contains the following retinal components such as fovea, macula, optic disc, veins, and artery. At the center of the retina, macula is located. The shape of the macula is oval in shape with pigmented area whose diameter is given as 5.5 mm (0.22 in.). When the macula is damaged, the vision becomes faulty. It is responsible for the central color vision which is high in resolution

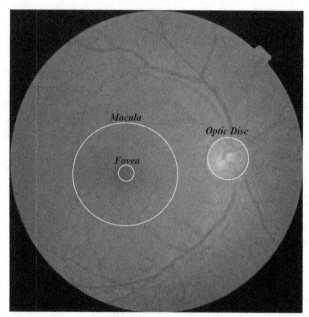

FIG. 4 Structure of retina.

that also feasible in good light. The next important component of retina is fovea which is pinpointed at the middle of the macula area. Fovea is culpable of providing the sharp central vision. The sharp central vision is also referred as foveal vision. This vision is very essential for the human's primary activities such as reading and driving related to eyes. Next, the optic nerve is the nerve that hooks the human eye up to the brain and is made up of never fibers with the count of more than 1 million. It is used to carry the signals that are discharged by light hitting the retina. Glaucoma is the disease caused by high eye pressures which will damage the optic nerve.

In the optic disc, all the central retinal vessels are emerged from its center. It is passed over the rim and radiates out to furnish the retina with light. Through the optic disc, the central artery of the retina is penetrated toward the retina. It supplies all the nerve fibers that form the optic nerve with blood. The central retinal vein is a vein that is passing through the optic nerve. The information is transmitted from the fovea by about half of the nerve fibers which are in the optic nerve, while the other halves of the nerve fibers which are in the optic nerve are transmitted from the rest of the retina. The retinal capture devices have been developed with the aid of scientific and technological advances that contribute significantly to the production of retina biometric authentication systems.

5 ANFIS-based retina biometric authentication system (ARBAS)

ANFIS stands for adaptive network-based fuzzy inference system [20]. It is also called as adaptive neuro-fuzzy inference system. By integrating the advantages of the two techniques of machine learning approach such as artificial neural networks with fuzzy logic based on Takagi-Sugeno's fuzzy inference method, it makes ANFIS to be a universal estimator. It is a technique used for data-driven that uses neural network for solving the problems related to function approximation. Usually, the data-driven approaches are based on clustering the training dataset with the collection of numerical samples belongs to the unspecified class of approximation.

ANFIS is a technique for data learning which is very basic in nature. Fuzzy logic is used by the ANFIS to attain the desired output by transforming the inputs which is given to the network using the processing elements of neural network which are highly interconnected. The weights are allocated to these connections for mapping the numerical inputs to the respective output. ANFIS networks have been successfully applied in the following research area such as pattern recognition, rule-based process control, classification tasks, and problems that are very similar to the abovementioned problems. The parameters of a fuzzy inference system (FIS) are tuned by applying the learning methods of neural network. The overall ARBAS framework undergoes two phases: training phase and testing phase.

5.1 Training phase

A fundus camera is also called as retinal camera. It is equipped with a camera attached with a sophisticated low-power microscope in order to take the photograph of the eye's inner surface. The retinal vasculature, macula, posterior pole (also named as fundus), optic disc, and retina form the interior surface of the eye. Based on the indirect ophthalmoscope, the optical design is done using fundus camera. The viewing angle is the optical acceptance angle of the lens used to describe the fundus cameras.

In fundus camera, a wide angle of view has an angle of view between 45 and 140 degrees, a normal angle of view has an angle of view of 30 degrees, and a narrow angle of view has an angle of view of 20 degrees or less. The normal angle of view is used to create a film image 2.5 times larger than life. The wide angle of view provides proportionately less retinal magnification. Fig. 5A–C shows the different view of retina at different angle of view such as 20, 40, and 60 degrees, respectively.

In training phase depicted in Fig. 6, fundus camera is employed in capturing the image of retinal fundus from a set of human eyes. In image preprocessing, the blood vessels in the retinal image of human eyes are segmented using Mathematical-Morphology-Based Edge Detection. Using Canny edge detection

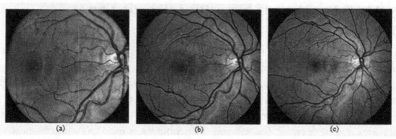

FIG. 5 Different view of retina at different angle.

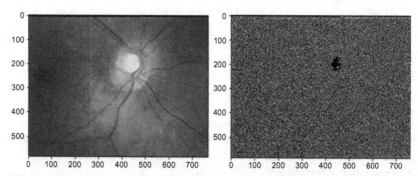

FIG. 6 Fovea extraction using Canny edge detection.

technique, edge of the fovea has been extracted. Once the edge has been extracted, the diameter of the fovea has been measured. Similarly, other features have been extracted and stored as a dataset. (See Fig. 7.)

Then, the segmented image is given as the input to the process of feature extraction technique for extracting the feature from the segmented feature to perform training process.

Once the feature has been extracted, it is converted to dataset for further processing. Once the dataset creation is finished with sufficient retinal images, it is given as an input to ANFIS for training. Once the training is completed, ANFIS trained model is ready for evaluation.

In order to demonstrate the working process of the ANFIS architecture, the network structure is shown in Fig. 8. Based on a first-order Sugeno model, the following two rules, which are fuzzy IF-THEN rules, are defined:

$$\text{Rule}_{(1)}: \textbf{IF}\, x\, \textbf{is}\, A_1\, \textbf{AND}\, y\, \textbf{is}\, B_1, \textbf{THEN}$$

$$f_1 = p_1 x + q_1 y + r_1$$

$$\text{Rule}_{(2)}: \textbf{IF}\, x\, \textbf{is}\, A_2\, \textbf{AND}\, y\, \textbf{is}\, B_2, \textbf{THEN}$$

$$f_2 = p_2 x + q_2 y + r_2$$

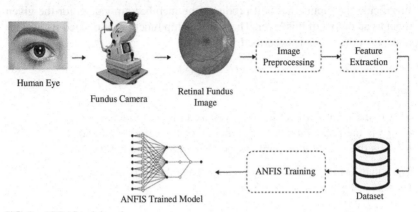

FIG. 7   ARBAS training phase.

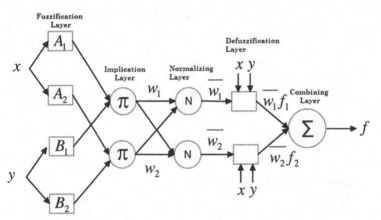

FIG. 8   ANFIS network structure.

where

- x and y are the variables that is given as input,
- f_1 and f_2 are the first-order polynomial that produces the output,
- A and B are the sets of fuzzy available in the antecedents part of IF-THEN rules, and
- p_1, q_1, p_2, and q_2 are the design parameters which is a constant that are determined during the training phase.

The step-by-step procedure involved at each and every individual layers in ANFIS structure is illustrated in detail in the forthcoming steps:

Step 1: Fuzzification Layer:

Each and every node in this layer contains a membership function which is adaptive in nature. Fuzzification Layer is the first layer which is used to fuzzificate the inputs that is it produces the membership values for the given input as an output of this layer. The membership function associated with every node, i, in this layer is described in Eq. (1).

$$O_i^1 = \mu_{A_i}(x) \tag{1}$$

where

- x is the input variable that is given as an input to node i,
- μ_{Ai} is the fuzzy membership function of the variable A_i, and
- A_i is the linguistic variable associated with this node function.

The equation to determine the bell-shaped membership function $\mu_{A_i}(x)$ is formulated as in Eq. (2) or in Eq. (3)

$$\mu_{A_i}(x) = \frac{1}{1 + \left[\left(\frac{x - c_i}{a_i} \right)^2 \right]^{b_i}}, \quad i = 1, 2 \tag{2}$$

or

$$\mu_{A_i}(x) = \exp\left\{ -\left(\frac{x - c_i}{a_i} \right)^2 \right\} \tag{3}$$

where

- x is the variable that is given as an input and
- $\{a_i, b_i, c_i\}$ is the set of parameters of the membership function to be tuned.

Step 2: Implication Layer:
  In this layer, all the nodes are fixed and labeled with the symbol "M" that represents the multipliers. The firing fuzzy strength w_i of each rule is determined by multiplying the incoming signals using the fuzzy AND operators and produce the product value as an output for all nodes using the formula in Eq. (4)

$$O_i^2 = w_i = \mu_{A_i}(x) \times \mu_{B_i}(y), \quad i = 1, 2 \tag{4}$$

Step 3: Normalizing Layer:
  In this layer, all the nodes are fixed and labeled with the symbol "N" that represents the normalization process. For each node, the normalized fuzzy firing strength of a rule is calculated using the formula that node's firing strength of a rule divided by the sum of firing strengths of all the rules. The following Eq. (5) is used to determine the output from that node which is the normalized firing fuzzy strength

$$O_i^3 = \overline{w_i} = \frac{w_i}{w_1 + w_2}, \quad i = 1, 2 \tag{5}$$

Step 4: Defuzzification Layer:

All the nodes are adaptive in this layer. The output, which is weighted consequent value, of this layer is determined using the node function given by Eq. (6)

$$O_i^4 = \overline{w_i}f_i = \overline{w_i}(p_ix + q_iy + r_i), \quad i = 1,2 \tag{6}$$

where

- $\{p_i, q_i, r_i\}$ is the set of parameters of the membership function to be tuned and
- w_i is the output of Layer 3

In this layer, parameters to be tuned are called as consequent parameters.

Step 5: Combining Layer:

There is only one node that is fixed in this layer. The overall output is calculated in this layer by performing the summation over all the signals that are incoming using the Eq. (7)

$$O_i^5 = \sum_i \overline{w_i}f_i = \frac{\sum_i w_if_i}{\sum_i w_i} \tag{7}$$

5.2 Testing phase

In testing phase depicted in Fig. 9, the image of retinal fundus is extracted from a human eye using fundus camera. Then, the blood vessels in the retinal image of human eyes are segmented using Mathematical-Morphology-Based Edge Detection. Then, the features are distilled from the image which is segmented to perform testing. The extracted features are into ANFIS trained model as an input and tell whether the given image is an authenticated user or unauthenticated user.

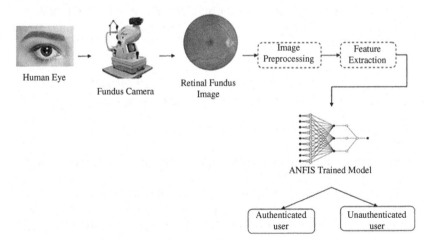

FIG. 9 ARBAS testing phase.

5.3 Performance metrics for authentication system

To measure the performance of biometric authentication system, accuracy is one of the most significant factors considered in the success of that system. Accuracy is a measure that represents how well the system can accurately match the individual's biometric information and avoid wrongly matching different people's biometric information.

To appraise the performance of the authentication system using biometrics and also compute biometric authentication accuracy, the following performance metrics are used:

- **True Acceptance Rate**

  True Acceptance Rate is abbreviated as TAR. It is also called as True Match Rate (TMR). It is a measure of the probability that an authorized user will correctly accept an access attempt by the biometric authentication system. It is represented as the percentage of times an authorized person instance is correctly recognized by the authentication system. For an authentication system to be more successful, this measure has to be maximized and can be calculated as in Eq. (8)

$$TAR = \frac{Number\ of\ authorized\ user\ instance\ that\ is\ correctly\ accepted}{Total\ number\ of\ authorised\ user\ instance} \quad (8)$$

- **True Rejection Rate**

  True Rejection Rate is abbreviated as TRR. It is also termed as True Non-Match Rate (TNMR). It is a measure of the likelihood that an unauthorized user will correctly reject an access attempt by the biometric authentication system. It is represented as the percentage of times an unauthorized user instance is correctly rejected by the authentication system. For an authentication system to be more successful, this measure has to be maximized and can be calculated as in Eq. (9)

$$TRR = \frac{Number\ of\ unauthorized\ user\ instance\ that\ is\ correctly\ rejected}{Total\ number\ of\ unauthorised\ user\ instance}$$

$$(9)$$

- **False Acceptance Rate**

  FAR is the abbreviation for False Acceptance Rate. It is also termed as Fraud Rate or False Match Rate or Type 2 errors. It is a measure of the likelihood that an unauthorized user will incorrectly accept an access attempt by the biometric authentication system. It is represented as the percentage of times an unauthorized user instance is incorrectly accepted by the authentication system. For an authentication system to be more successful, this measure has to be minimized. The formula to compute FAR is shown in Eq. (10)

$$FAR = \frac{Number\ of\ unauthorized\ user\ instance\ that\ is\ incorrectly\ accepted}{Total\ number\ of\ unauthorised\ user\ instance}$$

$$(10)$$

- **False Rejection Rate**
  FRR is the abbreviation for False Rejection Rate. It is also called as Insult Rate or False Non-Match Rate (FNMR) or Type 1 errors. It is a measure of the probability that an authorized user will incorrectly reject an access attempt by the biometric authentication system. It is represented as the percentage of times an authorized user instance is incorrectly rejected by the authentication system. For an authentication system to be more successful, this measure has to be minimized. The formula to compute FRR is shown in Eq. (11)

$$FRR = \frac{Number\ of\ authorized\ user\ instance\ that\ is\ incorrectly\ rejected}{Total\ number\ of\ authorised\ user\ instance}$$

$$(11)$$

- **Equal Error Rate**
  EER is the abbreviation for Equal Error Rate. It represents the overall accuracy of the authentication system using biometrics. The lower the EER value, the higher the accuracy of the authentication system using biometrics. When the EER values are related to the FRR and FAR, they are determined by the point at which the FAR and the FRR are equal in value. It is also called as Crossover Error Rate (CER).

- **How do the FAR and FRR impact on each other?**
  The graph depicted in Fig. 10 shows how the FAR and FRR impact themselves. FRR is inversely proportional to FAR and vice versa. It can be managed by a parameter called confidence threshold (sometimes referred as sensitivity). With the increase in the value of the sensitivity (which is marked on the X axis of the graph plot) of a biometric authentication system, FARs will drop and at the same time FRRs will raise. Conversely, when the value of the sensitivity is decreased, FARs will rise and at the same time FRRs will drop. The CER is the point where FAR line and FRR line intersect with each other in the graph that gives the overall accuracy of the authentication system using biometrics. In order to boost the accuracy of the authentication system using biometrics, the sensitivity can be increased.

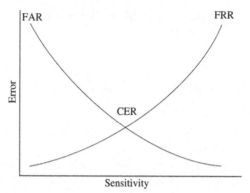

FIG. 10 FAR vs FRR.

5.4 Experimental setup

In order to perform personal authentication using retina biometrics, the VARIA database can be used. It contains set of 233 images of retina which has been collected for the purpose of authentication. These images are collected from 139 different individuals. With the help of a TopCon TRC-NW100 which is nonmydriatic fundus camera, the retinal images have been acquired. The resolution that has been set for the centered optic disc is 768 × 584. The VARIA database folder contains a directory and text file. The directory contains all the acquired retinal images. The text file which is named as index.txt groups the images that are acquired from an individual [21, 22]. The experiments were performed using Python.

Out of 233 retinal images in the VARIA database, 70% of the VARIA database (163 retinal images) has been taken for training and remaining 30% of the VARIA database (70 retinal images) has been taken for testing. Seventy retinal images in the testing dataset have been divided in the following way, and testing has been performed for different combination (Table 1).

From the above result, ARBAS achieves the False Acceptance Rate (FAR) that is 2.86% in an average manner. At the same time, it achieves the False Rejection Rate (FRR) that is 2.82% in an average manner. Also, the overall accuracy obtained by the retinal authentication system is 97.16%.

6 Conclusion

In recent years, many authentication systems based on various biometrics have been developed, such as iris, finger, palmprint, face, and ear. Among the different biometrics, an efficient biometric retina identification using ANFIS-based Retina Biometric Authentication System (ARBAS) for person's authentication has been suggested and proved it on a real-time dataset named as VARIA database with 70% for training and 30% for testing. Based on the output of different

TABLE 1 Experimental result.

Number of authenticated image in testing dataset	Number of nonauthenticated image in testing dataset	TAR%	TRR%	FRR %	FAR %
30	40	100.00	97.50	0.00	2.50
31	39	96.77	97.44	3.23	2.56
32	38	96.88	97.37	3.13	2.63
33	37	96.97	97.30	3.03	2.70
34	36	97.06	97.22	2.94	2.78
35	35	97.14	97.14	2.86	2.86
36	34	97.22	97.06	2.78	2.94
37	33	97.30	96.97	2.70	3.03
38	32	94.74	93.75	5.26	6.25
39	31	97.44	96.77	2.56	3.23
40	30	97.50	100.00	2.50	0.00
	Average	**97.18**	**97.14**	**2.82**	**2.86**

experiments, it is concluded that ARBAS achieves the FRR and the FAR with the percentage of 2.82% and 2.86%, respectively. The overall accuracy obtained by the retinal authentication system is 97.16%.

References

[1] D. Harikrishnan, N. Sunil Kumar, R. Shelbi Joseph, K. Nair, R. Nishanth, A.J. Joseph, FPGA implementation of fast & secure fingerprint authentication using trsg (true random and time-stamp generator), Microprocess. Microsyst. 82 (2021) 103858, https://doi.org/10.1016/j.micpro.2021.103858.

[2] G. Chen, F. Wang, X. Yuan, Z. Li, Z. Liang, A. Knoll, NeuroBiometric: an eye blink based biometric authentication system using an event-based neuromorphic vision sensor, IEEE/CAA J. Autom. Sin. 8 (1) (2021) 206–218, https://doi.org/10.1109/JAS.2020.1003483.

[3] M.K. Morampudi, M.V.N.K. Prasad, M. Verma, U.S.N. Raju, Secure and verifiable iris authentication system using fully homomorphic encryption, Comput. Electr. Eng. 89 (2021) 106924, https://doi.org/10.1016/j.compeleceng.2020.106924.

[4] P.N. Ali Fahmi, E. Kodirov, D.C. Ardiansyah, G. Lee, Hey home, open your door, I'm back! authentication system using ear biometrics for smart home, Int. J. Smart Home 7 (1) (2013) 173–182.

[5] A. Ponticello, Towards Secure and Usable Authentication for Voice-Controlled Smart Home Assistants, Diss. Wien, 2020.

[6] H. Li, et al., VocalPrint, in: Proceedings of the 18th Conference on Embedded Networked Sensor Systems, Nov. 2020, pp. 312–325, https://doi.org/10.1145/3384419.3430779.

[7] K. Mohan, P. Chandrasekhar, K.V. Ramanaiah, Object-specific face authentication system for liveness detection using combined feature descriptors with fuzzy-based SVM classifier, Int. J. Comput. Aided Eng. Technol. 12 (3) (2020) 287–300.

[8] B. Dappuri, V. Srija, B. Dhanne, Palm print biometric authentication system for security applications, IOP Conf. Ser. Mater. Sci. Eng. 981 (2020) 042083, https://doi.org/10.1088/1757-899X/981/4/042083.

[9] Z. Ivanova, V. Bureva, Generalized net model of a biometric authentication system based on palm geometry and palm vein matching using intuitionistic fuzzy evaluations, Notes Intuitionistic Fuzzy Sets 26 (4) (2020) 71–79, https://doi.org/10.7546/nifs.2020.26.4.71-79.

[10] J.A. Alzubi, Blockchain-based Lamport Merkle Digital Signature: authentication tool in IoT healthcare, Comput. Commun. (2021), https://doi.org/10.1016/j.comcom.2021.02.002.

[11] M. Ashiqul Islam, M. Sagar Hossen, M. Hossain, J. Nime, S. Hossain, M. Dutta, An Online E-Cash Scheme With Digital Signature Authentication Cryptosystem, Sustainable Communication Networks and Application, Springer, Singapore, 2021, pp. 29–39.

[12] N. Altwaijry, Keystroke dynamics analysis for user authentication using a deep learning approach, Int. J. Comput. Sci. Secur. 20 (12) (2020) 209–215, https://doi.org/10.22937/IJCSNS.2020.20.12.23.

[13] P. Porwik, R. Doroz, T.E. Wesolowski, Dynamic keystroke pattern analysis and classifiers with competence for user recognition, Appl. Soft Comput. 99 (2021) 106902, https://doi.org/10.1016/j.asoc.2020.106902.

[14] E. Ichtiaroglou, Gait Verification Using Deep Learning Models, Accelerometers and Gyroscope Data, 2020.

[15] G.K. Chaitanya, K. Raja Sekhar, Verification of pattern unlock and gait behavioural authentication through a machine learning approach, Int. J. Intell. Unmanned Syst. (2021), https://doi.org/10.1108/IJIUS-09-2020-0048.

[16] T. Thivakaran, S. Padira, A. Kumar, S. Reddy, Fusion based multimodel biometric authentication system using ear and fingerprint, Int. J. Intell. Eng. Syst. 12 (1) (2019) 62–73, https://doi.org/10.22266/ijies2019.0228.07.

[17] S.K. Behera, P. Kumar, D.P. Dogra, P.P. Roy, A robust biometric authentication system for handheld electronic devices by intelligently combining 3D finger motions and cerebral responses, IEEE Trans. Consum. Electron. 67 (1) (2021) 458–467, https://doi.org/10.1109/TCE.2021.3055419.

[18] V.M. Antonova, K.A. Balakin, N.A. Grechishkina, N.A. Kuznetsov, Development of an authentication system using voice verification, J. Commun. Technol. Electron. 65 (12) (2020) 1460–1468, https://doi.org/10.1134/S1064226920120013.

[19] M.D. Abramoff, M.K. Garvin, M. Sonka, Retinal imaging and image analysis, IEEE Rev. Biomed. Eng. 3 (2010) 169–208, https://doi.org/10.1109/RBME.2010.2084567.

[20] J.-S.R. Jang, ANFIS architecture, IEEE Trans. Syst. Man Cybern. 23 (3) (1993) 665–685.

[21] M. Ortega, M.G. Penedo, J. Rouco, N. Barreira, M.J. Carreira, Personal verification based on extraction and characterisation of retinal feature points, J. Vis. Lang. Comput. 20 (2) (2009) 80–90, https://doi.org/10.1016/j.jvlc.2009.01.006.

[22] M. Ortega, M.G. Penedo, J. Rouco, N. Barreira, M.J. Carreira, Retinal verification using a feature points-based biometric pattern, EURASIP J. Adv. Signal Process. 2009 (1) (2009) 235746, https://doi.org/10.1155/2009/235746.

Chapter 6

Gender recognition from facial images using multichannel deep learning framework

R. Ramya[a], A. Anandh[a], K. Muthulakshmi[a], and S. Venkatesh[b]
[a]*Department of Computer Science and Engineering, Kamaraj College of Engineering and Technology, Madurai, India,* [b]*Microland, Bengaluru, India*

1 Introduction

The major reason for drastic development in all fields is because of human thinking to incorporate the abilities and intelligence to each physical object. Emergence of an innovative idea is domain independent. There is a chase always to find a novel or an improved solution to the existing problem. Two such technologies which help researchers on their chase are artificial intelligence and machine learning. The focus of machine learning is to build a model from input data and produce an expected output [1]. The input formats to such ML models could be a text, number, geographical location, images, audio signals, time series, etc. Once the input is processed, the model's learning will be classified into supervised learning and unsupervised learning based on its feature labels and properties. The supervised ML models will generate the results either by prediction or by classification. Random forest, support vector machines, neural networks, decision trees, logistic regression, and LDA are few classification algorithms. The output of unsupervised models could either be the formation of a new cluster or the formation of a new pattern. K-Means, K-medoids, BIRCH, and DBS are few clustering algorithms.

Fine-tuning algorithms are used to evaluate the models as well as to improve the accuracy of the output. Few evaluation metrics that are used in the industries include accuracy, precision, and F1 score. The most complex existing problems have a nonlinear model and they are represented by n-D matrices [2]. The algorithms used to solve complex problems have also become complex. When there is a complex problem, the data involved to solve the problem will be huge which resulted in a huge feature set. In machine learning models, the input feature set will be created and passed to the models [3, 4]. But for a huge feature set, there is

Machine Learning for Biometrics. https://doi.org/10.1016/B978-0-323-85209-8.00009-2

105

a need for a model which will extract the features automatically and that is important for classification also.

A subset of machine learning called deep learning has emerged and solved most of the complex classification problems [5]. This automatic way of feature extraction from the raw data is called feature engineering. Training data helps the system to learn and also determines the overall accuracy. When a testing sample is presented, the system must classify it into the corresponding class. Though DL models take a long time to get trained with the input data, it takes only less time with the test data to predict the output. It is commonly stated that a DL model does not require a human programmer to provide the instructions on the steps to execute. They always tend to extract high-level features from the input dataset.

A neural network is termed as the basic building block of a deep learning model. Each neuron of the network will act like a human brain. They are trained using the back-propagation method. It has a single or few hidden layers to solve the given problem. A single-layer neural network model is called a perceptron model. It is also called a shallow neural network. Convolutional neural network, feed-forward neural network, and recurrent neural network are few networks that are used widely among ML engineers. CNN has its application on signal and image processing [6]. Feature extraction is applicable to all forms of input data and specifically, a DL model can extract n-number of features from an image. Feature fusion combines the required features from a high-dimensional feature input. They also describe the image with rich internal information and lower the computational complexity. Agriculture, automobile industry, defense, healthcare, and many such industries make use of the deep learning algorithms for image analysis. Super-human accuracy will be delivered by a deep learning model with image restoration, image classification, object detection, and image segmentation.

An amazing area of research called computer vision (CV) gains high level of understanding from digital images and videos [7]. They supersede the CNNs with their accuracy of image classification. The three major areas where CV stabilized its success are surveillance, quality assessment, and face recognition. There exists is a subfield of deep learning called transfer learning. It is nothing but the reuse of an algorithm generated for one task and the use of it for another task with a small tweak. It is widely used when enough sample training data are not available and the existing input data can be transferred. Industries always prefer such transfer learning models instead of building a CNN from scratch. Two common methods that use transfer learning on predictive modeling are develop model approach and pretrained model approach. Several pretrained transfer learning models are available on the internet from various research institutions and tech giants. Oxford VCG, Google Inception, and Microsoft ResNet are the famous models that apply transfer learning to image data [8]. Though we have such advancements, still industries are facing cyberattacks and threats.

Customer experience and satisfaction have been improved by ideas like cashless, cardless, and touch-free, and they equally have fears of threats. There are some of the issues like network intruders, fraudulent transactions, illegal immigration, and flight terrorism where the specialists have to stay alert for 24*7. These security compromises are eradicated by stable biometric techniques. Fingerprint, iris, facial recognition, palm, and vein detections are some of the highly convenient prevailing systems that help businesses/individuals for unique access. They are designed for the recognition of the unique physiological and behavioral features of an individual. Biometric inputs are captured as images and computer-driven image recognition systems automatically recognize and classify the subjects. Soft biometrics are generally used to identify a subject's traits namely height, gender, hair color, and skin color [9].

Gender identification is the key mechanism on the distribution of rights, property registrations, pension eligibility, and marriages. Various automated gender recognition systems prevail to classify the subjects and every system has its own unique solution with its own limitations. Due to the gaining importance of face identification systems on the security field, gender recognition system makes use of it. Complex training data and manipulation of complex features from the training facial image data accurately predict the gender. The images can be analyzed using various features that are extracted using machine learning algorithms [10] or by using a deep learning framework [11].

Several days or even more weeks may be taken by deep convolutional neural network models to train on very large datasets. The need for lots of new data is evaded by the introduction of transfer learning. A model which was trained on a task can be used to handle a new similar task. In transfer learning, the training data which are labeled already are plentiful in an old task, and less data are enough for a new task. The process of training the model on a new task is very fast and a more accurate and effective model can be obtained through this transfer learning. Multichannel deep learning framework (MC-DLF) was introduced in the proposed system. The proposed system extracts two feature sets from the preprocessed input image set. One set of feature extraction is via the transfer learning method and the other is via a shallow CNN. Prominent features from the newly constructed sets will be fused and then pipelined to an SVM classifier. This ensemble boosts the prediction accuracy and forms a stable gender recognition system.

2 Literature review

A gait analysis was done by Zhang et al. [12]. Gait-based soft biometrics, such as age and gender prediction, were included in their gait analysis using a joint CCN-based framework. This method was found out to be efficient in terms of training time, testing time, and storage. The joint CNN-based framework can also be used for a gait-recognized abnormal behavior detection using the sequences of silhouettes.

Tapia and Arellano [13] preserved the gender information using a generative adversarial network (GAN)-based algorithm while generating synthetic images. A latent vector was used to encode the gender information within the conditional GAN algorithm. A gender classification algorithm (CNN) was used to test the synthetic images. A novel person-disjoint gender-labeled dataset was created. This dataset was introduced to train deep learning-based gender classification systems.

Jonsson and Soderberg [14] proposed a method to spot spontaneous facial expressions using a deep convolutional neural network. Instead of an emotion-specific classification, this work projected a broader classification as positive, neutral, and negative. The system also focuses on individual images rather than video sequences because it is believed that facial expressions on a video are limited than single images and it has been very difficult to fetch the commencement and end of a facial expression on a video sequence. Multiclass SVM loss function and cross-entropy loss function have been analyzed on the classifier optimization. This neural network model with less computational cost will classify the images with high accuracy. The number of labels has been reduced from eight to three. This condensation has been achieved after a label binning method. The paper dealt with practical application considerations and use cases.

A three-phase transfer learning framework has been proposed by Zen et al. [15] to analyze the emotions from facial features. A set of classifiers and vectors learned from auxiliary sources were represented in phase 1. The user unlabeled data mapped with an associated classifier using a regression function was concentrated on phase 2. Though the tasks and adopted features from the source are different, the approach outperforms the user-independent classifiers. Phase 3 concentrated on parameter transfer methods which in turn identified a set of parameters. The performance evaluation has been conducted on a smart watch-based gesture recognition dataset and on CK+ and PAINFUL datasets. The performance has been evaluated using the F1 score. It has been established that computational cost is far lesser when compared to the further domain-adoption algorithms.

Identification of local patches on the images was initiated by the work of local deep neural network of gender recognition. This localization reduces the computational cost of training time since the original method uses 100 s of patches per image. The nine-patch model was proposed and applied on LFW and Adience databases by Liao et al. [16]. Patch extraction regions have been defined appropriately and pixel values are normalized to a standard Gaussian distribution. The classification depends on the highest posterior of the averaged nine patches. It concludes that the mouth region provides the best estimates on age classification whereas eyes for gender classification. Of the nine patches, the second-row patches such as 4th, 5th, and 6th contain the eye portion pixels, hence a higher classification rate. A five-fold cross-validation method has been used as an optimization technique. The posterior obtained from the neural network is divided by nine as the same weightage as there are nine patches extracted from the image. The results have been established with improvement when three sets of inputs, original image, nine-patched images, and the second-row images fed to the neural network when compared to the single original image fed as input.

Afshin Dehghan et al. proposed a method called DAGER using CNN. The entire dataset has been processed and estimates age, gender, and emotions as the first output layer. A sight-bound dataset was used, and when compared to Adience database approach instead of five-fold, the model has been applied on all folds without further fine-tuning. They have applied the model on real-time APIs like Kairos and Face++. The model accuracy has been obtained using confusion matrix. The deep training approach on each task—age, gender, and emotion recognition—has a separate network with inexpensive computation cost. The experiments have been conducted separately for each task and the classification was based on the combined output results.

The inclusion of multimodal 2D and 3D facial expression recognition proposed by Li et al. [17] has dealt with deep convolutional neural network methodology. The probability of applying the given approach on gender recognition improves the accuracy. The 3D curvatures, normal vectors, principal curvatures, and texture maps are the six kinds of 2D facial attributes from which a set of conditioned and textured 3D face scans was obtained. Three restrictions such as parameter-shared/unshared feature extraction, optimality of linear SVM prediction, and effectiveness of learning-based fusion are discussed as issues on validation about the effectiveness of DF-CNN. The experiment's results publish that the combined deep features that are 32-dimensional can accomplish better results than the combined deep features that are 16-dimensional and 64-dimensional. Two standard 3D face datasets such as BU-3DFE and Bosphorus have been used here and the best results were achieved on visualization and quantification space.

Pedestrian parsing was performed by Raza et al. [18] using a deep decomposition neural network method. Foreground pedestrial full-body images were extracted from the input image using the binary mask which was created as the output of pedestrian parsing. A stacked, sparse autoencoder with a SoftMax classifier was used to predict the gender of various pedestrians' views such as frontal views, mixed views, and back views. This gender prediction method can be applied to part-dependent body appearances.

A mixed structure that comprises of convolutional neural network (CNN) and extreme learning machine (ELM) was introduced by Duan et al. [1] for integrating two classifiers to handle gender and age classification in the MOORPH-II dataset. Several measures were adopted here to lower the risk of overfitting.

Arora and Bhatia [19] introduced a network using Adam optimization and back-propagation to identify gender from faces. An accuracy of 98.5% was reached in just 50 epochs on the CASIA dataset using grouping of the convolutional and max-pooling layers. Prediction using other biometric personas such as fingerprint, palm, and iris can be performed by extending the CNN network.

To recognize the gender from face pictures, Azzopardi et al. [20] planned a completely unique approach that fuses domain-specific and trainable options. Above all, this work used the SURF descriptors extracted from 51 facial landmarks associated with eyes, nose, and mouth as domain-dependent options, and therefore the COSFIRE filters as trainable options. The planned approach seems to be terribly durable with relevance to the well-known face variations, together with totally different poses, expressions, and illumination conditions.

Rai and Khanna [21] conferred that a gender classification technique uses the (2D) pair of PCA, Gabor filter, and SVM for classifying the gender from occluded and non-occluded face pictures. The present work explores two approaches, i.e., fusion at the feature level and fusion at the classifier level. Experimental result shows that each of the planned approaches offers a suitable result on non-occluded face image information.

Common experimental analyses do not take into consideration that the face pictures given as input to the neural networks are usually precious by solid corruptions not forever outlined in typical datasets. During this work, Greco et al. [22] projected an associate experimental framework for gender recognition "in the wild." An associate experiment on the MIVIA-Gender dataset was performed to investigate the consequences of mixed image corruptions happening within the wild. The experimental analysis demonstrates that the hardiness of the thought of strategies is often more improved since all of them are precious by a performance drop on pictures collected within the wild or manually corrupted.

The investigation into age and gender identification has been receiving more attention from researchers since social and multimedia networks are becoming more popular nowadays. Recently, Duc-Quang et al. [23] published method has yielded quite good results in terms of accuracy but has also been proven to be ineffective in real-time applications because the models were too complicated. A lightweight model that can classify both age and gender can be proposed in this work.

Age and gender identification became a serious part of the network, security, and care. It is of standard use in age-specific content access for kids. Social media uses it in delivering bedded ads and selling to increase its reach. Face recognition has developed to a good extent that we have to map it to any in obtaining additional helpful results having completely different approaches. Rafique et al. [24] projected deep CNN to enhance age and gender declaration from which important results will be obtained and a big improvement will be seen within the output.

Mathivanan and Poornima [25] have suggested a comparison of the existing different gender classification algorithms. These existing algorithms were used to identify the genders very easily. With the help of the best classification algorithm, the genders are easily classified. Different constraints such as gender, ethnic origin, texture, pose, intensity, gait shape, face, iris, lip movement, and fingerprint were frequently used to recognize the gender of a person. The accuracy and reliability were the constraints that are used to improve the gender identification algorithms based on the analysis. The histogram of the LBF methodology identified the genders very easily and secured more accuracy than the existing methodology.

Gurnani et al. [26] proposed a new tactic SAF-BAGE that illustrates a new way to train a neural network. The performance was further enhanced to classify facial soft-biometrics. The dominant attributes such as mouth, eyes, and nose were used as the salient regions. Facial soft-biometrics were classified using these attributes. These salient regions played a substantial role to perform classification using class activation maps (CAM). The fully connected layers that are present before the final output classification layer were substituted with global average pooling (GAP) with a SoftMax layer in AlexNet of CAM. The output layer weights on the feature maps were projected back on the feature maps to recognize the significance of the image by giving this simple structure.

Cheng et al. [27] suggested a multipatch-based gender recognition method using convolutional neural network. This policy outstrips the prevailing single-input techniques by dropping the errors that are stemming from face rotation or occlusion. Estimating the capability of outsized patches, effective aggregation of complementary patches, and proposing a gender classification system that can handle occlusions and view changes were the contributions of this work. A new database AAF is provided to validate the robustness of this technique across all ages for gender classification.

Saeed et al. [28] prompted a brand-new methodology to handle coarse level features that were extracted from an LR image using grayscale, medical X-ray image reconstruction methodology. Unit of time image reconstruction is finished using the assistance of machine learning-based methodology. Granular level feature extraction methodology produced an acceptable quantity of training set from a restricted quantity of training image sets was projected by this work. However, a high volume of training pictures was needed for the convolutional neural network (CNN) to reconstruct the unit of time pictures. These coarse-grained level options comprise the impact of several adjacent points along the direction. A polynomial regression model is employed for the unit of time worth restoration. This image restoration provided reasonable results for the dataset of dental radiographs and also the structural similarity index is regularized.

Afifi and Abdelhamed [29] suggested a new methodology for gender classification that intends at identifying the gender of a person. Although high accuracy was obtained by using the state-of-the-art ways for this task, there is still an area for enhancement in general, unrestricted datasets. During this work, a tendency to advocate a replacement strategy was impressed by the performance of humans in gender recognition. Rather than handling only the face image as a feature, the tendency to trust the mixture of isolated facial elements and discourse features was used to make decision about a foggy face. Then, a tendency has been adapted to train deep convolutional neural networks tailed by score fusion using AdaBoost to conclude the ultimate gender category. Four difficult datasets were introduced to exhibit their efficaciousness in attaining higher accuracy with progressive ways. Additionally, this work gifted a replacement face dataset that strengthens the face occlusion and illumination challenges. These were believed to be a reserve for performing gender recognition.

Cornia [30] explored the utilization of prominence that is similar to the human sensory structure to classify gender and countenance soft-biometric for facial pictures. This work proposed an approach—SAF-BAGE—that located the face first and then increased the bounding box (B-Box) margin and computed the prominence map victimization with reweighted, magnitude relation of prominence map. It increased the input of cropped face and extracted the convolutional neural network (CNN) predictions on the increased reweighted, prominent face. In this work, CNN used the AlexNet model that is trained already using ImageNet.

Qawaqneh et al. [31] proposed a deep CNN model to accomplish an estimation of ages using facial images. VGG-Face CNN is adapted and adjusted to accomplish an estimation of age. The model was applied on the Adience dataset which is the latest and challenging age estimation benchmark dataset that encompasses unrestricted facial images. GoogLeNet was trained using a huge dataset that contains millions of training pictures; its performance to estimate the age is not reasonable as compared with the system that uses VGG-Face. Not only does the amount of training images and the number of subjects in a training dataset affect the age estimation, but also the pretraining of the used CNN concludes the performance of the network for estimating the age.

3 Preliminaries

3.1 Deep learning

The impact of cutting-edge technologies in every aspect of life cannot be escaped. Two major technologies at the core of this impact are deep learning and machine learning. AGI (artificial general intelligence) is the furthermost technique of deep learning. These changes initiating agents revise the environment in which human beings live and communicate, like the industrial revolution, cybersecurity, and monitoring. They are at the intermediary stage; they are getting into our day-to-day life of healthcare advancements, monitoring climate change, agricultural yield improvements, smart devices, and power grid creation.

Machine learning is one piece of the puzzle of artificial intelligence and its algorithms used to build a mathematical model based on training data to make decisions in the future about test datasets. We often see things like ML as a single technology, but it will underpin a host of different things; often we will be using them without even knowing ML is there because underlying ML is a simple concept that complex systems get better and more closely aligned to their objective over time.

Deep learning is a field that is a subclass of machine learning methods as shown in Fig. 1 based on an artificial neural network (ANN). ANN is a structure that mimics the biological brain of living creatures. ANN comprises artificial neurons connected together. These neurons are arranged in layers. Input data travel on a layered architecture, maybe after passing through the layers several times. Various layers transform the given input into various forms with the help of activation functions.

Deep learning is a process of machine learning using artificial neural networks that consist of three main layers arranged hierarchically. The input to the network passes through the input layer, the data are transformed and activated on the hidden layer (also called as computation layer), and the desired output will evolve through the output layer. The process continues for each layer in the hierarchy for building more complex information from the given training data. It is a method of learning that is very useful for many real-world applications like stock prediction, multiclass classification, etc.

The number of hidden layers that are utilized in the architecture, through which data are transformed, is referred to as "deep." Such learning architectures are usually built with a greedy layer-by-layer approach. Various deep learning architectures such as deconvolutional network, deep convolutional neural network, deep belief network, and RNN. Generative adversarial network, deep

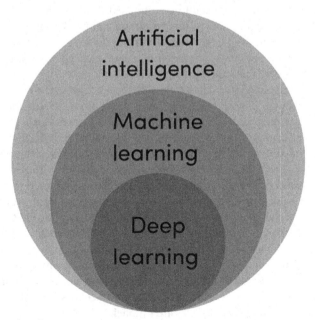

FIG. 1   Deep learning.

residual network, and neural tuning machines are used in various fields. These architectures use multiple layers to extract more features that are prominent.

CNN is one of the popular types of ANN. Normal ANNs are used in applications that operate on numerical data that are highly structured whereas CNN operates on images. It is a deep-feed forward network. The feed forward network is superior to the perceptron. A CNN typically has about 10 convolutional, rectilinear activation, and subsampling triplet layers (CRS) followed by 2 fully connected (FC) layers. CNNs are mainly used in image-related recognition and classification. CNNs perform less preprocessing as compared to other image processing algorithms.

In deep learning, every layer converts the input into a more abstracted and fused representation by learning the information on its own. The neurons on each layer make this abstraction possible. There are various cells on a neural network. They are input cell, noisy and backfed input cell, output cell, match input/output cell, recurrent cell, memory cell, convolutional cell, hidden cell, and probabilistic hidden cell. It can learn how to place features in each of the levels.

3.2 Pretrained networks

Deep neural networks (DNN) are the proven effective way for analysis tasks as they can change the mere features at a low level to dense features at a high level. Though DNN outperforms shallow neural networks for converting the features at a low level to features at a high level, there is a constraint that many network factors or hyperparameters need to be estimated. With the help of pretrained, off-the-shelf deep CNN models, this constraint can be eliminated. These pretrained, off-the-shelf deep CNN models retain optimum generalization capability for recognition problems. It is better to use a fine-tuned pretrained model, a transfer learning method, for recognition tasks.

With a diverse and large dataset, the CNN learns how to extract the features during pretraining. Transfer learning uses layers from the network that are trained already on a large dataset, which can be fine-tuned for a new dataset. With transfer learning, fine adjustment of a pretrained network is performed. Randomly initialized weights have been used to train a fresh network from the scratch. Former is easy and fast than the latter and it converges much faster, trains faster, and gives accurate and better prediction results. Using this, learned features can be easily transferred to the new task that has a small set of training images. This technique works very well in reality because it allows the network to use the features it learned in advance, mixes and matches them in novice combinations, and uses it to classify a new set of images. In fact, it is generally accepted that one should never train a CNN from scratch anymore.

We used the pretrained network as a feature extractor in which layer activations are used as features. These activations extracted as features are fed into SVM, another leading learning classifier model.

In the literature, various pretrained networks like ZFNet, VGGNet, GoogLe-Net, AlexNet, and ResNet readily exist for use to perform the recognition tasks. By performing fine adjustment of the pretrained networks that resulted in a better success rate, various features related to expression can be extracted. GoogLeNet and AlexNet are used in this study. While using both the networks for learning the detailed information, 0.01 is used as a learning rate in the final classifier layer.

3.3 AlexNet

AlexNet is the first successful CNN for a large dataset, ImageNet [32]. This dataset has nearly 15 million images with 22,000 categories, from which Alex-Net used a subset (1000 categories and 1000 images per category). In the ImageNet Large Scale Visual Recognition Challenge 2012, AlexNet is the winner. Its layout as depicted in Fig. 2. is relatively simple as compared to other recent architectures. It has five convolutional layers, three fully connected layers along with max-pooling and dropout layers. These typically included repeating a few convolutional layers, each followed by max pooling with limited dense layers. But there was no rule to fix the size of the filter and to decide how many convolutions to use before a max pooling. The traditional activation function, tanh, is given by Eq. (1).

$$f(x) = \tanh(x) = 2 * \frac{1}{1 + e^{-2x}} - 1 \qquad (1)$$

This tanh function is a saturating nonlinearity, which is slow to train as the exponential function is computationally expensive. So, a nonsaturating, nonlinearity ReLU as given by Eq. (2) is used by AlexNet, which is faster to train and computationally efficient.

$$f(x) = \text{ReLU}(x) = \max(0, x) \qquad (2)$$

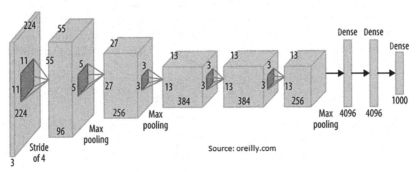

FIG. 2 Architecture of AlexNet.

ReLUs are said to be six times faster and they do not need input normalization to prevent saturation. But a local response normalization called brightness normalization is done to achieve generalization. Local response normalization (LRN) is a contrast improvement procedure for feature maps in ConvNets. It can also be just brightness normalization depending on the implementation details and this is especially significant for ReLU units which have unbounded outputs. This normalization results in a form of lateral inhibition, that is found as real neurons. AlexNet uses ReLU instead of tanh for adding the nonlinearities, which boosts up the speed for the same accuracy level. To deal with the overfitting issue, it uses dropout. To reduce overfitting and to learn robust features, the output of every hidden neuron is initially fixed to zero with a probability of 0.5. The LRN operation is inspired by a lateral inhibition process in real biological neural networks, which generates some kind of competition between neurons in a less, local neighborhood. A dropout operation is applied only to the first two fully connected layers of AlexNet architecture as the number of iterations that are required to converge is increased by two every time. The neurons that are dropped out will not participate in a forward pass, hence in back-propagation. Thus, it reduces the coadaptations of neurons, as each neuron cannot rely on other neurons. A pooling layer is used to summarize the neighboring neuron's output in the same kernel map. To decrease the size of the network, it overlaps the pooling layers. When we notice the AlexNet system, the initial layer has a filter of size 11×11, and the following layer has a 5×5 filter. There is max pooling after every convolutional layer.

AlexNet models were trained using stochastic gradient descent that minimizes the cross-entropy loss function with particular values for momentum as well as weight decay. Learning rate of entire layers is initially set to 0.01 and then they are adjusted manually when a validation error rate is not improving against the present learning rate.

3.4 GoogLeNet

In the ImageNet Large Scale Visual Recognition Challenge 2015, GoogLeNet [33] is the winner. It is from Google and is named to pay tribute to Prof. Yan Lecun's LeNet. It has a total of 22 layers as depicted in Fig. 3. It uses small 1×1 convolutions in the middle of the network. These convolutions are used

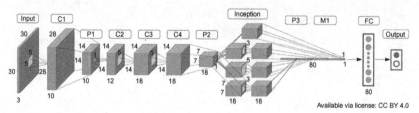

FIG. 3 Architecture of GoogLeNet.

for carrying out a dimensionality reduction in a nonlinear way in contrast to PCA, a linear reduction way. In this way, these convolutions reduce the bottle-necks in computation.

The pretrained GoogLeNet is augmented with the inception module that has more nonlinearity. This inception module is used as the regional classifier. It improves the regional proposal step by merging the multibox predictions with a selective search approach. There are some SoftMax layers in the middle for training purposes, providing regularization, and combating the gradient vanish-ing problem. These are used as auxiliary classifiers. GoogLeNet is designed to capture sparse correlation patterns in the feature map stack and provide compu-tational efficiency. It regularizes the training with batch normalization and thereby decreases the auxiliary classifier's importance. While decreasing the spatial resolution, it increases the number of feature maps.

It is one of the models that explored the concept that the layers used in CNN need not be arranged up sequentially. By using the inception module, it proved that a different layer structure can lead to performance and computational ben-efits of feature extraction. Collective parameters in the network are 6.7977 mil-lion where the majority of the parameters are due to the inception blocks of the network. The number, in fact, is pretty huge which in turn makes GoogLeNet a very complex and high-capacity deep network. As an alternative for fully con-nected layers at the end, GoogLeNet uses global average pooling so that it is less prone to overfitting and saves a large number of parameters. Like max-pooling layers, GAP layers are used to decrease the spatial dimensions of a 3D tensor. However, GAP layers accomplish a more extreme form of dimensionality reduction, where a tensor with a dimension of $h \times w \times d$ is reduced in size to have a dimension of $1 \times 1 \times d$. To decrease each $h \times w$ feature map to a sin-gle number, GAP layers calculate an average of every hw values.

4 Proposed system

Fig. 4 shows the outline of the proposed multichannel deep learning framework (MC-DLF). After preprocessing, LDP images are built from the facial images.

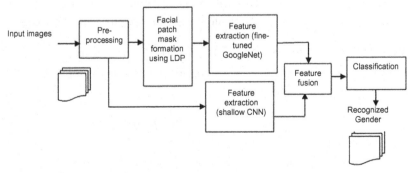

FIG. 4 Proposed Framework.

LDP-featured images are organized into a size of 220*170. Using the featured images, feature extraction is done using finely adjusted pretrained AlexNet/ GoogLeNet and a shallow CNN. Feature fusion is performed using CCA/ DCA. Then, the feature set that is fused is given as input to the SVM classifier to recognize the gender of the given image.

4.1 Steps

The steps involved in our proposed framework are shown below.

Algorithm Steps

(a) LDP images are constructed from the facial images after preprocessing.
(b) Images are organized into a size of 220*170.
(c) Two feature sets were extracted from the preprocessed images. One set of feature extraction is done via a transfer learning method and the other is done via a shallow CNN, i.e., features are extracted using finely adjusted, pretrained AlexNet/GoogLeNet and a shallow CNN.
(d) The feature fusion is done using CCA/DCA.
(e) Then, the fused feature set is given as input to an SVM classifier to recognize the gender of the given image.

4.2 Featured image formation

Instead of using the raw facial images to learn the facial features, featured images are used as they represent some prominent features at the initial level. The process of featured image formation is explained in the subsequent sections.

4.3 Local directional pattern (LDP) image formation

4.3.1 Edge direction magnitude computation

For each pixel in the input facial image, edge direction magnitude is computed using the Kirsch masks, K_{ij}^z, in all the eight different compass directions as represented in Fig. 5. The results obtained after applying Kirsch mask in all the eight compass directions is shown in Fig. 6. Each direction represents edge magnitude. Fig. 7 illustrates the input image and its equivalent LDP image.

4.3.2 Highest edge direction magnitude identification

The maximum edge direction magnitude, E, from the input image I, of size n * p, is computed using Eq. (3).

$$E_{i,j} = \max_{z=1,2,\ldots,8} \sum_{l=-1}^{1} \sum_{k=-1}^{1} K_{ij}^z * I_{l+i,k+j} \qquad (3)$$

	North West	North	North East
	-3 5 5	-3 -3 5	-3 -3 -3
	-3 0 5	-3 0 5	-3 0 5
	-3 -3 -3	-3 -3 5	-3 5 5
	5 5 5		-3 -3 -3
West	-3 0 -3	Pixel	-3 0 -3 East
	-3 -3 -3		5 5 5
	5 5 -3	5 -3 -3	-3 -3 -3
	5 0 -3	5 0 -3	5 0 -3
	-3 -3 -3	5 -3 -3	5 5 -3
	South West	South	South East

FIG. 5 Kirsch edge masks that are used in different compass directions.

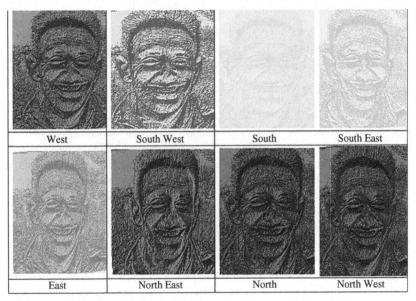

FIG. 6 Kirsch edge responses obtained in eight compass directions.

FIG. 7 Image and its corresponding LDP image.

where i and j from 2 to $n-1$ and 2 to $p-1$ respectively. It is calculated based on an eight of the Kirsch kernel series, k in all the compass directions. It depends on the mask that produces the most important edge magnitude.

4.3.3 LDP image computation

Let $Kirsch_i$ be the responses that are got after applying all the eight Kirsch Kernels, K_i, $i = 1, 2 \dots 8$. Let the highest edge magnitude be represented as $Kirsch_{\max}$. LDP value for all the pixels is computed using Eq. (4).

$$LDP = \sum_{i=0}^{7} b(Kirsch_i - Kirsch_{\max})*2^i$$
$$\text{where } b(x) = \left\{ \begin{array}{l} 1; \, x > 0 \\ 0; \, \text{otherwise} \end{array} \right\}$$

(4)

As the image is generated by considering all the eight directions, it results in a robust featured image.

5 Shallow CNN

The structure of the shallow CNN that is employed in this work is depicted in Fig. 8. CNN comprises three convolutional layers along with three pooling layers. In Table 1, the parameters employed by every CNN layer are enumerated. For transforming the featured image set into a learnable 3D filter set, a convolutional layer is employed. To decrease the dimension of the feature map and to eliminate the redundant details, a pooling layer is employed to accomplish down-sampling.

The layers minimize the space complexity of parameters used and they also eliminate the problem of overfitting. These layers are used in such a way that they can learn more discriminative and optimal features adaptively. The group of filters that are used in convolutional layers processes the local parts of the input. These filters result in strong responses when dealing with some parts of the face while suppressing the other parts, resulting in crucial local structures. After these several filtering in the convolutional layer, down-sampling is done to the filtered results in the max-pooling layer to make it strong against position variance.

The normalization layer is employed in between to improve the training process and to decrease the initialization dependence of the network. It normalizes the gradient values that flow through the network.

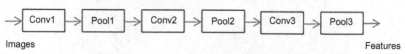

Images   Features

FIG. 8 Architecture of shallow CNN.

TABLE 1 Parameters that are used in shallow CNN.

Parameters	Conv1	Pool1	Conv2	Pool2	Conv3	Pool3
Filter size	3*3	2*2	3*3	2*2	3*3	2*2
No. of filters	16		32		64	
Stride	1	2	1	2	1	2
Padding	1	0	1	0	1	0

6 Feature fusion

In a recognition system, fusion can occur either at the level of feature or the level of a classifier. As the feature vectors contain rich information about the input images, fusion at the level of feature is considered superior as compared to the fusion at the level of a classifier.

The aim of this feature fusion step is to associate diverse feature vectors into a distinct feature vector that has a more discriminative ability. Fusion at the level of feature can be carried out using summation or concatenation of the transformed feature vector set. The summation method is employed here as it lowers the number of dimensions, hence the processing time.

We used two types of feature fusion techniques, such as canonical correlation analysis (CCA) and discriminant correlation analysis (DCA). The given two techniques operate at the feature level.

6.1 Canonical correlation analysis (CCA)

It aims to find out the associations among the two different feature sets [34]. CCA is used to recognize the basis of general statistical variations between several modalities. It does not assume some specific systems of directionality that is suitable for neuroscience applications. Let X and Y are two feature vectors of size "n." From X and Y, the covariance matrices S_{xx} and S_{yy} and the between-set covariance matrix S_{xy} are calculated by Eq. (5).

$$S = \begin{pmatrix} \text{var}(x) & \text{cov}(x, y) \\ \text{cov}(y, x) & \text{var}(y) \end{pmatrix} = \begin{pmatrix} S_{xx} & S_{xy} \\ S_{yx} & S_{yy} \end{pmatrix} \tag{5}$$

Then, the nonzero eigenvalues, G_1 and G_2 are computed using Eq. (6).

$$G_1 = S_{xx}^{-\frac{1}{2}} S_{xy} S_{yy}^{-1} S_{yx} S_{xx}^{-\frac{1}{2}} \quad G_2 = S_{yy}^{-\frac{1}{2}} S_{yx} S_{xx}^{-1} S_{xy} S_{yy}^{-\frac{1}{2}} \tag{6}$$

Then, the projection matrices W_x and W_y are found out, which represents the arranged eigenvectors that correspond to the nonzero eigenvalues. Lastly, to increase the pairwise association between two feature vectors, the linear combination of the transformed feature vector is found out using Eq. (7).

$$X^* = W_x^T X \quad Y^* = W_y^T Y \tag{7}$$

Thus, the objective function of CCA is to maximize Corr (Xa, Xb) subject to $a^T \sum_X a = 1$ and $b^T \sum_Y b = 1$.

6.2   Discriminant correlation analysis (DCA)

Correlation analysis aims to fuse the discriminated information that is captured by the feature vectors of different domains. It is intended to find the transformation that increases the pairwise association among two feature sets [35]. It also removes the association between classes by restricting the correlations to be inside the class. The major advantage of this approach is that it considers the structure of the class during fusion. DCA is generally applicable for recognizing faces in surveillance systems. It is used to avoid the low-resolution issue from the captured images by increasing the pairwise association among low- and high-resolution images. Here, we used it for gender classification.

Let n be the total samples, c be the number of classes, p and q be the number of features in feature vectors X and Y respectively. The n data matrix columns must be split into c distinct classes, where n_i columns are a part of ith class as in Eq. (8).

$$n = \sum_{i=1}^{c} n_i \tag{8}$$

Let x_{ij} be the feature vector of jth sample in ith class of X. Let $\overline{x_i}$ and $\overline{x}$ be the mean of x_{ij} feature vectors in ith class and the entire feature set. Then, the between-class scatter matrix, S_{bx}, defined by Eq. (9) is found out.

$$S_{bx}(p \times p) = \phi_{bx}\phi_{bx}^T \tag{9}$$

where

$$\phi_{bx(p \times c)} = \left[\sqrt{n_1}(\overline{x_1} - \overline{x}), \sqrt{n_2}(\overline{x_2} - \overline{x}), ..., \sqrt{n_c}(\overline{x_c} - \overline{x}) \right]$$

To diagonalize the between-class scatter matrix S_{bx} and to reduce the size of the data matrix X, from p to r, transformation matrix W_{bx} is found using Eq. (10).

$$W_{bx}^T S_{bx} W_{bx} = I \tag{10}$$

where I is the identity matrix.

The transformed feature vector is given by Eq. (11).

$$X' = W_{bx}^T X \tag{11}$$

where X is of size $p \times n$ and the resultant X' is of size $r \times n$. Similarly, the transformed feature vector, Y' for the second feature set Y is found using the above approach, i.e., a transformation W_{by} to diagonalize the between-class scatter matrix S_{by} and to decrease the size of the data matrix Y, from q to r.

To make one set of features have a nonzero association with the equivalent features in another set, the between-set covariance matrix of the transformed feature vectors X' and Y' is diagonalized.

The covariance matrix between sets of the converted feature vectors X' and Y' is given by Eq. (12).

$$S'_{xy} = X'Y'T \tag{12}$$

To diagonalize S'_{xy}, singular value decomposition is used to find the transformations W_{cx} and W_{cy}. So, the final transformed feature sets are found using Eq. (13).

$$\widetilde{X} = W_{cx}^T X' \text{ and } \widetilde{Y} = Y' \tag{13}$$

7 Experimental results and discussion

The following describes the dataset used and discussions about the experimental results that are obtained using our proposed approach. Initially, the featured LDP image database is formed for all the facial images that are available in Adience benchmark dataset. Then, the feature extraction is done from the input images using CNN, AlexNet, and GoogLeNet. Then, the feature fusion is done using CCA/DCA. For database formation, feature extraction, and feature fusion, Matlab is used. The total number of features extracted using CNN is 36,288. The number of features that are extracted using fine-tuned GoogLeNet and AlexNet is 1000. Then, the fused features are given as input to an SVM classifier using a Weka tool to obtain the result.

7.1 Adience dataset

In 2014, the Adience dataset was introduced by Eidinger et al. [36] in Age and Gender Estimation of Unfiltered Faces. It consists of 26,580 photos across 2284 subjects with a binary gender label and one label from eight different age-groups, partitioned into five splits. The key principle of the dataset is to capture the images as close to the real-world conditions. The images in the dataset include all the variations in appearance, pose, lighting condition, and image quality, to name a few. Images are captured from Flickr albums, collected by automatic upload from iPhone5 (or later) smart phone devices, and given to the general public under the Creative Commons (CC) license.

8 Single-channel approach

Initially, the experiments are done in such a way that each of the facial images and its corresponding LDP-featured image are fed as input individually into each of the three networks namely, GoogLeNet, AlexNet, and shallow CNN.

Fig. 9 shows the accuracies obtained in the single-channel approach. From the results, it is inferred that LDP image when it is fed into GoogLeNet performs better as compared to others.

9 Proposed MC-DLF approach

Table 2 and Fig. 10 illustrate the accuracy achieved when using the proposed MC-DLF approach where the original image and its equivalent LDP-featured image are given as input. From the results, it is inferred that shallow CNN and GoogLeNet along with CCA yield better results.

Table 3 illustrates the performance comparisons of the suggested MC-DLF approach, when it is assessed by various kernel functions using SVM.

The comparison between the suggested approach and other state-of-the-art methodologies is shown in Table 4.

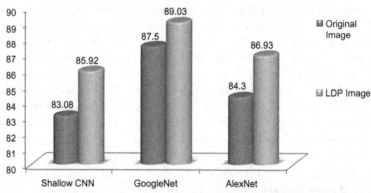

FIG. 9 Accuracy (in %) obtained using the single-channel approach.

TABLE 2 Accuracy obtained (in %) using our MC-DLF approach.

Shallow CNN and AlexNet (CCA)	Shallow CNN and AlexNet (DCA)	Shallow CNN and GoogLeNet (CCA)	Shallow CNN and GoogLeNet (DCA)
93.93	94.43	97.89	96.7

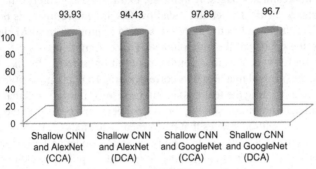

FIG. 10   Accuracy (in %) obtained using our MC-DLF approach.

TABLE 3 Performance of features assessed with various kernel functions—MC-DLF approach.

Kernel functions	Accuracy (%)
Polynomial	97.89
Normalized polynomial	90.56
RBF	90.32

TABLE 4 Comparison with state-of-the-art approaches.

Authors	Methodology used	Accuracy
Gurnani et al. [26]	SAF-BAGE without saliency module	83.4 ± 1.6%
	SAF-BAGE with saliency module	91.8 ± 1.2%
Gil and Hassner [37]	Single crop	85.9 ± 1.4%
	Multicrop	86.8 ± 1.4%
Dehghan et al. [38]	Convolutional neural network	91%
Proposed work	Multichannel—deep learning framework	97.89%

10   Summary

In this work, two feature sets were extracted from the preprocessed input image set. One set of feature extraction is via a transfer learning method and the other is via a shallow CNN. LDP images are constructed from the facial images after preprocessing. LDP-featured images are organized into a size of 220*170.

Moreover, a bigger model can be trained, and also the training time is reduced. So, from the featured images, features are extracted using finely adjusted, pretrained AlexNet/GoogLeNet and a shallow CNN. Feature fusion is done using CCA/DCA. Then, the fused feature set is given as input to an SVM classifier to recognize the gender of the given image. This ensemble boosts the prediction accuracy and forms a stable gender recognition system. In the MC-DLF approach, the original image and its corresponding LDP image (featured image) are used for extracting the features. From the results, it is inferred that when the featured images are used as input, the system performs better. As the proposed approach uses featured images that performed edge analysis, it recognizes gender at its best by removing the ambiguity caused by nonedge-based features. As the LDP-featured images modeled the edges and shapes, they characterize the classification task better. The salient, learned features are extracted by giving the LDP featured images as input into the proposed approach. Thus, these learned features are more amenable for effective classification.

References

[1] M. Duan, K. Li, C. Yang, K. Li, A hybrid deep learning CNN–ELM for age and gender classification, Neurocomputing 275 (2018) 448–461.
[2] J. Schmidt, M.R.G. Marques, S. Botti, M.A.L. Marques, Recent advances and applications of machine learning in solid-state materials science, NPJ Comput. Mater. 5 (2019) 1–36.
[3] I.H. Sarker, A.S.M. Kayes, P. Watters, Effectiveness analysis of machine learning classification models for predicting personalized context-aware smartphone usage, J. Big Data 6 (2019) 1–28.
[4] R. Ramya, K. Mala, C. Sindhuja, Student engagement identification based on facial expression analysis using 3D video/image of students, Taga J. 14 (2018) 2446–2454.
[5] G. Nguyen, S. Dlugolinsky, M. Bobák, V. Tran, Á.L. Garcí, I. Heredia, P. Malík, L. Hluchý, Machine learning and deep learning frameworks and libraries for large-scale data mining: a survey, Artif. Intell. Rev. 52 (2019) 77–124.
[6] M. Xin, Y. Wang, Research on image classification model based on deep convolution neural network, EURASIP J. Image Video Process. 40 (2019) 1–11.
[7] V. Wiley, T. Lucas, Computer vision and image processing: a paper review, Int. J. Artif. Intell. Res. 2 (1) (2018) 28–36.
[8] E.-Y. Huan, G.-H. Wen, Transfer learning with deep convolutional neural network for constitution classification with face image, Multimed. Tools Appl. 79 (2020) 11905–11919.
[9] A. Abdelwhab, S. Viriri, A survey on soft biometrics for human identification, in: Machine Learning and Biometrics, 2018, https://doi.org/10.5772/intechopen.76021. book chapter.
[10] A. Anandh, K. Mala, R. Suresh Babu, Combined global and local semantic feature–based image retrieval analysis with interactive feedback, Measur. Control 53 (1–2) (2020) 3–17, https://doi.org/10.1177/0020294018824122.
[11] R. Ramya, K. Mala, S. Selva Nidhyananthan, 3D facial expression recognition using multichannel deep learning framework, Circuits Syst. Signal Process. 39 (2020) 789–804, https://doi.org/10.1007/s00034-019-01144-8.
[12] Y. Zhang, Y. Huang, W. Liang, Y. Shiqi, A comprehensive study on gait biometrics using a joint CNN-based method, Pattern Recogn. 93 (2019) 228–236.

[13] J.E. Tapia, C. Arellano, Soft-biometrics encoding conditional GAN for synthesis of NIR periocular images, Futur. Gener. Comput. Syst. 97 (2019) 503–511.

[14] A. Jonsson, E. Soderberg, Recognizing Spontaneous Facial Expressions using Deep Convolutional Neural Networks, Master's thesis, 2018, p. E25.

[15] G. Zen, L. Porzi, E. Sangineto, E. Ricci, N. Sebe, Learning personalized models for facial expression analysis and gesture recognition, IEEE Trans. Multimedia 18 (4) (2016) 775–788.

[16] Z. Liao, S. Petridis, M. Pantic, Local deep neural networks for age and gender classification, Comput. Vis. Pattern Recognit. (2017).

[17] H. Li, J. Sun, Z. Xu, L. Chen, Multimodal 2D+3D facial expression recognition with deep fusion convolutional neural network, IEEE Trans. Multimedia 19 (2017) 2816–2831.

[18] M. Raza, M. Sharif, M. Yasmin, M.A. Khan, T. Saba, S.L. Fernandes, Appearance based pedestrians gender recognition by employing stacked auto encoders in deep learning, Futur. Gener. Comput. Syst. 88 (2018) 28–39.

[19] S. Arora, M.P.S. Bhatia, A robust approach for gender recognition using deep learning, in: 9th International Conference on Computing, Communication and Networking Technologies (ICCCNT), 2018, pp. 1–6.

[20] G. Azzopardi, A. Greco, A. Saggese, M. Vento, Fusion of domain specific and trainable features for gender recognition from face images, IEEE Access 6 (2018) 24171–24183.

[21] P. Rai, P. Khanna, An efficient and robust gender classification system, in: International Conference on Computational Intelligence and Communication Networks (CICN), 2015.

[22] A. Greco, A. Saggese, M. Vento, V. Vigilante, Gender recognition in the wild: a robustness evaluation over corrupted images, J. Ambient. Intell. Humaniz. Comput. (2020).

[23] V. Duc-Quang, T.-T.-T. Phung, C.Y. Wang, J.-C. Wang, Age and gender recognition using multi-task CNN, in: AsiaPacific Signal and Information Processing Association Annual Summit and Conference (APSIPA ASC), 2019.

[24] I. Rafique, A. Hamid, S. Naseer, M. Asad, M. Awais, T. Yasir, Age and gender prediction using deep convolutional neural networks, in: International Conference on Innovative Computing (ICIC), 2019.

[25] P. Mathivanan, K. Poornima, Biometric authentication for gender classification techniques: a review, J. Inst. Eng. (India): B 99 (2017) 79–85.

[26] A. Gurnani, K. Shah, V. Gajjar, V. Mavani, Y. Khandhediya, SAF- BAGE: salient approach for facial soft-biometric classification—age, gender, and facial expression, in: IEEE Winter Conference on Application of Computer Vision, 2019, pp. 1–9.

[27] J. Cheng, Y. Li, J. Wang, Y. Le, S. Wang, Exploiting effective facial patches for robust gender recognition, Tsinghua Sci. Technol. 24 (3) (2019) 333–345.

[28] K. Saeed, S. Datta, N. Chaki, A granular level feature extraction approach to construct HR image for forensic biometrics using small training DataSet, IEEE Access 8 (2020) 123556–123570.

[29] M. Afifi, A. Abdelhamed, AFIF4: deep gender classification based on AdaBoost-based fusion of isolated facial features and foggy faces, J. Vis. Commun. Image Represent. 62 (2019) 77–86.

[30] M. Cornia, A deep multi-level network for saliency prediction, in: Pattern Recognition (ICPR), 23rd International Conference on IEEE, 2016.

[31] Z. Qawaqneh, A.A. Mallouh, B.D. Barkana, Deep convolutional neural network for age estimation based on VGG-face model, Comput. Vis. Pattern Recognit. (2017). arXiv preprint arXiv:1709.01664.

[32] A. Krizhevsky, I. Sutskever, G.E. Hinton, ImageNet classification with deep convolutional neural networks, in: Proceedings of the 25th International Conference on Neural Information Processing Systems, 2012, pp. 1097–1105.

[33] C. Szegedy, W. Liu, Y. Jia, P. Sermanet, S. Reed, D. Anguelov, D. Erhan, V. Vanhoucke, A. Rabinovich, Going deeper with convolutions, in: Proceedings of the IEEE Conference on Computer Vision and Pattern Recognition, 2015, pp. 1–9.

[34] Q.S. Sun, S.G. Zeng, Y. Liu, P.A. Heng, D.S. Xia, A new method of feature fusion and its application in image recognition, Pattern Recogn. 38 (2005) 2437–2448.

[35] M. Haghighat, M. Abdel-Mottaleb, W. Alhalabi, Discriminant correlation analysis: real-time feature level fusion for multimodal biometric recognition, IEEE Trans. Inf. Forensics Secur. 11 (2016) 1984–1996.

[36] E. Eidinger, R. Enbar, T. Hassner, Age and gender estimation of unfiltered faces, IEEE Trans. Inf. Forensics Secur. 9 (12) (2014) 2170–2179. Special issue on Facial Biometrics in the Wild.

[37] L. Gil, T. Hassner, Age and gender classification using convolutional neural networks, in: Proceedings of the IEEE Conference on Computer Vision and Pattern Recognition Workshop, 2015.

[38] A. Dehghan, E.G. Ortiz, G. Shu, S.Z. Masood, DAGER: deep age, gender and emotion recognition using convolutional neural network, Comput. Vis. Pattern Recognit. (2017). arXiv:1702.04280.

Chapter 7

Implementation of cardiac signal for biometric recognition from facial video

M. Kavitha and R. Jai Ganesh

K. Ramakrishnan College of Technology, Trichy, India

1 Introduction

The term "Biometric" relates to the utilization of organic, physical, or social characteristics of an individual to personality or confirms his/her character. A biometric is characterized as a "life measure" and biometric innovation utilizes pictures of human body parts, caught through cameras and filtering pictures. Multimodal biometrics involves the combination of at any charge biometric modalities [1]. Paintings abuse the reasonableness of physiological signal electrocardiogram (ECG) to assist in human distinct verification. Signal looking after techniques for exam of ECG are mentioned. A take a look at set of ECG narratives prepared from 50 topics ECG from Physionet are evaluated on proposed recognizable evidence framework, deliberate on layout coordinating and flexible thresholding. The coordinating choices are assessed on the premise of relationship between's highlights. The benefits of utilizing ECGs for biometric acknowledgment include comprehensiveness, perpetual quality, uniqueness, power to assaults, liveness identification, persistent confirmation, and information minimization. Annals of the cardiovascular potential at the outside of the body are slanted to commotion due to improvements. In any case, even without interference, the ECG sign may destabilize concerning a biometric format that was fabricated some time previously. The purpose at the back of that is the fast impact that the frame's body structure and cerebrum technological know-how have at the coronary heart paintings. In this manner, a valuable part of ECG biometrics studies is the evaluation of the wellsprings of intra-challenge changeability.

Biometrics Personal Identification Tool by Electrocardiogram: This work manages the reliability of the electrocardiogram (ECG) of physiological signs to assist with human ID. On a planned defining proof basis, focused on layout

Machine Learning for Biometrics. https://doi.org/10.1016/B978-0-323-85209-8.00004-3

alignment and flexible quantization, a test collection of 250 ECG accounts organized from 50 subjects' ECGs from Physionet was tested. There was an unnecessary risk of short changes with time various biosignals that can also threaten biometric protection. Due to developments, information of the cardiovascular ability on the outside of the frame is biased to controversy. Irrespective, even without disruption, in terms of a biometric layout that was established some time earlier, the ECG sign can destabilize. The explanation behind it is the rapid influence of the physiology of the body as well as the science of the brain on the function of the heart. The evaluation of the exemplars of intra-subject alterability is a key piece of ECG biometrics research along those same lines.

Related work by Lacewell et al. [2] involved a study on strategies of picture combinations to acquire the most precise data. To create a precise intertwined picture, DWT was utilized for highlight extraction and a genetic calculation is utilized to obtain a more upgraded, consolidated picture. Jun-Ying Gan et al. [3] proposed a proficient calculation for combination and acknowledgment of face and iris highlight dependent on wavelet change. The DWT strategy was utilized to decrease the measurement, remove the commotion, save space, and improve proficiency. Arun Vivek et al. [4] discussed the investigation of multimodal biometric frameworks. The component extraction methods were utilized for three modalities. The separated data from every methodology was put away as format. Jun-Ying Gan et al. [5] proposed an examination on face and iris highlight acknowledgment dependent on 2DDCT and the Kernel Fisher Discriminant Analysis technique for include combination. This new methodology was provided for multimodal biometric distinguishing proof. Ashish Mishra et al. [6] clarified the various sorts of multimodal biometric framework, distinctive choice combination methods utilized in the framework. This examination talked about the achievability and points of interest over a unimodal biometric framework. Sheetal Choudhary et al. [7] introduced a multimodal biometric acknowledgment framework coordinating palmprint, unique mark and face dependent on score level combination. The element vectors were separated freely from the preprepared pictures of palmprint, unique mark, and face. Lillin Shen et al. [8] had plans to improve the precision of individual ID, when just a single example was used as layout, by incorporating numerous hand-based biometrics. To make combination a lot simpler, the equivalent feature, called combination code, and choice level combination system were utilized. Two combination cases—face and palmprint, and FKP and palmprint—were taken as guides to confirm the viability.

Gemma Piella et al. [9] introduced another methodology for evaluating quality in picture combination and contrasted diverse picture combination strategies or with locate the best boundaries for a given combination calculation. Deepak Kumar Sahu1 et al. [10] proposed PCA-based picture combination and furthermore centers around picture combination calculation dependent on wavelet change to improve goal of the pictures in which two pictures to be melded are immediately decayed into subimages with various recurrence and afterward the data combination is performed lastly these subimages are reproduced into result picture with abundant data. Manjusha Deshmukh et al. [11] presented a written survey on a portion of the picture combination procedures for picture combination like, crude combination.

Distantly estimating physiological action can give considerable advantages to both the clinical and the full of feeling processing applications. Recent exploration has proposed various procedures for the inconspicuous recognition of pulse (heart rate, or HR) utilizing human face chronicles. These methods rely upon inconspicuous concealing changes or developments of the face in light of cardiovascular activities, which are invisible to the human eye, yet can be identified by mechanized cameras. A couple of theories have been proposed, such as signal getting ready and artificial intelligence (AI). In any case, these systems are differentiated and particular datasets, and there is consequently no concurrence in terms of method execution. In this article, we portray and evaluate a couple of methodologies described recorded as a hard copy. At each stage, estimations are dismembered and investigated subject to their introduction using a public database.

For centuries, people have used body features to view each other, such as face, speech, and development. During the 19th century, Alphonse Bertillon, chief of the criminal ID section of the police headquarters in Delhi, established and then scripted using different body estimates to identify criminals. Likewise, as his thought gained ubiquity, it was obscured in the late 19th century by an undoubtedly greater and more feasible discovery of the peculiarity of fingerprints. Not long after this, several essential divisions of legislative issues understood the idea of first "exchanging" criminals' fingerprints and placing them in a database. Afterwards, the additional fingerprints could be "lifted" at the scene of the crime and synchronized with fingerprints in the database to identify the individuals. Given the fact that biometrics emerged from its widespread use in law enforcement to identify criminals, today it is increasingly used in numerous—anti staff applications to create individual identification. The proposed system uses an essential video acquisition webcam and uses sign-making plans to adjust the color of facial images that could be performed with the assistance of heartbeats for subsequent improvements. There is no need for the suggested biometric to have difficulty with any important sensor. It is full and unceasing, distinctively thinking of the manner in which a heart works for any living person. And it is extremely difficult to falsify; it will be ultra-stable in standards by comparison to its traditional accomplices. This article suggests a method for the use of this new biometric for verification of an individual by using more than enough signal care for procedures with a mostly classification-based selection system [12].

2   Biometric identification system based on facial video

A block diagram of the proposed heart signal from face video biometric for human identification is shown in Fig. 1. The steps are discussed below.

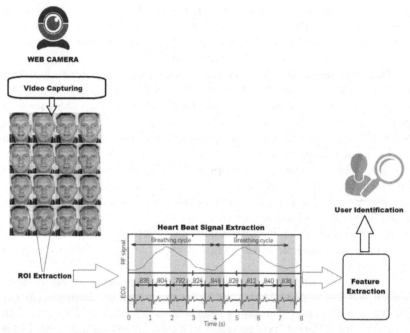

FIG. 1 Proposed block system.

2.1 Face detection and video acquisition

The proposed shape calls for coming across facial video utilizing a red, green, and blue (RGB) camera. As limitless frameworks for facial video primarily based totally heartbeat sign evaluation used direct webcam for video getting, right here the shape pick a webcam primarily based totally video getting method [13]. The heartbeat sign is withdrawn from the facial video through following camouflaging adjustments in RGB masterminds within side the steady video follows [14]. This is delicate through acquiring a Region of Interest (ROI) from the face through choosing 60% width of the face locale perceived through the modified face sector method. The fashionable of the red, green, and blue areas of the entire ROI is recorded because of the RGB lines of that chart. Quantifiable imply of those three RGB lines of every part is settled and recoded for every packaging of the video to get the heartbeat sign. The signal appears distorted and loose confirmed up diversely akin to the heartbeat sign were given through ECG [15]. This is an immediate end result of the impact of outside lighting, practical head-development, and the displaying of blood as a damper to the coronary heart siphoning stress to be moved from the focus of the chest to the face. Thus, we use a denoising channel through perceiving the pinnacle within the eliminated coronary heart signal and discarding the ways off RGB follows. The impact of the denoising method on a distorted heartbeat sign received from RGB is depicted in Fig. 2. The signal is then moved to the accompanying module.

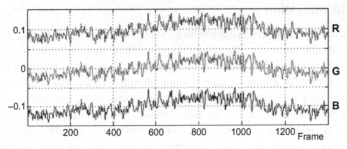

FIG. 2 Noisy heartbeat signal obtained from RGB traces.

2.2 Feature extraction

We have remotes our capabilities from radon pictures, as those snapshots are confirmed up within side the ECG primarily based totally recreation plan of to bring appropriate results. To make such pictures we want a route plot, which may be created with the aid of a rehashed heartbeat sign acquired from a facial video. The quantity of the replication reciprocals to the quantity of the castings within side the video [16]. From the figure, it is going to while all is said in carried out be visible that the heartbeat sign is repeated and associated within side the second a part of the signal to make the route plot for a 20 s in period video stuck in a 60 accommodations for every ensuing setting. The chart is going likely as a dedication to an alternate module. The capabilities used in the proposed machine are achieved by making use of a method referred to as Radon alternate to the made path diagram [17]. Radon alternate is an essential alternate processing projections of a photograph community alongside decided headings and is normally used to redesign snapshots from a scientific CT filter. A projection of a -dimensional photograph is lots of line integrals. Anticipate f (a, b) is a dimensional photograph providing photograph power in the (a, b) arranges. The Radon change (R) of the image, $R(\theta)$ [f(a, b)], can be portrayed as follows:

$$[f(a,b)] = \int_{-\infty}^{\infty} f(a'\cos\cos\theta - b'\sin\sin\theta, a'\sin\sin\theta - b'\cos\cos\theta)dy' \ldots\ldots\ldots$$

$$(1)$$

where θ is the point shaped by the distance vector of a line from the line vital with the important pivot in the Radon space, and:

$$[a'b'] = [\theta - \sin\sin\theta \sin\sin\theta \cos\cos\theta][a\,b] \qquad (2)$$

We utilize the notable distance metric of Minkowski to gauge the pair distance for $m \times n$ pixels sof the Radon picture R by:

$$d_{st} = \sqrt[p]{\sum_{i=1}^{n} |Rsi - Rti|p} \qquad (3)$$

where R_s and R_t are the row vectors representing each of the row vectors of R.

2.3 Identification

We use the selection tree primarily based totally framework for the ID. This is a flowchart-like shape which includes three styles of areas: (i) internal attention has a tendency to a take a look at on a section; (ii) branch-addresses the final results of the take a look at; and (iii) leaf attention factor has a tendency to a category mark coming as a desire coming approximately to isolating all of the highlights with inside the internal attention focuses. Prior to using the tree (the trial stage), it has to be prepared. At the supply stage, the element vectors of the arranging records are used to element focuses and approach the selection tree. At the trial stage, the phase vector of a trial records encounters the assessments within side the center focuses at final receives a social occasion name, in which a celebration addresses a topic to be seen. The arranging/trial breakup of the records is clarified within side the primer results.

2.4 Algorithm for implementation

Step 1 Input data: EEG_data;
Step 2 Output data: model result, features result;
Step 3 Set parameters No of Populations, No of Generations, and threshold;
Step 4 Model Selections;
Step 5 Generate randomly model populations using Epochs, lstm cells, Activation, Dropout, Optimize and repeat this step until No of Populations;
Step 6 Learn model populations using input data in lstm and then save only 20% of top results for next generation, and repeat this step until No of Generations;
Step 7 If (result RMSE > threshold) {;
Step 8 Crossovers ();
Step 9 Mutate ();
Step 10 Repeat GA-Model Selection;
Step 11};
Step 12 Else;
Step 13 Save model result;
Step 14 Feature Selections:
Step 15 Generate randomly feature populations using Input data;
Step 16 Learn feature populations using input data and model result and save only 20% of top results for next generation, and repeat this step until No of Generations;
Step 17 If (result RMSE > threshold) {;
Step 18 Crossovers ();
Step 19 Mutate ();
Step 20};
Step 21 Else;
Step 22 Save features result.

3   Results and discussions

3.1   Experimental environment

To test the presentation of the framework, we have utilized the freely accessible information base of MAHNOB-HCI. This information base has been gathered and contains facial recordings caught by a straightforward camcorder (like a webcam) associated with a PC. The information base remembers information for two classes: Feeling Elicitation Experiment (EEE) and Verifiable Tagging Experiment (ITE). Among these, the video cuts from EEE are frontal face video statistics and affordable for our trial. Subsequently, we chose the EEE video cuts from MAHNOB-HCI statistics base as were given facial chronicles for our biometric spotting proof structure. Portrayals of a few video cuts from MAHNOB-HCI statistics base are confirmed in Fig. 3. The information base produces 3810 facial recordings from 30 subjects. Notwithstanding, not these recordings are reasonable for our trial on account of brief span, document missing, and blocked face (brow) in certain recordings. Subsequently, we chose 351 recordings appropriate for our investigation. These recordings were received from 18 subjects (16–20 chronicles for each subject). We used the underlying

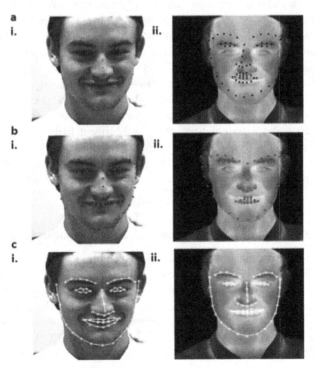

FIG. 3   Face capture of facial video clips.

20 s of every video for trying out and 80% of the difficult and speedy statistics for making plans in a novel overlay test.

3.2 Performance evaluation

In the wake of growing the selection tree from the association data, we made the affirmation effects from the trial data. The functions of each test were given from the heartbeat signal from facial video (HSFV) have been remotes within side the selection tree with locate the excellent healthy from the game-plan set. The presentation of the proposed HSFV biometric modified into assessed through the cutoff facilities that could be False Positive Identification Rate (FPIR) and False Negative Identification Rate. The FPIR proposes the chance of a check misleadingly apparent as a subject. In the occasion that True Positive, True Negative, False Positive and False Negative IDs among N range of basics in an assessment.

One significant factor may be mentioned from the effects that the TPIR and exactness price have a considerable difference in characteristics. This is in mild of the reality that the true wonderful and certifiable bad starters and triumphs are basically superb in numbers and the gadget accomplished excessive velocity of veritable bad approval as regarded via way of means of expresses and affectability estimations. This recommends that the proposed biometric, besides offering excessive capability, might also additionally require development in each the phase extraction and the organizing rating figuring. Notwithstanding the manner that contact primarily based totally ECG and PCG biometrics were given over 90% precision on a few neighborhood facts bases, we assume their short evaluation towards our shape is choppy closer to their civility, as they use substantial contact-primarily based entirely sensors, which provide cautious evaluation of heartbeat signals, while we, the usage of our without touch sensor (webcam), get handiest value determinations of these heartbeat hails which are gotten through touch primarily based totally sensors. This shows that it seems desirable if our sans touch shape, in any event on this essential improvement of its unexpected improvement, would not beat the ones contact-primarily based totally systems.

3.3 Comparison of physiological datasets for emotion recognition

During the experimental setup, the inclusion of emotion will look very difficult, whereas the bio signal data can be included with the EEG signal for processing. From this it is to propose that an alternative source for getting the data. Here an open set data was used for utilization. Table 1 shows the list of datasets according to the research data. On the other side, not cleared experimental data were intended to create a dataset included in MAHNOB-HCI. Here the MAHNOB-HCI dataset was used for an open dataset with observer tagging for valence for continuous emotion recognition.

TABLE 1 Comparison for emotion recognition with different dataset numbers.

Database number	Part number	Natural/Induced	Sound	Video	Peripheral	EEG	Labels
MIT	17	Natural	No	No	Yes	No	No
VAM	19	Natural	Yes	Yes	No	No	No
SEMAINE	20	Induced	Yes	Yes	Yes	No	No
DEEP	32	Induced	No	Yes	Yes	Yes	No
MAHNOB-HCI	28	Induced	Yes	Yes	Yes	Yes	Valence

The MAHNOB-HCI dataset included 20 videos that were used to elicit prolonged emotions. The participants aided in video collection in the preliminary analysis by recording their feelings through self-assessment. The 20 source videos in the excerpt contain disgust, laughter, excitement, terror, sorrow, and neutral emotions. Each video clip lasted roughly 34–117 s. There were 27 stable people in the study: 13 men and 16 women. The EEG signals were collected using 32 activation electrodes that were located according to the Biosemi Active II and 10–20 Foreign System requirements. The attendees' faces were shot in 720 × 580 video at 60 frames per second and coordinated with the EEG signal. The dataset output is listed in detail in Table 2. A total of 239 records were made, each with its own label and details. Fig. 4 provides an example of the annotation labeling test result using the MAHNOB-HCI dataset. The solid line depicts the shift in goal valence over time, while the dotted

TABLE 2 MAHNOB-HCI dataset.

Number of testers	Total 27: male 15; female 12
Recorded value	32-channel EEG, peripheral physiological signals, face and body video using 6 cameras, eye gaze and audio
Report	Stimulation, excitation, superiority, and predictability, emotional keywords
Rating range	1–9
Videos number	20
Method of selection	Online streaming

System parameters Vs Output Results

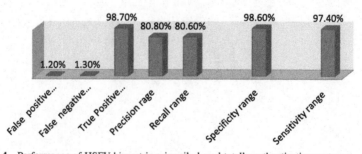

FIG. 4 Performance of HSFV biometric primarily based totally authentication system.

line depicts the valence expected by GA-LSTM. Annotation marking thresholds ranged from 0.1 to 0.1. Fig. 5A depicts changes in positive valence across time, while Fig. 5B depicts changes in negative valence over time. The GA-LSTM and goal results are often identical. The unusual thing is that the GA-LSTM valence tends to move to the neutral value faster than that of the target valence just after a positively or negatively valence statement. The explanation for this is that the annotation data are unbalanced. Since there are more optimistic annotations than negative annotations, the model is influenced more, and negative valence or arousal cannot be correctly regressed. Besides that, good feelings are almost impossible to mark with facial expressions, whereas negative feelings are difficult to label due to major individual variations. As a consequence, the process of marking by facial expression is sensitive to negative expression of emotion.

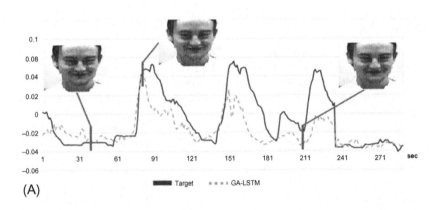

(A)

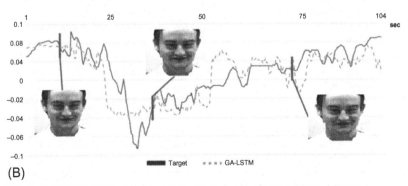

(B)

FIG. 5   MAHNOB-HCI test results. (A) Positive valence and (B) negative valence.

4 Conclusions and future work

This chapter presents heartbeat signal from face video as a new biometric characteristic for person verification. Using the Transformation matrix on a waterfall methodology of the reproduced HSFV, features were extracted. The bilateral Minkowski distances were derived as features from the Radon picture. A decision tree-based supervised method was used for authentication. The suggested biometric, as well as its authentication mechanism, proved its biometric recognition capability. However, a number of problems must be investigated and resolved before this biometric may be used in real systems. For example, in a real scenario, it is required to establish the effective length of a video that may be taken for authentication. By managing the face spoofing, combining face with HSFV may generate intriguing results. Processing time, characteristic optimization to decrease the disparity between accuracy and acceptance rate, and experimenting with alternative metrics for computing the matching score are all things that must be looked at. These might be potential future areas for expanding on the existing research.

References

[1] A.K. Jain, A. Ross, Introduction to biometrics, in: A.K. Jain, P. Flynn, A.A. Ross (Eds.), Handbook of Biometrics, Springer, US, 2008, pp. 1–22.
[2] C.W. Lacewell, M. Gebril, R. Buaba, A. Homaifar, Optimization of image fusion using genetic algorithms and discrete wavelet transform, in: Radar Signal and Image Processing, vol. 10, IEEE, 2010.
[3] J.-Y. Gan, J.-F. Liu, Fusion and recognition of face and iris feature based on wavelet feature and KFDA, in: Proceedings of the 2009 International Conference on Wavelet Analysis and Pattern Recognition, Boarding, IEEE 12–15 July, 2009.
[4] S.A. Vivek, J. Aravinth, S. Valarmathy, Feature extraction for multimodal biometric and study of fusion using gaussion mixture model, in: Proceedings of the International Conference on Pattern Recognition, Informatics and Medical Engineering, March 21–21, IEEE, 2012.
[5] J.-Y. Gan, J.-H. Gao, J.-F. Liu, Research on face and iris feature recognition based on 2DDCT and Kernel Fisher Discriminant Analysis, in: Proceedings of the 2008 International Conference on Wavelet Analysis and Pattern Recognition, Hong Kong, 30–31 Aug, 2008.
[6] A. Mishra, Multimodal biometrics it is: need for future system, Int. J. Comput. Appl. 3 (4) (2010).
[7] S. Chaudhary, R. Nath, A fusion mutimodal biometric recognition system based on palmprint, fingerprint & face, in: International Conference on Advances in Recent Technologies in Communication and Computing, IEEE, 2009, pp. 596–600.
[8] L. Shen, Z. Ji, Y. Li, L. Bai, Coding Gabor features for multi-modal biometrics, in: Chinese Conference on Pattern Recognition, IEEE, 2010.
[9] G. Piella, H. Heijmans, A new quality metric for image fusion, in: Proceedings 2003 International Conference on Image Processing (Cat. No.03CH37429), 2003, p. III-173, https://doi.org/10.1109/ICIP.2003.1247209.
[10] D.K. Sahu, M.P. Parsai, Different image fusion techniques –a critical review, Int. J. Mod. Eng. Res. 2 (5) (2012) 4298–4301. ISSN: 2249–6645.

[11] M. Deshmukh, U. Bhosale, Image fusion and image quality assessment of fused images, Int. J. Image Process. 4 (5) (2010) 484–508.

[12] C. Hegde, S. Manu, P. Deepa Shenoy, K.R. Venugopal, L.M. Patnaik, Secure authentication using image processing and visual cryptography for banking applications, in: 16 th International Conference on Advanced Computing and Communications. ADCOM 2008, 2008, pp. 65–72.

[13] H.-Y. Wu, M. Rubinstein, E. Shih, J. Guttag, F. Durand, W. Freeman, Eulerian video magnification for revealing subtle changes in the world, ACM Trans. Graph. 31 (4) (2012) 65. 1–65:8.

[14] Y.N. Singh, Evaluation of electrocardiogram for biometric authentication, J. Inf. Secur. 03 (01) (2012) 39–48.

[15] L. Biel, O. Pettersson, L. Philipson, P. Wide, ECG analysis: a new approach in human identification, IEEE Trans. Instrum. Meas. 50 (3) (2001) 808–812.

[16] M. Nawal, G.N. Purohit, ECG based human authentication: a review, Int. J. Emerg. Eng. Res. Technol. 2 (3) (2014) 178–185.

[17] M.A. Haque, R. Irani, K. Nasrollahi, T.B. Moeslund, Physiological parameters measurement from facial video, IEEE Trans. Image Process. (2014).

Chapter 8

Real-time emotion engagement tracking of students using human biometric emotion intensities

Sumitav Acharya[a] and Motahar Reza[b]

[a]Department of Computer Science and Engineering, National Institute of Science and Technology, Berhampur, India, [b]Department of Mathematics, GITAM Deemed to be University, Hyderabad, India

1 Introduction

Knowing human deportment is a token of the judgment that demonstrates the visual evidence of facial movement or expression. Human emotion intensities [1] are another type of character which can be measured by some visual discernible of few parts of facial movements. As we know, FACS (Facial Action Coding System) is the most acknowledged model to track facial behaviors [2]. FACS is used to understand and measure the anatomical system, which refers to the collection of encodings of different facial movements compounding the basic AUs (Action Units) and creates the emotion categories [3, 4]. One of the prominent issues rising nowadays revolves around student concentration capabilities [5]. Students of this generation are more inclined toward short-term pleasure resources. With emerging technologies comes comfort, which eventually proves to be a distraction for the fickle-minded students. Another point being with the advancement of technology, the methodology and tactics to deliver learnings to a student are becoming innovative. Here comes a challenging situation for the teachers to deliver their best and get to know if students are getting the delivered learnings from their end. Student commitment comes into existence when the student participates in the learning atmosphere and equally supports the teacher's efficiency and, it turns out to be the most promising trait contributing to smooth and productive teaching and learning process [4, 6].

This chapter derived behavioral attributes from multiple images of our custom-made "Distracted" dataset that uses understanding from FACS [2] database. Then we output the extracted information to a file with one column signifying respective pixel values supporting whether a face is classified as

Machine Learning for Biometrics. https://doi.org/10.1016/B978-0-323-85209-8.00008-0

distracted or not. Initially, annotations are done to identify the features contributing to a Boolean array using specified action units. The model is a concatenation of Custom-Deep Emotion Network using Convolutional Neural Network [7], and the other one is the Reversed-Neural network to maintain the uniformity. In the first phase, the images are preprocessed using various preprocessing techniques [8], and then annotation results in significant pixel values. In the second phase, the pixel values are examined using the proposed model, which goes through several layers of training and then outputs the trained model. Now, this trained model is loaded into the application and shows up the classification for a respective face in real-time. Extracting behavioral attributes of the students determines their engagement index. The engagement index is directly proportional to their level of understanding. In this era of digitization, smartphones are acting as one of the resources for extracting data, be it keystroke dynamics, touch dynamics, or Gait Recognition. These all track the behavior of the users, and then the content is displayed according to that. These existing factors bring to us tracking human emotion intensities to solve Behavioral Biometrics in students in the classroom [9, 10]. If there's any fault in the system, whole learning goes to waste. One of the eminent issues is being handled using Behavioral tracking of the students [11, 12].

Although there exist multiple approaches focusing on student engagement tracking given that they are based on part-based methods, i.e., analyzing different movements in a face. Our primary goal is to associate prominent features out of face using Action Units, those contributing a distracted face, and then classifying according to that. Our model's multipurpose methodology supports various booming concerns related to student concentration [4], be it in class or even while attending the virtual classroom, which equally helps the futuristic aspect of our model. We further extend our goal to be not limited to only student distraction, but this methodology can also be used to track a user's engagement while watching videos. The below flowchart takes one through our proposed work.

2 Related work

As we know, behavioral biometrics deals with recognizing persons based on their unique behavioral traits. It opens up a horizon of traits like what we see in our day-to-day authentication strategies ranging from voice recognition, keystroke dynamics to human signature recognition. These strategies are majorly equipped in many of the modern applications to track the behavior of their users. But here, we have considered tracking the behavior of an individual through their emotions via facial emotion recognition. Thus, tracking the engagement of students via their emotions is one such application we have discovered. The existing art of methods represents the flow of engagement detection which is being divided into three main categories: Automatic, Semi-Automatic, and Manual. In general, machine-based systems promote observational strength, i.e., through pupil movements, facial emotions features can be extracted to identify an engaged student in a class. Now engagement detection focuses more on the methods like Facial Expression, Part-based methods which states the techniques to analyze a face through different action units also known as FACS and appearance-based methods.

The research conducted by Zewe Serpell and Yi-Ching Lin [13] examined whether humans can analyze an engaged face or not and then based on the observations used the signals to automate the process. Another article contributed by Mikhaylov D.M. and Samoylov A.S [14] monitors the faces based on the template matching technique. Also, they suggested some modifications on top of it considering template averaging, face loss at image edges, lost face recovery etc. Omid Mohamad Nezami et al. [15] present a deep learning-based model to improve engagement recognition from images that overcome the data sparsity challenge by pretraining it. Recently, prediction on student's emotion or candidates' behavioral competency is analyzed to using the real-time image processing based on an artificial intelligence [16, 17].

3 Methodology

Our workflow revolves around three layers of phases. The initial phase deals with obtaining image data and preprocessing [8] it. The second phase deals with annotating essential features based on the FACS database for a distracted face (will be seen in detail in the below explanation) and then preparing pixel values *vs* label database followed by applying the feature extraction technique. The third and final phase involves training our model on top of our extracted dataset and then classifying based on real-time images using an application that triggers a real-time camera (Fig. 1).

3.1 Preprocessing steps for initial dataset preparation

Preprocessing is an enhancement of images to subdue unwanted damages further increasing the image's feature necessary for further processing [8].

The algorithm states that the imperfect pixel is often substituted as an average of nearby pixel values. Given that there exist multiple techniques to preprocess a damaged image ranging from Gaussian Blur technique, Fourier transform (mostly used in image filtering, compression, and reconstruction), to geometric transformation (where the locations of the pixels are altered) etc.

Our dataset consists of multiple 364*321 resolution images based on the input images we performed various preprocessing steps, i.e., Re-sizing, Normalization, Gaussian Blur technique, etc.

1. Every input image was resized up to 48*48 to maintain uniformity across the model. The background objects under a particular threshold were considered an input for the second stage of preprocessing.

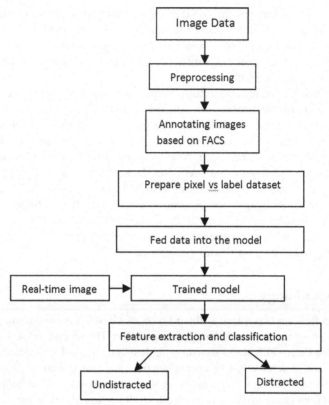

FIG. 1 Block diagram to explain the methodology.

2. Then we perform normalization on the images that change the range of pixel intensity values.
3. Then the Gaussian Blur technique was applied to remove unwanted noise.

3.2 Feature extraction technique

In our work, we have used Boosted LBP (Local Binary Pattern) as the feature extraction technique because it takes less computational time as compared to the standard LBP method. In this approach, the Chi-square distance between the corresponding LBPs of two facial images is majorly used for classification. This technique gave an accuracy of 96.72% on my dataset.

3.3 Interpreting FACS database

Facial Action Coding System is a technique of part-based methods where facial parts are considered to analyze human emotion. Firstly, the standard was revealed by an anatomist Carl-Herman Hjortsjö and later embraced by Ekman and Wallace V. Friesen and declared in 1978 [5, 18]. Thus, FACS is considered to be one of the very few procedures possible for evaluating emotions in real-time, before this, Facial Electromyography (FEMG) was used [6]. However, other measures like psychometric tests are there but they must be completed after a motive has been presented. After registration of this innovative strategy mostly, the examiners were using manual coding video registrations of members according to the action units described by the FACS [2]. But now, it holds the capability to automate the entire analysis process, thus helping with a lot of effort and money to these researchers. Nowadays, the coding system is widely used across many respected domains. Moreover, it is majorly being used by computer animators, gamers, and computer scientists involved in facial identification tasks.

The coding system also helps the interviewers to analyze the facial behaviors while communicating with the candidate. Using FACS [7], the examiners can easily break down emotion into multiple action units like for what we have considered in our classification is to have the action units for a distracted face. So for the same, we have considered Inner Brow Raiser + Upper Lid Raiser + Blink + Head with respective AU (1 + 5 + 45 + 53). Also, there are 14 head postures and actions, nine eye forms, 5 diverse action units, 9 action descriptors (i.e., movements for which the anatomical basis is unspecified), 9 gross behaviors, and 5 visibility codes. So, anyone wishing to make an emotion-based classification can study the database to classify according to their need such as EMFACS and the FACS [19] Investigators' Guide. Concerning the studies in this review, there were inconsistencies with how affective (i.e., emotional) response is inferred from AU activation. Specifically, there were instances where AUs, as well as emotion-based inferences, were not used in agreement with FACS [2].

Let us explore some of those in the database:

Now for the distracted dataset, we used the following action units that dominantly describe a distracted face (Figs. 2 and 3).

3.4   Step-wise algorithm

1. **Preparing the dataset**
   1.1 Initial Preprocessing
   1.2 **data[]**<- load from csv with labels
   1.3 Splitting the test and train data
   1.4 Converting string of pixels data to an array
   1.5 Generating reversed images for every data assuming emotions are symmetric
2. **Defining the model**
   2.1 Defining **Model 1** to train distracted dataset
   2.2 Defining **Model 2** to train the symmetric-distracted dataset

ACTION UNIT	DESCRIPTION	FACIAL MUSCLE	SAMPLE
1	Inner Brow Raiser	Frontalis, pars medialis	
5	Upper Lid Raiser	Levator palpebrae superioris	
2	Outer Brow Raiser	Frontalis, pars lateralis	

FIG. 2 Sample FACS database.

Action Units	Label
1+5+45+53 (Inner Brow Raiser+ Upper Lid Raiser+Blink+Head Up)	
41+42+43+54+64 (Lid Drop+Slit+EyesClosed+HeadDown +Eyes Down)	

FIG. 3 Distracted dataset sample.

3. **Train two models, one on normal images, another on reversed images, and finally a neural network on predicted values from these models, i.e., the third one**
4. **Prediction**
   3.1 pred_tr [] <- prediction on training data
   3.2 pred_te [] <- prediction on test data

5. **Enumerating on the dataset to save the trained model to reduce complexity**
6. **Trains a Conventional Neural Network on previously predicted values by the two models as the third model.**
7. **Real-Time classification**
    7.1 Loading the saved models
    7.2 Predicting on top of a captured frame
        7.2.1. Recognizing the face
        7.2.2. Prediction using the loaded models

3.5   Training and real-time classification

After deriving bottleneck features out of the dataset, we train the labels based on pixel values. So pixel values, in a sense, denote the region which predominantly signifies a particular behavioral trait (distracted/not). Encoding the images in our custom made dataset. Three columns extracted one is the label and the second column is a string (pixel values) accompanied by prognostication. You just have to operate through this dataset to train it and then test it over the given dataset. The architecture of the model is mentioned in Fig. 4.

Apart from this, one thing that has been done is that two models have trained one on the normal image with the same architecture and the other one being the reversed image to maintain the symmetricity. This becomes very helpful when the real-time setting input isn't stable. After the same is concatenated with the primary one, the prediction is made over the two classes.

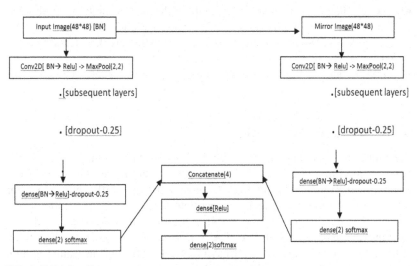

FIG. 4 Model architecture.

For training purposes, we granted the batch size of 64 with each of 25 epochs. And for the last one where both models concatenate, the batch size is 32 and each of 3 epochs.

As the model in Fig. 4 promotes symmetricity by concatenating mirror and normal images, each image goes through succeeding layers of convolution [20] of size 128*128 and a dense layer of 64, maintaining a dropout of 0.25 in each designated layer. Ultimately, after we get the demanded classification from the last layer using softmax as an activation function, we again concatenate the four, and a final prediction is made on top of softmax [8, 20]. Eventually, after prognosticating for each image, we preserve the model to eradicate future execution expenses. In real-time prediction, the GUI triggers the camera, and in the backend, the model is loaded, boosting response and overcoming time concerns. The later part will be reviewing the arrayed GUI results.

3.6 Advantage and disadvantages of the approach

First, listing down the pros of our strategy:

- In this chapter, we have concatenated two layers of models to advance accuracy. One is the custom deep emotion network and the second, Reversed-NN model to handle the symmetricity considering the real-life scenarios.
- Our model exceeds the existing models to classify a distracted face in a live classroom with an average accuracy of 95.7%.

The shortcomings:

- I believe that the detriment of our model is the heterogeneity of our dataset. For future work, we have to consider wide varieties of dataset covering human faces from different regions and then extracting their facial features on top of it.
- Figuring out the model accuracy on top of the diverse dataset.

4 Results and discussions

The workflow was implemented using Python-3.7.9 leveraging various Computer Vision libraries like OpenCV, Tensorflow, and Keras. The entire work is done and examined using Intel Core i5 4th Gen 4210U processor. For real-time prediction, the model has been interfaced with GUI. It follows like you opening the application and it asks you to launch the Webcam, and real-time prediction goes on with that. The GUI serves as a standalone application to trigger the model for real-time behavioral tracking of students using Emotion Intensities. Figs. 5 and 6 explain the GUI results.

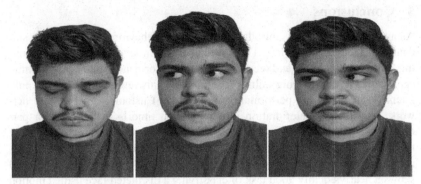

FIG. 5 GUI results of distracted images in real-time.

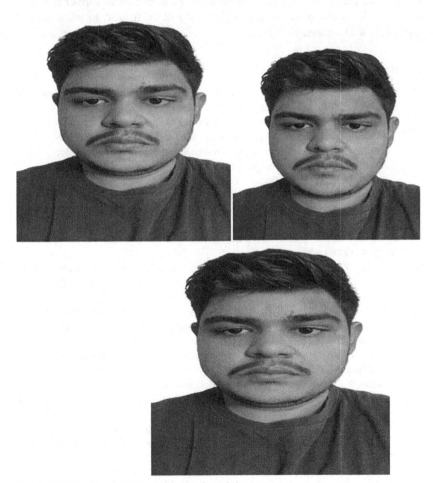

FIG. 6 GUI results of undistracted images in real-time.

5 Conclusions

An adequate solution was introduced to track the behavioral attributes of a student while studying in a class. This solution opens up several applications ranging from authenticating and recording student performance, enhancing training capabilities to diminishing failure measures. By this research, we do not only intend to heighten the performance through the Custom-Deep Emotion network, but also the deterioration in computation time is striking. Major part of the study concentrates on deriving the prevailing features out of a face using the FACS database and then mapping it with Behavioral Biometrics by implementing the model to distinguish the designated classes. The technique adopted shows a nearly equally good task of classifying a distracted face using emotion intensities with a significant gain in model performance. Our approach lacks in considering the diverse dataset to automate the entire process, further enhancements made in our model and this domain will be fruitful to track student engagement in a class.

References

[1] Y. Tian, T. Kanade, J.F. Cohn, Recognizing action units for facial expression analysis, IEEE Trans. Pattern Anal. Mach. Intell. 23 (2) (2001) 97–115.

[2] Y. Tong, W. Liao, Q. Ji, Facial action unit recognition by exploiting their dynamic and semantic relationships, IEEE Trans. Pattern Anal. Mach. Intell. 9 (10) (2007) 1683–1699.

[3] J. Chen, Z. Chen, Z. Chi, H. Fu, Facial expression recognition in video with multiple feature fusion, IEEE Trans. Affect. Comput. 9 (2018) 38–50.

[4] A. Paul, D. Mcvitty, The meanings of student engagement: implications for policies and practices, in: A. Curaj, L. Matei, R. Pricopie, J. Salmi, P. Scott (Eds.), The European Higher Education Area, Springer, Cham, 2015, https://doi.org/10.1007/978-3-319-20877-0_232.

[5] F. Bougourzi, K. Mokrani, Y. Ruichek, F. Dornaika, A. Ouafi, A. Taleb-Ahmed, Fusion of transformed shallow features for facial expression recognition, IET Image Process. 13 (9) (2019) 1479–1489.

[6] M.M. TaghiZadeh, M. Imani, B. Majidi, Fast facial emotion recognition using convolutional neural networks and Gabor filters, in: 2019 5th Conference on Knowledge Based Engineering and Innovation (KBEI), Tehran, Iran, 2019, pp. 577–581.

[7] S. Adatrao, M. Mittal, An analysis of different image preprocessing techniques for determining the centroids of circular marks using Hough transform, in: 2016 2nd International Conference on Frontiers of Signal Processing (ICFSP), Warsaw, 2016, pp. 110–115.

[8] A. Mahfouz, T.M. Mahmoud, A.S. Eldin, A survey on behavioral biometric authentication on smartphones, J. Inf. Secur. Appl. 37 (2017) 28–37.

[9] A. Buriro, B. Crispo, F. Delfrari, K. Wrona, Hold and sign: a novel behavioral biometrics for smartphone user authentication, in: Proceedings of IEEE Security and Privacy Workshops (SPW), San Jose, CA, 2016, pp. 276–285.

[10] B.L. Tait, Behavioural biometrics authentication tested using eyewriter technology, in: Proceedings of 2019 IEEE 12th International Conference on Global Security, Safety and Sustainability (ICGS3), London, United Kingdom, 2019, pp. 1–9.

[11] M. Frank, R. Biedert, E. Ma, I. Martinovic, D. Song, Touchalytics: on the applicability of touchscreen input as a behavioral biometric for continuous authentication, IEEE Trans. Inf. Forensics Secur. 8 (1) (2013) 136–148.

[12] E.A. Clark, J. Kessinger, S.E. Duncan, M.A. Bell, J. Lahne, D.L. Gallagher, S.F. O'Keefe, The facial action coding system for characterization of human affective response to consumer product-based stimuli: a systematic review, Front. Psychol. 11 (2020), https://doi.org/10.3389/fpsyg.2020.00920.

[13] J. Whitehill, Z. Serpell, Y.-C. Lin, A. Foster, J. Movellan, The faces of engagement: automatic recognition of student engagement from facial expressions, IEEE Trans. Affect. Comput. 5 (2014) 86–98.

[14] D. Mikhaylov, A. Samoylov, P. Minin, A. Egorov, Face detection and tracking from image and statistics gathering, in: Proceedings—10th International Conference on Signal-Image Technology and Internet-Based Systems, SITIS, 2014, pp. 37–42.

[15] O. M Nezami, M. Dras, L. Hamey, D. Richards, S. Wan, C. Paris, Automatic recognition of student engagement using deep learning and facial expression, in: U. Brefeld, E. Fromont, A. Hotho, A. Knobbe, M. Maathuis, C. Robardet (Eds.), Machine Learning and Knowledge Discovery in Databases: European Conference, ECML PKDD 2019, Würzburg, Germany, September 16–20, 2019, Proceedings, Part III, Springer, Cham, 2020, pp. 273–289. Springer Nature, (Lecture Notes in Computer Science (including subseries Lecture Notes in Artificial Intelligence and Lecture Notes in Bioinformatics)).

[16] Y. Su, Y. Suen, K.E. Hung, Predicting behavioral competencies automatically from facial expressions in real-time video-recorded interviews, J. Real-Time Image Proc. (2021), https://doi.org/10.1007/s11554-021-01071-5.

[17] J. Zhou, J. Ye, Sentiment analysis in education research: a review of journal publications, Interact. Learn. Environ. (2020) 1–13.

[18] M.A. Abu, A. Halim, A. Rahman, A study on image classification based on deep learning and tensorflow, Int. J. Eng. Res. Technol. 12 (4) (2019) 563–569.

[19] G. Ou, Y.L. Murphey, Multi-class pattern classification using neural networks, Pattern Recogn. 40 (1) (2007) 4–18.

[20] S. Liu, W. Deng, Very deep convolutional neural network based image classification using small training sample size, in: Proceedings of 2015 3rd IAPR Asian Conference on Pattern Recognition (ACPR), Kuala Lumpur, 2015, pp. 730–734.

Chapter 9

Facial identification expression-based attendance monitoring and emotion detection—A deep CNN approach

Priyanshu Sarmah[a], Rupam Das[a], Sachit Dhamija[a], Saurabh Bilgaiyan[b], and Bhabani Shankar Prasad Mishra[b]

[a]School of Electronics Engineering, KIIT, Deemed to be University, Bhubaneswar, India, [b]School of Computer Engineering, KIIT Deemed to be University, Bhubaneswar, India

1 Introduction

The COVID-19 pandemic has affected the health of people worldwide and brought challenges in the field of education. Educational institutions are closed worldwide in order to comply with social distancing norms. Institutions attempted to alleviate this problem by moving their classes online to maintain the continuity of classes and lectures. Many pieces of software for video-conferencing among teachers and students were made available to educational institutions for conducting online classes. While such steps have promoted online learning, classes online come with their own set of problems. This chapter aims to illustrate technological frameworks to solve some key challenges.

A teaching method used by teachers and lecturers in a traditional classroom setup is student feedback to alter teaching strategy. In a physical classroom setting, the teacher can gauge the comprehension of a concept or lack thereof by the students from their responses and facial expressions. These "reactions" from the students provide the teachers with information that they use to change the pace or structure of a lecture to understand the students better. Naturally, this process cannot occur effectively during an online lecture that requires functioning computer hardware and a fast Internet connection. Malfunctioning Web-cams and microphones, as well as unreliable access to the Internet, impede this process. It is common for the video feed during online lectures to be pixelated, jittery, or remain turned off due to poor Internet connectivity. Students

Machine Learning for Biometrics. https://doi.org/10.1016/B978-0-323-85209-8.00001-8

155

may refrain from notifying the teacher that they have not understood a concept instead of saying they have. In such a situation, teachers do not get any feedback from the students' expressions on whether it would be better to explain a concept again or continue the lecture. To tackle this issue, technology to detect facial expressions could provide some basic information about the students' reactions to aid teachers during online lectures.

Emotion recognition is a technology that can detect the emotions of a person. While the psychological aspects are difficult to understand by technological means, essential emotion recognition can be performed by detecting and classifying facial expressions. Six basic facial expressions are accepted and used in emotion-detection algorithms—Anger, Happiness, Sadness, Surprise, Disgust, and Fear. These expressions have different and distinct characteristics and appearance figures based on which classification of an expression is performed [1]. Facial expression detection technology can enable teachers in an online learning scenario to compensate for the lack of student feedback during online classes. This implementation would also help students feel more in tune with the study matter as concepts they found hard to understand in online learning would be repeated by the teachers.

Another issue that crops up during online classes is that of marking the attendance of students. Schools and colleges integrate attendance as a part of education and provide credits based on it. In a physical class, the teacher could mark the students who were in class as a present. Students who genuinely suffer from hardware malfunction or unreliable Internet connectivity can also leave their Webcams turned off to at least join the online lecture. The teacher cannot accurately distinguish between these problems to mark some students present and others absent for the online lecture. A solution to this challenge would be to use facial recognition methods to identify the student correctly without relying on the teacher manually.

Facial recognition is a technology that is a biometric mode of authentication of people. This technology has continued to improve exponentially owing to rapid improvements in image-processing algorithms [2]. Facial recognition algorithms perform analysis on faces, obtain unique identification features for each face, and then identify (and thus proceed to authenticate) faces by corresponding the identification features from a database of registered faces. This process is not only fast and convenient but also can be fine-tuned to achieve high accuracy. This technology can be utilized in frameworks to automatically mark attendance and authentication in accessing and appearing for examinations online. This process relieves the teacher from having to identify students and manually mark attendance. If integrated into the student's computer, this technology can perform authentication without putting excess load on an unreliable Internet connection by performing face recognition on the student's computer and sending only the necessary data online instead of pictures or videos. Thus, it can mark attendance for students who do not have access to high-speed Internet.

This chapter illustrates effective models for identification using facial recognition technology using the histogram of oriented gradients (HOG) as well as a convolutional neural network (CNN)-based approach to facial expression-based emotion detection.

The authors propose a framework utilizing HOG and CNN models to enable a smoother experience in online education, helping teachers and students alike to concentrate on academics rather than solve technical problems during the mass adoption of e-learning facilities.

2 Related work

Marking attendance by facial recognition is a tested practice. An apt example would be the work of Budi et al. [3], where they implemented a comprehensive framework detailing image acquisition, face detection, attendance registration, and attendance monitoring. They developed a mobile application to be used by the lecturer for clicking pictures of students and upload them to a computer that then identifies the students and registers attendance for the recognized faces [3]. For face detection, they used Haar cascade classifiers to crop and group the faces according to the classes. For the students who were registered to the attendance system, lecturers could monitor attendance by obtaining a simple report of attendance [3]. The authors emphasize time efficacy and reduction of staff workload. They compared the time taken for attendance registration through their application to traditional methods like roll-calling and sign sheets being handed down. Tested on a selected number of students for a week, they found that taking pictures to register attendance outperformed manual methods [4]. Similarly, the staff is no longer required to convert attendance data to digital form [3]. Their proposed work lessened printing and labor costs as well as human error involved while registering attendance.

Allagwail and Elbkosh [4] implemented a facial recognition system where the training dataset was increased using the symmetrical feature of faces. From every image, they separated the left and right halves of the face, mirrored the halves, and attached these mirrored halves to the original halves of the face [4]. The HOG algorithm was used for feature extraction in both training and testing sets with symmetrical samples of each face. Upon using their framework on the original and symmetrical samples, they obtained 96% and 100% accuracy for those samples, respectively [4]. Asmara et al. [5], in their paper, compared the Viola-Jones cascade classifier and HOG performance in face detection. For HOG, they extracted the faces in the images by finding contours in the edge map, followed by extracting HOG descriptors to train a linear support vector machine (SVM) [5]. They performed both positive and negative (pictures with no faces) training. The Viola-Jones classifier selected Haar-like features, creating the integral image and calculating feature values followed by AdaBoost feature selection before performing multilevel classification [5]. Their training set contained images of faces in various poses, illuminations, occlusions, scale (size of the face), and heavy makeup. Their implementations had mixed results due to these variants but had an average accuracy of 71.11% for the Viola-Jones classifier and 79% by using HOG features in [5]. Ahmad et al. [6] used histogram equalization and median filtering to improve image quality. Then, they utilized HOG for feature extraction before using principal component analysis (PCA) to reduce dimensionality and an SVM classifier for face detection. They used the Yale database to evaluate performance, which was 98.64% accuracy [6].

Several studies, experiments, and algorithms were used to detect people's emotions from static images, video feeds, a combination of video and audio, and those involving body language. Jaiswal and Nandi [7] proposed a CNN-based model with 1×1 convolutions to reduce dimensionality before the last convolutions to lessen computational complexity, taking inspiration from an "inception module." An inception module contains multiple smaller network architectures with fewer filters to reduce dimensionality. They performed extensive techniques to reduce complexity, including batch normalization, separable convolutions, global average pooling, and finally downsampling the images for enhanced feature extraction and improved accuracy. Their CNN model contained 10 convolutional layers, excluding ReLU and pooling layers [7]. They calculated a reduction in time complexity of 50% with their proposed model compared to the vanilla model without considering the classification part [7]. Their proposed model required 146,000 parameters and 9 h of training to achieve an average of 74% validation accuracy [7].

Happy et al. [8] proposed a learner monitoring system to monitor user activity automatically. Their framework depended wholly on visual cues to perform analyses to determine alertness, attention levels, and emotional state. They used local binary pattern features and block histogram features to detect facial expression changes, however minute, both local and global [8]. The detected emotions were classified into six emotion classes. Alertness level was determined using the PERCLOS standard. They used Haar-like features and a Kalman filter for efficient face detection followed by affine and perspective transformations to account for rotations and tilts of the detected faces [8]. They detected the eyes using local binary pattern-based features and the state of eye closure using a support vector machine classifier. Their work represents a comprehensive study on measuring various aspects of learners during online learning to promote more effectiveness in online learning.

More recently, deep learning-based implementations have become popular. Fatima et al. [9] used mini-Xception-based convolution models trained on the ImageNet dataset. Using the FER-2013 dataset, their model achieved over 95% accuracy. Minaee et al. [10] have used the Japanese Female Facial Expression (JAFFE), FER-2013, Cohn-Kanade (CK+), and the Facial Expression Research Group (FERG) image datasets to train their attention-based convolutional network. This proposed network had less than 10 layers to achieve 98% accuracy on their proposed model using the CK+ dataset and 92.8% accuracy on the

JAFFE dataset. Liliana [11] used the CK+ dataset with two other emotion classes, "contempt" and "neutral" emotions, to train a convolutional network achieving an average accuracy of 92.81%. Geetha and Joseph [12] used discrete wave transform (DWT) and fuzzy to enhance images of the CK+, Karolinska Directed Emotional Faces (KDEF), and Oulu-CASIA datasets. They used a modified mouth map to detect the mouth. They modified eye maps to construct eye geometry before using TensorFlow to classify and test the results of their proposed model [12]. They achieved an incredible 98.1% accuracy on their model using the KDEF dataset [12]. Wang et al. [13] used FERPlus (an extended version of FER-2013), SPEW, and AffectNet datasets to run a region attention network (RAN)-based model. They achieved an accuracy of 59.5% on the AffectNet dataset, 56.4% on the SFEW (static facial expression in the wild) dataset, 86.9% on the RAF-DB (Real-world Affective Faces Database) dataset, and the highest accuracy of 89.16% on the FERPlus dataset [13].

3 Proposed work

3.1 Facial recognition

Implementing the proposed framework requires using the student's Webcam to capture the student's image for attendance registration during the lecture classes. A practical implementation of facial recognition of attendance registration is installing software on the student's computer to function during an online lecture. This software would be able to check the presence of the student at predefined time intervals. The software does not require that the image of the student's face be transferred over an Internet connection. For the initial setup, a student must scan his face through the Webcam and reference the software for future referral. For every lecture, the student needs to log in. During the proceedings, the Webcam would take pictures of the student at predefined intervals. The ones who were successfully identified by the algorithm would be marked "present" for the lecture. This would be reflected in the database record for the corresponding student for that particular lecture. Any image-based attendance system could be devised following the basic principles of taking attendance. Our framework automates the process, making it more efficient and less cumbersome due to the nonrequirement of transferring the images over the Internet, simply displaying the results.

After the end of the lecture, the lecturer is required to confirm the final attendance. It required that the student present in front of the screen for most of the duration during the lecture. The teacher can set the time interval for the pictures to be taken and not disclosed to the students. Suppose the number of pictures taken by the Webcam is 10. It is required that the student is detected as present in it for at least 75% of the pictures. If this criterion is met, then the student would be marked as present. Here, in case of occasional false detections, such as detecting false positives (i.e., an error of mistakenly identifying an object as a human face) or detection of false negatives (i.e., incapability to detect human faces). Generally, the impact of false positives is harmless to the student for attendance registration unless a student complains about a misrecognized face or falsely detecting an object as a face. The lecturer is, however, suggested verifying the list of identified faces for every lecture session.

3.1.1 Face acquisition, processing, and recognition

The first step of this pipeline process is to locate all the faces from an image before distinguishing, classifying, and recognizing them. We find the image/ video locations, and then, it is passed to the next step of the process. For this process, we are implementing the HOG.

The key concept behind the HOG algorithm is that computer vision algorithms can easily recognize the appearance of an object, especially the characterization of shape based on the distribution of intensity gradients in an area. It does not require knowledge of corresponding edge or gradient intensity positions [14]. The image is divided into tiny regions containing a one-dimensional histogram of gradient directions representing the physical orientations of edges based on intensity [14]. Combining the one-dimensional histograms of all regions provides the final form of the HOG. Since it is so dependent on light intensity in the image to determine edges, contrast normalization of the whole image is a good approach before using the image. An application-based procedure for the implementation of HOG is described in the following.

To locate faces in the given image, we convert the image to gray scale as color data are unnecessary to locate the faces. Fig. 1 demonstrates this step.

Subsequently, every pixel of the image is examined and compared to the surrounding pixels, as shown in Fig. 2. This step aims to compare the darkness of the current pixel to the one right next to it, i.e., the contrast between pixel intensities is taken into account.

Arrows indicate the direction of light flow, i.e., the darkest pixel among the surrounding pixels is selected. When the aforementioned step is repeated for

FIG. 1   The grayscale version of an image containing the face of a person.

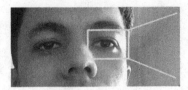

FIG. 2   Comparing pixel intensities.

each pixel, the pixels in the image are replaced with arrows. These arrows or gradients indicate the light flow from light areas to dark ones. When we consider the direction in which brightness changes, the dark images and the bright images end up equal representation.

As saving every pixel of the image is a tedious and computationally expensive process, the image is 16 × 16 pixels squares, the gradients pointing to each direction are numbered and counted. Arrows replace the square pixels of the image pointing to the direction of the gradient. We obtain a basic face structure of minimalistic representation, as shown in Fig. 3. Then, we locate the image areas that are found to be similar to the HOG pattern that has been extracted from faces that were trained earlier.

There exists a problem arising out of the fact that the pose and positioning of a single face would register differently to a computer. Fig. 4 is an example of the same.

Humans can recognize that both these pictures are of the same person, but a computer cannot. To counter this issue, the second step of the process wraps the images in such a way so that the lips and the eyes of a student image can be located in the sample space. An algorithm known as the "face landmark estimation" is used for this purpose. Sixty-eight points at specific locations of the face are termed landmarks, as shown in Fig. 5. The algorithm finds these points and distinguishes them.

HOG face pattern generated
from lots of face images

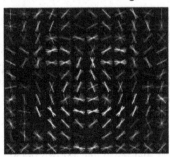

FIG. 3   The HOG face pattern.

FIG. 4   One face in different poses and lighting.

FIG. 5   The 68 landmarks we will locate on every face.

After recognizing the mouth and the eyes, the image is accordingly warped, sheared, and rotated to place the vital elements at the best position, as shown in Fig. 6.

This process allows the eyes and the mouth to be approximately the same position in the image, making it convenient to process the faces in the images. A few basic measurements are extracted, and then, the closest measurements are taken from the known faces. With the help of deep learning, the algorithm determines the essential parts of measurement. We train deep convolutional neural networks that create 128 measurements, as shown in Fig. 7. The training process works by three faces at a time:

- The face of a known person is loaded.
- A different picture of that particular known person is loaded.
- A picture of a different person is loaded.

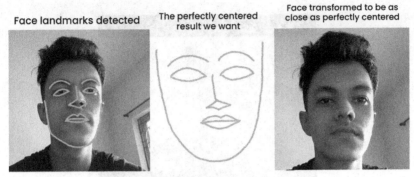

Face landmarks detected **The perfectly centered result we want** **Face transformed to be as close as perfectly centered**

FIG. 6 Rotation and shearing of detected facial landmarks.

128 Measurements Generated from Image

0.097496034368908	0.045223236083984	0.5973086936941	0.12369467318058
0.1252924674129	0.1281466782033	-0.070026844759914	0.058418422609568
0.03080943978723	0.06030917912716	0.11478432267904	0.89727545702558
0.0050505059068403	0.17521631717682	0.08962149173021	-0.0085843298584223
0.0974868340187	0.1981477253139	0.14841195040971	0.022388197481632
0.0066401711565094	0.10801389058365	0.123757817745	0.020696049556136
0.214131525158882	0.065554238855839	0.049525424808066	0.050584398210049
0.048540540039539	0.073130600154	0.13227833807468	0.07237545236379
0.212567175024778	0.1226262897253	0.5101629719138	-0.034365277737379
0.0514187717437	-0.029626874253154	0.1413292139768	0.045013956725597
0.016741496771574	0.0067503909160292	0.528127679228	-0.013955107890009
0.2121365014314	0.1595809660044	1.3407498500	0.1780OS5713387
0.061606746166945	0.1411424748516	0.0048638740554452	-0.0726000274321 56
0.061989940702915	0.033135158494114 9	-0.0394910750223 87	0.005051128275228
0.10904195904732	0.061901587992907	0.11443792283535	0.0148239535833
0.019414527341723	0.1504264324903 5	0.07199795544147 5	0.043765480012003
0.15245945751667	1.0568545013666	00146835956735 1	0.120622654D02
0.122166685780 02	0.1272865384817 1	0.05223154733777	0.0127744954079 39
0.089308121613	0.7428703457117 1	0.081752359367096	0.069833300612392
0.087945111095905	0.0653652325272 56	0.031709920614958	0.11638788878918
0.021407851949834	0.005176188122481 1	0037022035568953	0.015535792916059
0.018298890441656	0.1474654375506 8	1.1009479314089	0.10281457751989
0.011014151386917	2.105599194765 1	0.1278313182307 6	0.082041338051128
0033679834963 28	0.004109122790096 2	0.18932339605045	0.031351584941149
0.5813925713300 7	0.1134576573967 9	0.094398014247417	0.061901587992907
0.024210374802351	0.021352224051952	0.11768248677254	0.15042643249035
-0.057223934680223	0.19372203946114	0.10034311562777	1.0568545013666
0.023535015061498	-0.036726233353152	0.040977258235216	0.12728653848171
0.0098039731383324	0.84853030741215	0.032084941864014	0.74287034571171
0.020220354199409	0.09463594853878	0.02097608521580 7	0.065365232527256

FIG. 7 The 128 measurements for each face generated.

The algorithm observes the measurements of the three generated images. The neural network is modified so that the same faces have closer measurements while different faces have further apart measurements. The training process to encode faces requires a lot of computing power and immense amounts of data. After the neural network is trained, it can generate the measurements of any face. For this purpose, we will use the pretrained OpenFace model instead of training a model from scratch.

Finally, the last step of this process is to identify the person from a database of known people, which can be done by using classification algorithms of machine learning, of which an example is shown in Fig. 8. We chose to use the SVM classifier to accomplish this task. The classifier is trained to take the 128 measurements from a new test image, and the closest match is returned as the output.

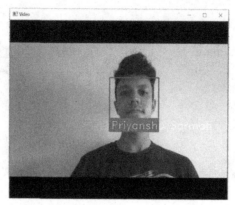

FIG. 8 Identification of face.

3.1.2 Evaluation

To assess the presence of utilized quality estimations versus our proposed framework, we utilized the extended Yale database B [15]. The Yale database contains 16,128 different images, each of 28 different people under varying lighting conditions and perspectives. These images are in gray scale. First, to assess how the contrast measure reflects the adjustment in the picture contrast, artificial contrast varieties of the faces in pictures are initiated. To evaluate how the contrast of an image affects the model's accuracy, contrast variations are artificially induced to the input image. Contrast essentially refers to the differentiation of how distinct a bright pixel is compared to a darker one. Ten percent of the inputted data are saturated at maximum and minimum intensities. When an image has higher differentiability among its pixels, the model finds it easier to process, and in turn, the results get better. So, there is a possibility that we can artificially add some contrast to the image for better performance.

Second, to assess how the proposed brightness measure reflects changes in image brightness, deviations in illumination are instigated. A crucial factor for the performance of the model is the image brightness. The image should be decently illuminated to maintain differentiability between the highlights, midtones, and shadows.

To test the model's performance, we artificially induced some changes in the brightness intensity of the image. Gamma parameter is the critical concept based on which we made adjustments in the illumination intensity. If $\gamma < 1$, the mapping is directed toward higher brightness and vice versa. To evaluate how the performance gets affected by a change in focus, sharpness, blurriness, we manipulated the smoothening of the image at various levels.

When the image's contrast is set around 0.4 through the gamma parameter, we can get optimum results. For the brightness, we get the best results for a measure of around 0.5. Focus measure lies at an optimum when the gamma value is set between 0.1 and 0.2. The sharpness of the image should be kept at around 0.7, while illumination at around 0.6 for best results. Thus, we can conclude that the face recognition model is dependent on various external conditions of the input image for its performance. When conditions are optimum, we obtain an accuracy of around 97.2%. However, the average accuracy was found to be 95.3%. In the real world, this framework is most likely to encounter indoor settings with average lighting. So, test images, like the one shown in Fig. 8, were taken to replicate such scenarios. The framework's accuracy drops to 75%–85% if the ambient lighting is too poor and the HOG algorithm cannot determine contrast gradients. There is also a significant drop in accuracy if there is a bright backlight behind the face. The Webcam automatically adjusts exposure in such situations, which darkens the face, rendering the framework unable to recognize faces. Table 1 compares the proposed framework with some other implementations of HOG.

3.2 Emotion recognition

The process of emotion detection is carried out by identifying facial expressions as this is a convenient aspect to monitor during online classes. A practical implementation of emotion detection is installing such software on the student's computer, which will function during an online lecture. This software would check the student's facial expressions at predefined time intervals and communicate to the teacher the mood or emotion that the student may have felt. In this manner, the software does not require that the image of the student's face be transferred over an Internet connection. Instead, the software runs the algorithm on the student's computer itself to obtain probability values for detected facial expressions. The probability values provide the likelihood of the student feeling an emotion based on their expressions. These numbers are sent over the Internet connection to the teacher's computer. It also provides the teacher the "dominant" facial expression, i.e., the emotion most likely felt by the student and for which the highest probability has been calculated. By adopting this measure, the framework can perform its intended function without requiring much bandwidth of what could be an unreliable Internet connection. This enables the

TABLE 1 Comparison of performance of some HOG implementations.

Sl. no.	Method	Accuracy (%)
1.	Allagwail and Elbkosh [4]	96.0
2.	Rahmad et al. [5]	79.0
3.	Proposed framework	97.2

teacher to continue receiving even a basic form of student feedback to enhance their lecture though they cannot see the students.

This implementation assumes seven basic emotions, to which the algorithm can classify detected facial expressions. These emotions are—Anger, Fear, Disgust, Neutral, Happiness, Sadness, and Surprise. To detect the facial expression and categorize it into one of seven emotion classes, the student's image needs to undergo preprocessing. This involves face detection, resizing, and cropping. Face detection is performed by Haar cascade classifiers, which was proposed by Viola and Jones in their 2003 paper [16]. Once the image is processed, a trained sequential model is loaded and classifies the detected facial expression into one emotion class. The model produces an output that contains detected probabilities for each emotion class for the detected facial expression.

Since training a custom neural network is a computationally intense process, this implementation uses transfer learning. Bottleneck features are created from a pretrained VGG-16 convolutional neural network (CNN). This network contained weights that were trained on the ImageNet database. Our sequential model uses these bottleneck features for training on the provided dataset.

3.2.1 Image gathering and preprocessing

The dataset used for detecting facial expressions is the FER-2013 (facial expression recognition) faces database created by Aaron Courville and Pierre-Luc Carrier [17]. Our dataset consists of 30,000 images of human faces with various facial expressions. Some colored pictures captured with various cameras and Webcams were also mixed in with this dataset. The pretrained convolutional neural network VGG-16 requires image input with 224×224 pixels and three RGB channels. In reality, the intended usage of the framework will encounter images with a much higher pixel density.

The following steps were performed during preprocessing:

- Convert the input 3-channel RGB image into a 1-channel grayscale image (where applicable). This is done so that there is no bias during training where colored images are mixed in with some grayscale images. Furthermore, the result of the model does not depend on the color of the image.
- In each image, human faces are detected by implementing cascade classifiers from the OpenCV library, which are based on Haar-like features. Cascade classifiers are trained using several positive (with faces or objects) images and arbitrary negative (without faces or objects) images. OpenCV contains several pretrained cascading classifiers used in image processing to detect frontal views of faces and the upper body.
- The images are cropped to the face detected by Haar cascade classifiers.
- The images are resized to the 224×224-pixel resolution, which is the requisite resolution for the VGG-16 model.

- Finally, to adhere to the 3-channel specification of VGG-16, the 1-channel (grayscale) images are converted to 3-channel images to use the weights of the pretrained model. Then, the images are saved to disk.

3.2.2 Haar cascade classifiers

Haar-like features are features in images that can be utilized for recognizing faces. Viola and Jones developed these by adapting the concept of Haar wavelets while developing the face detector for their model using cascading classifiers [16]. Haar-like features are used on smaller sections of an image and categorize them. A Haar feature looks at rectangular sections or regions of the image adjacent to each other and computes pixel densities in every region. One Haar feature is obtained by computing the difference between the sum of pixel densities of two adjacent same-sized rectangular regions A and B, as shown in Fig. 9 [16]. Haar cascade classifiers make use of the AdaBoost learning algorithm. This enables the classifier to select a small number of essential features from a large set.

Properties that we have utilized in the recognition of human faces using Haar features are:

(1) Nose bridge and eyes: adjacent rectangles for the nose bridge region and the eyes can produce a Haar feature since it is usually seen that the nose bridge area is brighter compared to the darker eyes, as shown in Fig. 10;
(2) The eye region is darker than the upper cheeks: adjacent rectangles for the eye region and the lower located upper cheeks are used for another Haar feature.

The regions of the image are under black and white adjacent rectangles. The sum of pixel densities lying under the white rectangles is subtracted from the sum of the pixel densities lying under the gray rectangles. In C in Fig. 9, the nose bridge region could occupy the central gray rectangle with the eye regions occupying the adjacent white rectangles. This filter has three rectangles where the sum of pixel densities in the laterally positioned white rectangles is subtracted from the centrally positioned gray rectangle. The filter used in D can subtract pixel densities between diagonally located regions [16]. In this manner,

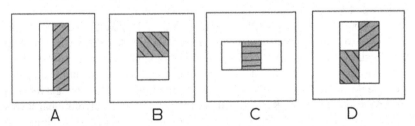

FIG. 9 Adjacent rectangles used for the extraction of Haar-like features.

FIG. 10   How the shaded rectangles correspond to the nose region.

using cascade classifiers that use Haar-like features is a convenient method to perform face detection on images.

3.2.3   VGG-16 network and modelling

The VGG-16 network structure was developed by Simonyan and Zisserman and entered into the ILSVRC—2014 competition, where it achieved an accuracy of 92.7% on the ImageNet dataset [18]. While it is similar to models preceding it that achieved high accuracies like AlexNet and LeNet, the depth of the VGG-16 network was increased. This network performs better with larger datasets and image-recognition-related tasks. This implementation has been used to express more characteristics of the dataset of facial expressions [19]. This allows it to learn and correctly classify expressions of faces with varying profile, tilt, and illumination. This makes it ideal for detecting the facial expressions of students who are sitting in front of cameras while attending online classes. Students may not always sit straight or be looking at the camera, for example, when solving a problem on paper. The training dataset contains faces in varied poses and expressions to account for this scenario.

The network architecture consists of 13 convolutional layers, three fully connected layers, and five pooling layers [19], a diagram of which is shown in Fig. 11. The size of the convolution kernel in the convolutional layers is 3×3 with stride fixed at 1. The size of the kernel in the pool layers is 2×2 with step size 2. The convolutional layers use the rectified linear unit (ReLU) as the activation function. The VGG-16 network receives input as a three-channel 224×224-pixel image. The first part contains two convolutional layers followed by a pooling layer. These convolution layers contain 64 kernels, each at 224×224 pixels.

The pooling layer resizes the image to 112×112 pixels. The second part contains two convolutional layers with 128 convolution kernels each. A pooling layer resizes the image to 56×56 pixels. The next part contains a set of three convolutional layers followed by a pooling layer. The convolutional layers increase the number of kernels to 256, and the pooling layer following it reduces the image size to 28×28 pixels. The fourth set of three convolutional layers increases the depth to 512 kernels, and a pooling layer resizes the image to 14×14 pixels. The fifth set also has three convolutional layers of depth

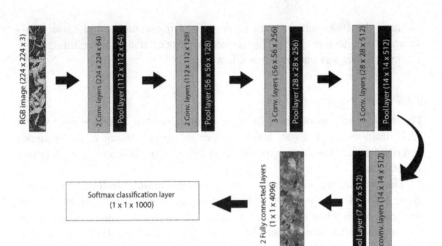

FIG. 11 Schematic architecture of the VGG-16 neural network.

512. The final pooling layer following it resizes the image to 7 × 7. Finally, we have two fully connected layers, each having 4096 nodes. The output layer uses a 1000-unit Softmax classification layer as the final layer in their configuration, representing the 1000 classes in the ImageNet dataset.

Due to hardware limitations involved in training a CNN, transfer learning is adopted. Transfer learning leverages the pretrained VGG-16 model's layers with ImageNet weights to train with a new dataset. However, it does not update the weights of the layers to produce the required bottleneck features. To create bottleneck features, only the first five sets of convolutional and pooling layers were utilized, i.e., the fully connected and classification layers were excluded from the VGG-16 architecture. The bottleneck features are stored in a NumPy array.

The sequential model utilized for training contains five dense layers, a dropout layer to adjust for overfitting, and a batch normalization layer. The first four dense layers contain 512, 256, 128, and 64 ReLU activation units. ReLU is a nonlinear activation function that can be represented as follows:

$$a = ReLU(b) = \begin{cases} b; & \text{if } b \geq 0 \\ 0; & \text{if } b < 0 \end{cases} \quad (1)$$

Here "a" and "b" represent output signal and input signal, respectively [19]. The output signal is 0 when the input signal is less than 0. This implies that the slope of "b" (the input signal) is constant for less than or equal to 0. This enables ReLU not only to avoid the vanishing gradient problem but also to improve performance during training. The fifth dense layer, i.e., the output layer, has seven Softmax activation units instead of ReLU. The Softmax layer will produce seven probability values corresponding to the seven emotion classes. This contrasts the 1000-unit Softmax layer utilized in Simonyan and Zisserman's network architecture [18]. The sequential model undergoes training after loading the weights and bottleneck features.

3.2.4   Testing and results

The test dataset was obtained from the original pool of 30,000 images with a 90:10 train-test split. Every image underwent preprocessing in the sequence described earlier: conversion to gray scale followed by face detection, cropping, and resizing.

The dropout rate was decreased to 0.7 to keep training loss low, for example, lower values for dropout rate, 0.4, significantly increased training loss for the last few epochs while also reducing testing accuracy. The batch normalization layer produced the best results when put after the third dense layer. The sequential model achieved 89.58% accuracy on the training dataset and 89.2% accuracy on the test dataset. During training, the learning rate was set to 0.001. The loss function used is categorical cross-entropy loss with the Adam optimizer.

Figs. 12 and 13 show graphs tracing the accuracy and categorical crossentropy loss, respectively, during our sequential model's training and test-validation process. It was found that beyond the 13th epoch, test-validation loss started to increase with no significant improvements in the corresponding accuracy. This is suggestive of overfitting as training accuracy continued to improve after epoch 13.

Tables 2 and 3 show Recall and Precision matrices, respectively, for the model while testing. Recall, also known as Sensitivity, may be defined as the ratio of predicted correct positive values by the model to the total number of positive values defined while training. Each number in the Recall matrix

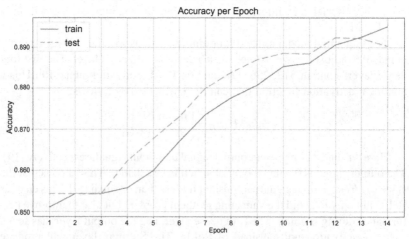

FIG. 12 Graph showing accuracy per epoch of training and validation.

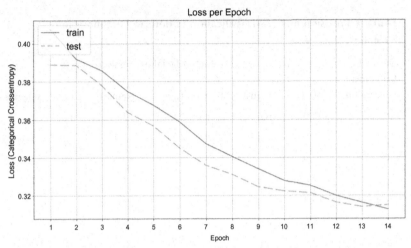

FIG. 13   Graph showing loss per epoch of training and validation.

TABLE 2 Recall matrix—classification of detected emotions into 7 classes.

Desired/ true facial expression	Detected facial expression						
	Anger	Disgust	Fear	Happy	Neutral	Sad	Surprise
Anger	91.7	4.2	0.0	0.0	2.5	0.0	1.7
Disgust	7.2	84.1	0.0	0.0	5.3	0.0	3.8
Fear	2.0	0.0	87.3	0.0	4.1	6.6	0.0
Happy	0.0	0.0	4.9	89.0	3.7	2.4	0.0
Neutral	0.0	17.9	0.0	2.8	79.3	0.0	0.0
Sad	0.0	14.6	0.0	0.0	1.1	83.0	1.3
Surprise	1.4	0.7	6.3	3.1	0.0	0.0	88.5

table represents this ratio. Recall implies that the ratio is defining how many correct values the model could predict. Precision may be defined as the ratio of correct predicted positive values to the total number of positive predicted values by the model. It is essentially the ratio defining how correct the predictions are. Each number in the Precision matrix table represents this ratio.

The Recall matrix shows that some emotion classes are slightly biased toward the "Disgust" emotion class. Several images from both "Sad" and "Neutral" emotion classes were categorized as "Disgust" emotion. The cause for this

TABLE 3 Precision matrix—classification of detected emotions into 7 classes.

Desired/ true facial expression	Detected facial expression						
	Anger	Disgust	Fear	Happy	Neutral	Sad	Surprise
Anger	93.0	0.0	0.0	4.8	2.2	0.0	0.0
Disgust	7.5	89.4	0.0	0.0	0.0	3.1	0.0
Fear	0.0	4.7	92.1	1.3	0.0	0.0	1.9
Happy	0.0	1.8	0.0	88.7	3.7	0.0	5.8
Neutral	6.2	0.0	0.0	3.4	80.6	2.3	7.5
Sad	3.9	0.0	8.2	0.0	10.1	77.8	0.0
Surprise	2.7	5.8	1.0	0.0	0.0	0.0	90.5

may be attributed to the relatively lesser number of images labeled "Sad" or "Neutral" compared to the number of images labeled "Disgust" in the training dataset. A further consequence of this can be seen in the recall value of images labeled "Neutral," i.e., 79.3, which is the lowest value among all the detected emotion classes. On the other hand, the "Anger" emotion class has the highest Recall of 91.4, perhaps because the number of images in the training dataset labeled "Anger" is the highest of any other emotion classes.

The values in the Precision matrix indicate that a higher number of images in the "Anger" emotion class were classified correctly. The higher number of training images for this class and the significantly different facial features on the faces of "Anger" images may be attributed as the cause. However, the "Sad" emotion class recorded the lowest precision value of 77.8, indicating a lesser number of predicted "Sad" images were correctly classified.

The sequential model achieved high accuracy while performing the 7-class classification problem, which involved classifying the detected facial expressions into 1 of 7 classes—Anger, Disgust, Fear, Happiness, Neutral, Sadness, and Surprise. The model and its weights were saved to disk to be implemented for emotion detection for any photo captured.

For real-world testing, several pictures of a small number of subjects were taken on low-resolution camera settings and laptop Webcams in 1280 × 720-pixel resolution, which is standard on most laptops. The subjects for these pictures were people who sat in front of a desk at a comfortable distance from the screen with natural indoor illumination. This was done to simulate the scenario of an online class where the student would be sitting on a chair with their Webcams affixed to a computer at desk level. The distance of the cameras or laptops from the subjects' faces varied between 75 and 90 cm. At the image's 1280 × 720-pixel resolution, this distance from the camera offered a good crop of the image to the 224 × 224-pixel resolution required for the model after face detection while preserving enough details in the image. Each of these images underwent preprocessing and generated bottleneck features before being inputted into the sequential model. The output of the sequential model provides a list of probabilities for each of the seven emotion classes. It is found that the model achieves high accuracy and correctly categorizes the facial expressions when the subject's face is well illuminated or illuminated enough to discern basic facial features. For dimly lit subjects, the model achieved lower accuracy for the detected emotion. Predicted dominant probabilities generated on a laptop powered by an Intel Core-i5 7200U processor with integrated graphics and 8GB memory were between 87% and 79%. These results were obtained consistently under 45 s, from image preprocessing to output (Fig. 14).

On comparing our framework to other appropriate implementations, such as the attention-based convolutional network by Minaee et al. [10], we find that our sequential model with VGG-16 weights has better accuracy of 89.2% as opposed to 70.02% on the same dataset, i.e., FER-2013. Wang et al. [13]

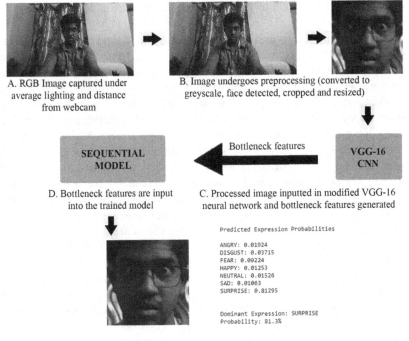

A. RGB Image captured under average lighting and distance from webcam

B. Image undergoes preprocessing (converted to greyscale, face detected, cropped and resized)

Bottleneck features

SEQUENTIAL MODEL

VGG-16 CNN

D. Bottleneck features are input into the trained model

C. Processed image inputted in modified VGG-16 neural network and bottleneck features generated

Predicted Expression Probabilities

ANGRY: 0.01924
DISGUST: 0.03715
FEAR: 0.09224
HAPPY: 0.01253
NEUTRAL: 0.01526
SAD: 0.01063
SURPRISE: 0.81295

Dominant Expression: SURPRISE
Probability: 81.3%

E. Predicted emotion probabilites generated as output

FIG. 14 Flowchart describing the process of emotion detection.

achieved an accuracy of 89.16% on the FERPlus dataset using the region attention network (RAN), which is very comparable to the proposed framework's accuracy of 89.2%. Other studies, however, have achieved better results by using other datasets like CK+, JAFFE, and KDEF. The proposed framework includes facial recognition, and emotion detection is a concept, the application of which would be beneficial in the online education scenario.

4   Conclusion and future work

This chapter proposes solutions to challenges brought about by the widespread adoption of online classes during the pandemic using facial recognition and emotion detection technology.

Facial recognition-based attendance registration is performed using HOG to achieve 97.2% accuracy in identifying faces under well-lit optimal conditions. The model is highly effective in the recognition of faces which is essential for users during online classes. This reduces the chances of false negatives and false positives while registering attendance. In distance learning, automating this process would relieve the lecturer of having to worry about attendance. Future scope involves enhancement by applying the framework in real-time attendance monitoring, which would be computationally expensive and require powerful hardware.

Emotion detection is performed by detecting facial expressions using Haar cascade classifiers, pretrained weights of the VGG-16 neural network, and a custom sequential model. Due to training limitations, a convolutional neural network, VGG-16 with pre-trained weights, is used to create bottleneck features for the images. These are then fed to the sequential model using ReLU activation, dropout, and a batch normalization layer with a learning rate of 0.001. Thus, the model classifies facial expressions from a preprocessed image into one of seven emotion classes—Anger, Disgust, Fear, Happiness, Neutral, Sadness, and Surprise. The model achieves 89.2% accuracy while testing on the test dataset. On performing testing in real-world conditions, the model achieves accuracies around 87%–79%, which is effective for the intent of this framework. In the future, there exists scope for improvement in the performance to increase accuracy to over 90%. Providing the dominant emotion detected from the student to the lecturer serves to have a basic form of "student reaction" to aid the teaching process of the lecturer. However, in the age of distance learning and unreliable Internet connections, optimized models which are not computationally demanding are a challenge. In the future, real-time emotion monitoring systems that can perform similar functions would serve enhanced utility in similar educational situations, e.g., classrooms, and would provide benefits to education. Real-time emotion detection models that can operate on a local machine instead of requiring high-bandwidth Internet and powerful computers can benefit online learning.

References

[1] J. Rani, K. Garg, Emotion detection using facial expressions—a review, Int. J. Adv. Res. Comput. Sci. Softw. Eng. 4 (4) (2014).

[2] Q. Zhao, M. Ye, The application and implementation of face recognition in authentication system for distance education, in: 2010 International Conference on Networking and Digital Society May 30 (vol. 1, pp. 487–489), IEEE, 2010.

[3] S. Budi, O. Karnalim, E.D. Handoyo, S. Santoso, H. Toba, H. Nguyen, V. Malhotra, IBAtS-image-based attendance system: a low-cost solution to record student attendance in a classroom, in: 2018 IEEE International Symposium on Multimedia (ISM) Dec 10, IEEE, 2018, pp. 259–266.

[4] Allagwail S., Elbkosh A., 2020. Face recognition with symmetrical face training samples based on histograms of oriented gradients. In: Third Conference for Engineering Sciences and Technology (CEST-2020).

[5] C. Rahmad, R.A. Asmara, D.R. Putra, I. Dharma, H. Darmono, I. Muhiqqin, Comparison of Viola-Jones Haar Cascade classifier and histogram of oriented gradients (HOG) face detection, in: IOP Conference Series: Materials Science and Engineering (vol. 732, No. 1, p. 012038), IOP Publishing, 2020.

[6] M.Z. Al-Dabagh, S.J. Rashid, M.I. Ahmad, Face recognition system based on wavelet transform, histograms of oriented gradients and support vector machine, Int. J. Comput. Digit. Syst. 10 (2020) 1–4.

[7] S. Jaiswal, G.C. Nandi, Robust real-time emotion detection system using CNN architecture, Neural Comput. Applic. 32 (15) (2020) 11253–11262.

[8] S.L. Happy, A. Dasgupta, P. Patnaik, A. Routray, Automated alertness and emotion detection for empathic feedback during e-learning, in: 2013 IEEE Fifth International Conference on Technology for Education (t4e 2013) Dec 18 (pp. 47-50), IEEE, 2013.

[9] S.A. Fatima, A. Kumar, S.S. Raoof, Real time emotion detection of humans using mini-xception algorithm, IOP Conf. Ser.: Mater. Sci. Eng. 1042 (1) (2021) 012027. IOP Publishing.

[10] S. Minaee, M. Minaei, A. Abdolrashidi, Deep-emotion: facial expression recognition using attentional convolutional network, Sensors 21 (9) (2021) 3046.

[11] D.Y. Liliana, Emotion recognition from facial expression using deep convolutional neural network, J. Phys.: Conf. Ser. 1193 (1) (2019) 012004. IOP Publishing.

[12] A. Joseph, P. Geetha, Facial emotion detection using modified eyemap–mouthmap algorithm on an enhanced image and classification with tensorflow, Vis. Comput. 36 (3) (2020) 529–539.

[13] K. Wang, X. Peng, J. Yang, D. Meng, Y. Qiao, Region attention networks for pose and occlusion robust facial expression recognition, IEEE Trans. Image Process. 29 (2020) 4057–4069.

[14] N. Dalal, B. Triggs, Histograms of oriented gradients for human detection, in: 2005 IEEE Computer Society Conference on Computer Vision and Pattern Recognition (CVPR'05), vol. 1, IEEE, 2005, pp. 886–893.

[15] A.S. Georghiades, P.N. Belhumeur, D.J. Kriegman, From few to many: illumination cone models for face recognition under variable lighting and pose, IEEE Trans. Pattern Anal. Mach. Intell. 23 (6) (2001) 643–660.

[16] M. Jones, P. Viola, Fast Multi-view Face Detection, Mitsubishi Electric Research Lab TR-20003-96. Jul 15;3(14):2, 2003.

[17] I.J. Goodfellow, D. Erhan, P.L. Carrier, A. Courville, M. Mirza, B. Hamner, W. Cukierski, Y. Tang, D. Thaler, D.H. Lee, Y. Zhou, Challenges in representation learning: a report on three machine learning contests, in: International Conference on Neural Information Processing Nov 3 (pp. 117-124), Springer, Berlin, Heidelberg, 2013.

[18] K. Simonyan, A. Zisserman, Very Deep Convolutional Networks for Large-Scale Image Recognition, arXiv preprint arXiv:1409.1556. Sep 4, 2014.

[19] H. Wang, Garbage recognition and classification system based on convolutional neural network VGG16, in: 2020 3rd International Conference on Advanced Electronic Materials, Computers and Software Engineering (AEMCSE) Apr 24, IEEE, 2020, pp. 252–255.

Chapter 10

Contemporary survey on effectiveness of machine and deep learning techniques for cyber security

P. Suresh[a], K. Logeswaran[a], P. Keerthika[b], R. Manjula Devi[b], K. Sentamilselvan[a], G.K. Kamalam[a], and H. Muthukrishnan[a]

[a]*Department of Information Technology, Kongu Engineering College, Erode, Tamil Nadu, India*, [b]*Department of Computer Science and Engineering, Kongu Engineering College, Erode, Tamil Nadu, India*

1 Introduction

Nowadays many organizations have requested workers to operate remotely and/or limit travel. Furthermore, hackers use this as an opportunity to step up their operations. When more workers continue to work from home, maintaining and holding tight security controls can be more difficult. Due to the increase of Internet-enabled devices, the surface of the attack also grows, which contributes to increased risk. In addition, attackers are growing well-advanced, creating zero-day vulnerabilities and malware that bypass security measures allowing them to remain without detection for long time. Zero-day vulnerabilities are threats that were not previously observed, but are also variants on an established attack [1]. Hence, cyber security is an essential task needed to be taken care by both corporate and individuals. With that in mind, advanced-level techniques are presented to help keep corporate IT environment and remote workers safe. Cyber security is vital as it helps to protect the secret information, protected health data, personally identifiable data, business data, and personal data from stealing and damage [2].

Cyber security risk is growing due to worldwide connectivity and utilization of cloud storage to store personal information and other data. Due to lack of configuration of cloud applications/services, organizations suffer from a cyber attack by increasingly sophisticated cyber criminals. Cyber threats are able to originate at any stage of a company. Social scams such as phishing and

Machine Learning for Biometrics. https://doi.org/10.1016/B978-0-323-85209-8.00007-9
177

ransomware can harm sensitive data [3]. Cyber security helps to protect the data and provide integrity of computer properties from all threat actors. It is also used for preventing and recovering from attacks on computers, networks, and applications. Assailants are using the sophisticated methods that are using artificial intelligence (AI) to break security measures [4]. The importance of the cyber security is on the rise because social media pages now publish personal information which could lead to identity theft. Since most of the sensitive data like credit/debit card and bank account numbers are stored using cloud such as Dropbox and Google Drive, data security is vital everywhere [5].

Nowadays an individual, a tiny business, or a big corporation depends on computers for all. When it is combined with the cloud computing, risks in cloud security, mobile phones, and the IoT, everyone gets affected due to risks in cyber security. Because of the growth of smart attackers and facilities available to hackers, cyber security has become one of the most challenging domains today. It is a collection of algorithms, technologies, and policies that work collectively to secure networks, resources, applications, and data by protecting their privacy, confidentiality, and accessibility. Malware, data breaches, social engineering, phishing, SQL injection, insider threats, Denial-of-Service (DoS) attacks, and advanced persistent threats are all common cyber security threats [6].

This book chapter covers various applications of ML and DL techniques used for cyber security. It also examines the use of ML and DL techniques in the design, operation, and growth of cyber security systems, also the future of research and development in this field. The various types of biometric applications that enhance the features of cyber security systems are also covered in this book chapter. This chapter discusses how ML and DL techniques are applied to the different attacks that harm systems, networks, applications, and data. It also provides a thorough analysis of ML and DL approaches to identify cyber attacks. It addresses the use of ML and DL techniques in cyber security architecture, as well as the training process for a variety of new applications.

1.1 Categories of cyber attacks

Criminals are becoming more sophisticated in their deeds, and here are few of the attacks that affect many communities every day. Cyber threats are ransomware attacks that hijack significant business tools in return for money to unlock them and secret operations in which hackers break through a system to steal precious data.

1.1.1 Malware

The term malware refers to malicious software such as ransomware, viruses, and spyware. It normally infiltrates networks by exploiting flaws in the system, such as clicking on questionable links in emails or downloading a dangerous program. Malware can acquire confidential information once within a network, generate more malicious software within the system, and even chunk access to critical network components [7].

1.1.2 Phishing

It is the act of sending malicious messages that appear to come from well-known, trustworthy sources. To assuage doubts and persuade victims to click on dangerous links, these messages use the same logos, names, and so on as a business. When a phishing connection is clicked, cyber criminals gain access to secret data such as login credentials and credit card numbers [8].

1.1.3 Social engineering

It is a method of psychologically influencing people into revealing secret data. Phishing is a kind of this in which criminals exploit people's natural interest or confidence to their advantage. Voice manipulation is a best example of social engineering where criminals acquire an individual's voice and manipulate it to call relatives or friends and ask for personal or secret data [9].

1.1.4 Man-in-the-middle (MitM) attack

MitM attacks occur when perpetrators impede the flow of information between two parties. Criminals, for example, may place themselves between a public Wi-Fi network and a user's computer. Cyber criminals may also display all of a victim's details without ever being caught if they don't have access to a secure Wi-Fi link [10].

1.1.5 Zero-day attack

These attacks are increasing more widespread by the day. These attacks take place between the declaration of network vulnerability and the application of a patch solution. Most organizations will reveal that they have discovered a problem with their network security in the name of openness and security, but some hackers will use this opportunity to launch attacks before the organization can issue a security fix [11].

2 Biometrics in cyber security

Biometrics is the perfect option for data protection and cyber security in the future. To gain entry to a secured device, biometric protection uses specific physical characteristics. Biometric protection uses methods like face, eye, and fingerprint recognition to authenticate an individual identity and monitor access to secret data instead of a password that could be compromised or leaked. Biometric scanners are hardware with specialized programs that collect data in order to validate a person's identity [12]. The collected data are compared with

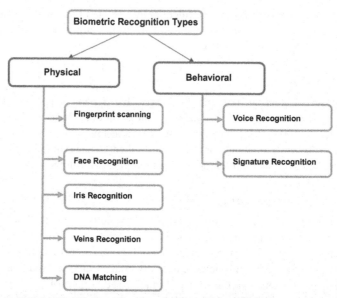

FIG. 1 Taxonomy of biometrics.

the database to accept or reject the access. The various forms of biometrics used in cyber security systems are depicted in Fig. 1.

However, in a world that is becoming increasingly paperless, more sophisticated methods of identifying and authenticating individuals have had to be created. This is especially true in light of the rising risks of global terrorism, cyber hacking, and complicated organized crime tactics. Biometric security has established itself as the most advanced technology available for authentication, identification, and verification. The basic principle of biometric authentication is that each individual is special and can be defined by intrinsic or behavioral characteristics. Biometric technology can recognize an individual based on their specific facial features, fingerprints, signatures, DNA, and then provide a safe and convenient method for authentication [13].

Biometrics is the study of an individual's physical and behavioral characteristics through measurement and statistical analysis. Biometrics is a means of distinguishing individuals based on one or more physiological or behavioral characteristics. This information is used to identify users and grant access. Users prefer biometric systems because information carriers are still with them and cannot be misplaced or forged [14]. They are known as trustworthy systems because, unlike username and password combinations, biometric credentials such as face and fingerprints are virtually not possible to use for unauthorized access in the event of a data breach.

2.1   Fingerprint scanning

A human fingerprint consists of ridges and valleys on the finger's surface which are distinctive for every person and used to identify a person. The upper skin layer segments of the finger are called as ridges and the lower skin layer segments are called as valleys. The various patterns of ridges and furrows, the minutiae points, decide the uniqueness of a fingerprint [15]. Fig. 2 depicts the methodology of fingerprint recognition system.

New technologies, such as optical and ultrasound, are being developed to capture the fingerprint for authentication during user recognition. To identify fingerprints, two key algorithms are used: minutiae matching and pattern matching. Minutiae matching matches the minutiae of the extracted minutiae to find variations in one user's fingerprint and another. Users can capture minutiae position and direction on the surface of the finger when they register with the device. Fingerprint recognition device validates user's identity by comparing a minute image that is displayed and the one given at the access time. Instead of comparing one specific point, pattern matching compares all of the finger's surfaces. It will focus on the thickness, density, and curvature of the surface of the finger. For this approach, the picture of the fingers surface will include the areas around a minutiae point, low curvature radius, and unusual ridge combinations [16].

Using fingerprint recognition devices has a wide range of advantages. This system is simple to run and set up. It necessitates low-cost equipment with low power consumption. This system does, however, have some drawbacks. Identification becomes more difficult if the surface of the finger has damaged and markings on it. The device often requires that the surface of users' finger has a point of pattern or minutiae to have matching images. This will be a stumbling block for the algorithm's security. Fingerprint authentication systems are commonly used in a wide range of applications such as mobile phones, laptop computers, and other devices. This type of systems is mainly utilized in legal systems to keep track of users' details and check their identities [14].

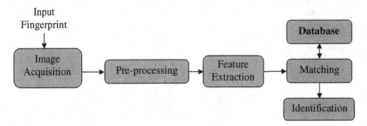

FIG. 2   Fingerprint identification process.

2.2   Voice recognition

Fig. 3 represents the process flow diagram of voice recognition methodology. A spoken phrase is compared to a digital prototype in speech recognition. It's used in security systems like access control and time monitoring to identify and authenticate users. The device generates digital templates that have a very high chance of being correctly interpreted. The physiological and behavioral features of a person's speech are unique to them. The size and shape of the throat, mouth, nasal cavity, larynx, and body weight influence physiological aspects. Language, educational level, and place of residence all influence behavioral characteristics, which can result in distinct intonations, accents, and dialects [17].

Usually two key parameters distinguish an individual's speech. To begin with, there is the physiological portion known as the voice tract. The voice accent, on the other hand, is a behavioral aspect. It is not possible to accurately mimic another person's voice in most of the cases when all of these variables are combined. Biometrics technology took advantage of these characteristics to develop voice recognition systems that use only a person's voice to verify their identity. Since the vocal tract is a special feature of a physiological characteristic, voice recognition will mainly focus on it. It performs admirably in terms of physical access control for users.

Voice recognition systems are simple to set up and require very little equipment. Microphones, telephone microphones, and even PC microphones are examples of this equipment. However, there are still some variables that can have an effect on the system's efficiency. For starters, user output when recording their voice to a database is critical. As a result, persons will be asked to say

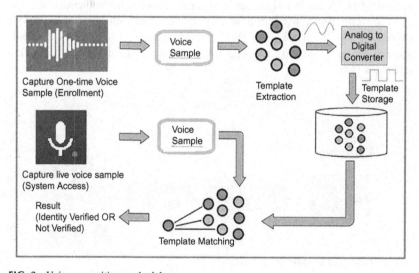

FIG. 3   Voice recognition methodology.

again a short pass and/or sentences; hence, the machine can more reliably analyze their voices. Unauthorized users are able to record approved users' voices and run them through the authentication process to gain device access control. Voice recognition systems will request persons to repeat random sentences/words generated by the device during the authentication to avoid the illegal access through recording devices [18].

2.2.1 Voice-speaker identification

The process of deciding the identity of an anonymous speaker is known as identification. The voice is verified with N patterns in a 1:N (many) match for speaker recognition. Speaker recognition systems can also be used to classify speakers in a conversation and check whether a user is already enrolled in a system, and so on, all without the user's awareness. In forensic applications, it's normal to start with a speaker identification method to generate a list of best matches, then go through a sequence of verification steps to find a definitive pattern.

2.2.2 Voice-speaker verification

It is the use of speech as a means of assessing a speaker's identity for access control. Here, 1:1 match occurs when a user's voice is matched to a single prototype called as voice print or voice model. Speaker authentication is often used to allow access to a system such as telephone banking. These systems work with the user's awareness and generally necessitate their involvement.

2.3 Facial recognition

It uses facial features for the identification and verification of a person's identity. Here, either two- or three-dimensional image of the face is captured using a high-resolution camera. The outline of the brows, eyes, nose, chin, lips, ears, and the distance between them are calculated, and the picture can be modified based on the rotation of the face, tilt, face expressions, and so on. A person's face image is stored in the database, which is required to compare the photographs of different people [19].

The face of a human is one of the simplest features which is used to recognize a user in a biometric security system. This technology is commonly used because it does not involve physical interaction between the user and the computer. For authentication, cameras check the user's face and compare it to a database. It's also quick to set up and doesn't need any costly hardware. The software for face scanning is commonly used in a number of security systems, including physical access control and device user accounts. It is, however, not as distinctive as its relatives, such as the retina, iris, or DNA. As a result, it's typically combined with other machine characteristics [20]. This technology has the most detrimental affective parameter because the user's age can change over time. This system collects information from users' faces and stores it in a database. It will assess the shape, and proportion of parameters on the user's face, such as the gap between the user's eyes, nose, mouths, ears, and jaw, as well as the scale of the user's eyes, mouth, and other facial expressions. One of the variables that changes during a user's facial recognition process is their facial expression. Smiling, weeping, and lines on the face are all examples [21].

2.4 Signature recognition

It is the process of verifying a person's identity by analyzing their handwriting style, specifically their signature. A pen and a special device connected to a computer are used to match and verify patterns. A high-quality device can record behavioral traits like signing speed, pressure, and time. An individual must write on the tablet several times to collect the data. Time, strain, speed, blows direction, signature path, and size are all extracted by signature recognition algorithms. These points are given different weights by the algorithm. Static and dynamic digital handwritten signature authentications are the two main styles [22].

2.5 Iris scanner and recognition

It is the process of scanning the pattern of the iris. The iris is translated into a digital code because it is distinctive. Since age spots and discoloration on the iris are likely, a black and white image is used. The iris of a human is a slim rounded structure in the eyes that regulates the size and diameter of the pupils. It also regulates the amount of light that reaches the retina in order to protect the retina of the eye. Iris color is a variable that varies from person to person and is determined by genetics. The color of one's iris determines the color of one's eyes [23]. Fig. 4 depicts the iris scanning and recognition process.

Iris comes in a variety of colors, including brown (the most common), gray, blue, gray, hazel, violet, and pink. The iris has its own patterns which contribute

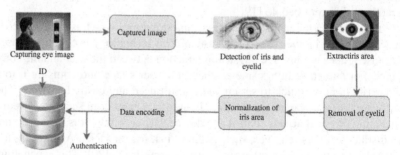

FIG. 4 Iris scanning and recognition.

to each person's uniqueness. Iris recognition systems use a variety of methods to search the iris. Around 200 points on the iris such as rings, furrows, freckles, and other features will be reviewed. The information from each person is stored in a database and compared when a user wants to access the system.

Iris recognition system is a widely used security system today. It is distinct and quick to recognize a user. Despite the fact that the device needs costly equipment, it is also the simplest and quickest way to classify a customer. During the verification process, there should be no physical interaction between the user and the device [24]. If the persons are using glasses or contact lenses during the authentication process, the device can continue to operate normally as no change in the features of the user's iris. And if users undergo eye surgery, it should theoretically have little effect on their iris features [25].

2.6   Veins recognition

Pattern recognition techniques are used in this technology, which is based on photographs of human vein samples found in the subcutaneous portion of the finger. Since vein models are situated underneath the skin's surface, they cannot be faked. Finger vein recognition works by capturing samples of finger veins and matching them to models using infrared rays. Fig. 5 shows the finger vein scanning and identification system.

The vein recognition device is a relatively new biometric technology. Blood vessels that bring blood to the heart are known as veins. The physical and behavioral characteristics of each person's veins are distinct. Biometrics takes advantage of this by using the distinctive features of the veins to distinguish the person. The veins in the users' hands are the main subject of vein recognition systems. Each human finger has veins that attach directly to the heart, and has its

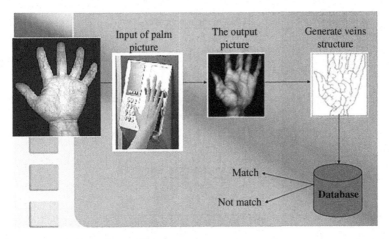

FIG. 5   Vein scanning and recognition.

own physical characteristics. The user's veins are found within the human body, unlike other biometric systems. As a result, the recognition system would use light transmission to capture images of the vein patterns within users' fingertips. The method involves passing near-infrared light through fingers to get more details and recording vein patterns with a camera [26].

Experts are paying more attention to vein recognition systems because they have many additional features that other biometrics technologies lack. It has a higher level of protection, allowing it to better secure information and access control [27]. By comparing the recorded database to the current data, the degree of accuracy is quite impressive and more. It also comes with a low cost of installation and supplies. The time required to verify each person is less than that required by other methods.

2.7   DNA biometrics system

Fig. 6 illustrates the DNA matching process. The most reliable way of biometric authentication is to use a person's DNA code. It's based on the human deoxyribonucleic acid chain's special series. The procedure starts with the preparation of a DNA sample like buccal smear, saliva, sperm, blood, and other tissues. The sample is analyzed, a profile of DNA is established, and their identities are verified by comparing them with another sample. Since everyone's DNA is different, it's difficult to mimic this trait. Each person's DNA carries a genetic trait inherited by his/her parents. This DNA is duplicated in every cell of the human body. The amount of variable number tandem repeat (VNTR) that repeats at a number of distinct samples can be calculated by DNA profiling. The DNA profile of a person is made up of quantities of VNTR. The system requires time as it has more complex steps to collect DNA from each individual. To begin, it must

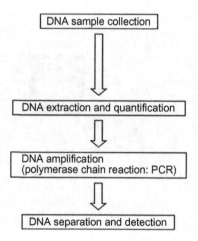

FIG. 6   DNA matching.

collect DNA from a physical sample given by each person. The samples must then be broken down into tiny fragments containing VNTR. Following that, each DNA fragment's size is calculated and arranged before being matched with other samples [28].

DNA biometric system is highly unique, the chances of more than one people having the similar DNA profile are very unlikely, and the technology is still relatively new and is seldom used in public. It necessitates the use of a lot of costly devices for the purpose of effectively breaking down DNA and analyzing the specific features of DNA in order to build a DNA profile. To collect users' DNA data, the system may also require physical samples (hair, blood, etc.) from them. Another element that contributes to the system's underutilization is time. To complete all of the processes of building and checking each person's DNA profile, the system takes a considerable amount of time. Unlike other biometric systems, it is not as widely used due to these drawbacks and barriers. In future, this unique and improved biometric technology will be used in everyday lives [29].

3 Cyber attacks versus machine learning

Machine learning excels at certain tasks, such as scanning vast volumes of data easily and analyzing it with statistics. Cyber security systems produce enormous amounts of data, so it's no surprise that the technology is so useful. Machine learning has emerged as a key component of cyber security. Machine learning proactively avoids cyber threats and enhances security infrastructure via pattern identification, real-time cyber crime visualization, and thorough penetration testing. In an era of massive amounts of data and a scarcity of cyber security expertise, machine learning appears to be the only option. Fig. 7 shows the block diagram of cyber security system using ML/DL methods [30].

Deep learning approaches are capable of identifying highly complex threats and independent of well-recognized signatures and standard patterns of attack being remembered. Rather, such strategies can separate suspicious behaviors from other common activities that may identify malware or security attackers.

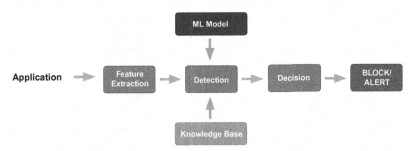

FIG. 7   Block diagram of cyber security system with ML.

DL is a subset of ML techniques and belongs to the group of AI. DL is a set of techniques for implementing ML which recognizes patterns such as recognition of images. The systems mainly classify the edges of objects, a structure, a type of object, and then an object itself. These algorithms can be improved to learn patterns using reinforcement learning such as Q-learning. Since malware attacks are rising in number and variety, it is very difficult to defend using conventional methods. DL methods provide the ability to create more advanced models to autonomously detect and identify malware. It will provide protection against small-scale attackers who use existing malware and large-scale attackers to target organizations or individuals using new types of malware [31].

Deep learning techniques can be applied for various purposes such as intrusion detection and prevention systems, malware detection, spam detection, network traffic monitoring, Web site defacement detection, and user behavior analytics. In these areas, DL has shown major advancements over other methods. Generally, deep leaning methods are classified into two major types such as supervised deep learning and unsupervised deep learning methods. Supervised DL algorithms include fully connected feed-forward deep neural networks (FNNs), convolutional feed-forward deep neural networks (CNNs), and recurrent deep neural networks (RNNs). Unsupervised DL algorithms include deep belief networks (DBNs) and stacked autoencoders (SAEs) [32].

4 Applications of ML and DL in cyber security

The taxonomy of ML models for cyber security systems is represented in Fig. 8. Machine learning has emerged as a key component of cyber security. Via pattern identification, real-time cyber crime visualization, and thorough penetration testing, machine learning proactively stamps out cyber threats and enhances security infrastructure. The following are the various approaches that can be applied to perform cyber security tasks [33].

4.1 Regression

It is also referred as prediction. The current data information is put to use in order to get a sense of the new data. It is used to detect fraud in cyber security. The characteristics (such as the total amount of suspicious transactions, location, and so on) decide the likelihood of fraudulent behavior. When it comes to the technical aspects of regression, there are two broad categories to consider: machine learning and deep learning.

4.2 Classification

The classification process is also simple. Assume you have two piles of photographs, each of which is categorized by form (e.g., dogs and cats). A spam filter that separates spam from other messages can be seen as an example in terms of

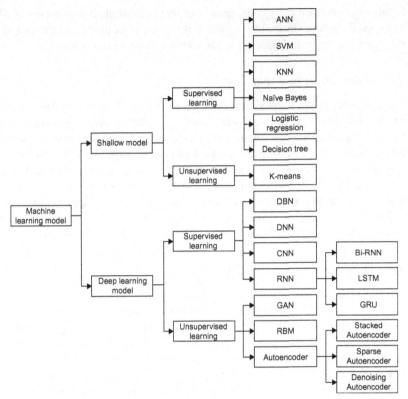

FIG. 8 Taxonomy of ML models for cyber security.

cyber security. Spam filters are most definitely the first ML solution to cyber security tasks. Where examples of particular groups are known, the supervised learning technique is commonly used for classification. At the start, all classes should be specified. When there is more data, deep learning methods perform better. However, they consume more energy, especially if they are used in production and retrain systems on a regular basis [34].

4.3 Clustering

Clustering and grouping are somewhat similar, with one big difference. There is no detail about the data's groups. There's no way of knowing whether or not this information can be classified. This is referred to as unsupervised learning. Forensic analysis is said to be the best task for clustering. An incident's cause, path, and consequences are all unknown. To find anomalies, all behaviors must be classified. It may be used to distinguish legitimate files from outliers in malware detection solutions (e.g., malware security or protected email gateways). User activity analytics is another interesting field where clustering can be used.

In this case, program users congregate in order to determine if they are assigned to a specific group. Generally, clustering is typically not used to address a specific cyber security task since it is just like a subtask in a pipeline [35].

4.4 Association rule learning

It is a rule-based ML method that can be used to find the relations. This theory can be used specifically for incident response in cyber security. Systems learn a form of response for a specific incident if an organization experiences a wave of incidents and provides different kinds of responses. Risk assessment software may also be advantageous if it assigns risk values to new vulnerabilities based on their definition. This system uses data from a historical vulnerability database to find out vulnerability association laws, which it then applies to vulnerability risk assessments. This system will define the attack rules based on the history database and can be applied to detect the attacks in the system [36].

4.5 Dimensionality reduction

It is one of the important processes which are highly required for cyber security systems in order to reduce the features for classification and increase the accuracy of the prediction model. It can assist in coping with it and eliminating unnecessary functionality [37]. It is a preprocessing step to minimize the attributes for reducing computation/training time. Generally, there are two important methods such as autoencoder and principal component analysis techniques used [38]. When it comes to cyber security, it is commonly used in face recognition solutions, such as those used in iPhone.

4.6 Generative models

Generative models have a different role than the ones described earlier. These models will simulate real data based on previous decisions, while certain tasks deal with current knowledge and related decisions. The basic task of offensive cyber protection is to create a list of input parameters in order to evaluate a specific application for injection vulnerabilities. It is a type of unsupervised learning method which can be trained with a phenomenon by considering huge existing samples and then produces new samples. The best examples of this kind are generative adversarial networks, deep autoregressive networks, and variational autoencoders [37].

5 Machine learning-based cyber security systems

5.1 Network protection system using ML

Network security is a set of solutions that concentrate on a particular protocol, such as Ethernet, wireless and virtual networks like SDNs. Intrusion detection system (IDS) solutions are often referred to as network security [39]. Initially, ML was mainly used for signature-based methods. ML in network security involves new solutions called network traffic analysis which analyze all traffic at all layers in detail and identify the anomalies and attacks. Few examples include regression to forecast network packet features and evaluate them to the standard classification to distinguish various types of network attacks including spoofing, scanning, and so on [40].

5.2 ML for endpoint protection

Endpoint detection and response (EDR) is the latest antivirus generation. It's preferable to learn attributes/features from the actions of processes. ML solution will be varied based on the type of endpoint like server, workstation, and IoT device. Endpoint has its own set of characteristics, but some tasks are universal, such as regression to forecast the next device call for an executable process and compare it to actual calls, classification to classify the applications/programs into categories such as malware and spyware, and clustering for malware security on stable email gateways [41].

5.3 Machine learning for application security

ML algorithms can be applied to various applications such as web applications, databases, and cloud applications to provide security. It is not possible to develop a common ML model that can efficiently deal with all threats in the near future [42]. Few examples of ML techniques used for application security are as follows. Regression can be applied to identify anomalies in web/HTTP requests, classification can be used to identify known types of attacks like injections, and clustering is used to detect Distributed Denial of Service (DDoS) attacks and mass exploitation [43].

5.4 ML for user behavior

User and entity behavior analytics (UEBA) uses huge datasets to model typical and atypical behaviors of humans and machines within a network. It is used to recognize suspicious activity, possible risks, and attacks that ordinary antivirus programs cannot detect by identifying such baselines. Since it analyzes different behavioral trends, it can detect nonmalware-based attacks [44]. UEBA also employs these models to determine the threat level, generating a risk score that can aid in determining the best course of action. UEBA is increasingly relying on machine learning to detect normal activity and warn of potentially dangerous anomalies that might indicate insider threats, lateral movement, compromised accounts, or attacks. When risks are viewed from the perspective of the consumer, the market has acknowledged the fact that a unique solution is needed.

Even UEBA tools, however, do not cover anything relevant to different user actions [45].

User behavior is a kind of dynamic layers and unsupervised learning problems that focuses on general attacks and the ability to train a classifier. In most cases, there is no labeled dataset or indication of what to look for. As a consequence, designing a general algorithm for all users is a difficult task in the user behavior industry. Regression and grouping may be used to identify anomalies in user behavior (e.g., login at an odd time), clustering can be used to isolate groups of users and detect outliers whereas classification can be applied to identify the different users [46].

5.5 ML for process behavior

Last but not least, there's the process area. In order to discover anything unusual, it's best to understand a business process when working with it. Business processes can be very different because fraud may rise in the banking and retail systems, as well as on a manufacturing plant floor. Both are very different and necessitate a great deal of domain awareness. To achieve results in machine learning, feature engineering is required. Similarly, each method has its own set of characteristics. In general, activities in the process field include regression, which predicts the next user behavior and detects outliers like frauds in credit cards, classification detects identified forms of fraud, and clustering compares business processes and detects outliers [47].

6 Deep learning-based cyber security systems

6.1 Intrusion detection/intrusion prevention (ID/IP) systems

ID/IP systems detect malicious activity in network, preventing intruders from gaining access to networks, and alerting the user. Recognized signatures and common forms of attack are commonly used to identify them. This is useful in the case of risks like data breaches. Usually, machine learning algorithms were used to perform this task at first. However, these methods caused the system to produce a high number of false positives, making protection groups' jobs more difficult and causing excessive fatigue [48].

DL, convolutional neural networks (CNNs) and recurrent neural networks (RNNs), can be used to make more advanced ID/IP systems by evaluating traffic more accurately and distinguishing malicious and nonmalicious network activities. Few of the impressive solutions include next-generation firewalls (NGFWs), web application firewalls (WAF), and UEBA. In order to identify known threats, ID/IP systems use rule-based and signature-based controls. Adversaries can easily evade conventional network ID/IP systems by changing malware signatures. Deep neural net-based systems have been used to tackle conventional security use cases like malware and spyware detection [49].

6.2   Malware detection

Standard firewalls detect malware by a signature-based detection scheme. The company keeps a database of identified threats that it updates on a regular basis to include new threats that have recently been introduced. While this strategy works well against such threats, it falls short of dealing with more sophisticated threats. DL algorithms can detect more complex threats without the need to recall existing signatures or attack samples. Instead, they learn about the network and can spot suspicious activities that may signify the existence of bad actors or malware [50].

6.3   Social engineering and spam detection

Social engineering attacks usually require psychological manipulation to persuade otherwise unaware consumers or staff to divulge confidential or sensitive information. Usually, social engineering includes an email or other contact that instills in the victim a sense of urgency, fear, or other related emotions, causing the victim to disclose confidential information or click a malicious connection [51]. Natural language processing (NLP) is a DL technique that can assist in the identification and control of spam and other forms of social engineering. It examines natural communication and language patterns and employs a variety of mathematical models to identify and block spam [52].

6.4   Network traffic analysis

When analyzing HTTPs traffic to search for malicious behaviors, deep learning algorithms have shown promising results. This is extremely useful in dealing with a range of cyber threats, such as SQL injections and DoS attacks [53]. Cyber attacks are mostly intended to steal consumer data, sales data, intellectual property records, source codes, and device keys from businesses. The adversaries use encrypted traffic to submit the stolen data to remote servers alongside normal traffic. Adversaries also use an anonymous network, making it difficult for security defenders to track traffic.

The correspondence among Alice and the destination server is depicted in Fig. 9. Alice initiates contact by requesting a route to the server. The AES-encrypted path is given by the TOR network. The path is randomly generated within the TOR network. The packet's encrypted route is highlighted in red. The simple packet is passed to the server until it reaches the exit node, which is the TOR network's periphery node. The packet is decrypted using the secret key at each receiver stage. The next destination relay address is exposed after decryption. This continues until the TOR network's exit node is reached, at which point the packet's encryption is terminated and a simple HTTP packet is forwarded to the destination server [54].

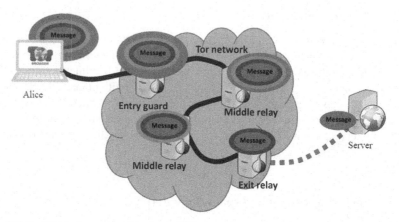

FIG. 9 Client-server communication in TOR network.

TOR was created with the purpose of preserving users' privacy. TOR traffic is blocked in an enterprise network by not allowing the TOR client to be installed or by blocking the entry node IP address. However, there are a variety of ways for adversaries and malware to gain access to the TOR network and use it to send data and information. Blocking IP addresses is not a smart tactic. Different IPs may be spawned by adversaries to carry out contact. The traffic packets can be analyzed to detect TOR traffic. This investigation may take place on the TOR node or between the client and the entry node. A tuple of source address, source port, destination address, and destination port makes up each flow.

6.4.1 Experimental data

The data for the data studies were obtained at the University of New Brunswick. Their data are made up of features gleaned from a review of university Internet traffic. Table 1 displays the metadata that were extracted from the data. Other flow-based parameters are also used in addition to these. Fig. 10 depicts a representative illustration from the dataset.

The protocol sector, as well as the source IP/port and destination IP/port, has been deleted from the instance. Deep feed forward neural network with N hidden layers is used to process all other functions. The neural network's architecture is described in Fig. 11.

The number of secret layers varies from 2 to 10. $N = 5$ was considered to be the best number. ReLU is used to trigger all of the secret layers. The secret layers are thick by default and have a dimension of 100. A sigmoid feature activates the output node. The DL module is trained in the backend using Keras and TensorFlow. The FFN was optimized using binary crossentropy loss. Different epochs were used to train the model. Fig. 12 depicts a training simulation for a

TABLE 1 Description of metainformation parameters.

Metainformation parameter	Parameter explanation
FIAT	Forward inter arrival time, the time between two packets sent forward direction (mean, min, max, std).
BIAT	Backward inter arrival time, the time between two packets sent backward (mean, min, max, std).
FLOWIAT	Flow inter arrival time, the time between two packets sent in either direction (mean, min, max, std).
ACTIVE	The amount of time a flow was active before going idle (mean, min, max, std).
IDLE	The amount of time a flow was idle before becoming active (mean, min, max, std)
FB PSEC	Flow bytes per second. Flow packets per second. Duration: the duration of the flow.

Source IP, Source Port, Destination IP, Destination Port, Protocol, Flow Duration, Flow Bytes/s, Flow Packets/s, Flow IAT Mean, Flow IAT Std, Flow IAT Max, Flow IAT Min, Fwd IAT Mean, Fwd IAT Std, Fwd IAT Max, Fwd IAT Min, Bwd IAT Mean, Bwd IAT Std, Bwd IAT Max, Bwd IAT Min, Active Mean, Active Std, Active Max, Active Min, Idle Mean, Idle Std, Idle Max, Idle Min, label

FIG. 10   Dataset instance.

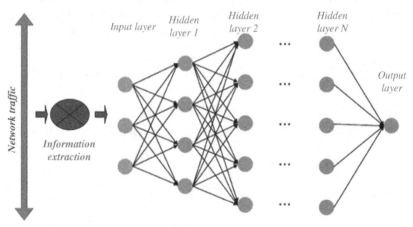

FIG. 11   Traffic detection using DL network.

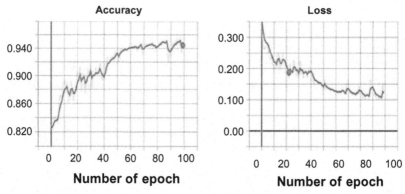

FIG. 12 Statics of the network training process.

run with increasing efficiency and minimizing loss value as the number of epoch increases.

The DL system's findings are compared with other estimators. The estimators' efficiency is measured using standard classification metrics such as recall, precision, and F-Score. The proposed DL-based framework did a good job of detecting the TOR class. For non-TOR category samples, it is shown that a DL-based method is minimizing false-positive cases [53]. Table 2 summarizes the findings.

Random forest (RF) and DL-based approaches outperform the others among various classifiers. The performance is based on 55,000 training scenarios. In contrast to traditional DL-based systems, the dataset used in this experiment is relatively limited. The output of both the DL-based and RF classifiers improves as the training data grow. A DL-based classifier, on the other hand, usually outperforms other classifiers for large datasets, and it can be generalized for similar types of applications. For example, if a classifier is needed to detect the application used by TOR, only the output layer needs to be retrained, while the other layers will remain unchanged.

TABLE 2 Performance of ML and DL models for traffic detection.

Classifier used	Precision	Recall	F-Score
Logistic Regression	0.86	0.86	0.86
SVM	0.91	0.91	0.91
Naïve Bayes	0.92	0.62	0.72
Random Forest	0.97	0.97	0.97
Deep Learning	0.96	0.96	0.96

6.5 Web site defacement detection

Defacement attacks alter the content of a Web site and, as a result, modify the appearance of the Web site. It is one of the most significant threats to business, enterprise, and government Web sites and web applications. Deep-learning-based solutions can perform detection by constructing detection profiles from both regular and defaced web pages as training data [54].

7 Conclusion and future scope

On the one side, machine learning isn't a magic bullet when it comes to defending the computer systems. There are undoubtedly numerous issues with interpretability, especially in the case of deep learning algorithms. However, with the increasing amount of data and dwindling number of experts, machine learning is the only solution. It works now and will be needed in the not-too-distant future. It's best to get started right away. Another noteworthy point to mention is that hackers are increasingly using machine learning in their attacks.

The integration of AI and cyberspace security will present an increasing number of application scenarios as AI and cyberspace security evolve at a rapid pace. There are a range of exciting and open topics for integrated cyber protection and AI technologies in the future. The cascading relation of malicious activities during an attack life cycle should be considered in future research like breach, manipulation, and data theft. There are the different metrics that are used to assess the success of DL in cyber security tasks. However, since different datasets were used for training and research, a fair assessment of all of the different methods was impossible. As a result, benchmark datasets are important for advancing deep learning in the cyber security domain. As a result, the aim of this survey is to create a useful body of work that will enable researchers to advance the state of ML and DL for cyber security systems.

References

[1] D.S. Berman, A.L. Buczak, J.S. Chavis, C.L. Corbett, A survey of deep learning methods for cyber security, Information (Switzerland) 10 (4) (2019), https://doi.org/10.3390/info10040122. MDPI AG.
[2] S. Mahdavifar, A.A. Ghorbani, Application of deep learning to cybersecurity: a survey, Neurocomputing 347 (2019) 149–176, https://doi.org/10.1016/j.neucom.2019.02.056.
[3] J. Jang-Jaccard, S. Nepal, A survey of emerging threats in cybersecurity, J. Comput. Syst. Sci. 80 (5) (2014) 973–993.
[4] H. Zheng, Y. Wang, C. Han, F. Le, R. He, J. Lu, Learning and applying ontology for machine learning in cyber attack detection, 2018. ieeexplore.ieee.org, (Accessed 1 April 2021). [Online]. Available: https://ieeexplore.ieee.org/abstract/document/8456049/.
[5] N. Sun, J. Zhang, P. Rimba, S. Gao, L.Y. Zhang, Y. Xiang, Data-driven cybersecurity incident prediction: a survey, IEEE Commun. Surv. Tutor 21 (2) (2018) 1744–1772.

[6] A. Lakshmanarao, M. Shashi, A survey on machine learning for cyber security, Int. J. Sci. Technol. Res. 9 (2020) 1. (Accessed 29 March 2021). [Online]. Available: www.ijstr.org.

[7] R. Das, T.H. Morris, Machine learning and cyber security, 2018, https://doi.org/10.1109/ICCECE.2017.8526232.

[8] V. Yadav, M. Verma, V. Dixit Kaushik, A biometric approach to secure big data, in: 2016 1st International Conference on Innovation and Challenges in Cyber Security, ICICCS 2016, Aug. 2016, pp. 75–79, https://doi.org/10.1109/ICICCS.2016.7542296.

[9] M.L. Gavrilova, et al., Emerging trends in security system design using the concept of social behavioural biometrics, in: Studies in Computational Intelligence, vol. 691, Springer Verlag, 2017, pp. 229–251.

[10] E. Proko, A. Hyso, D. Gjylapi, Machine Learning Algorithms in Cyber Security, RTA-CSIT, 2018.

[11] D. Dasgupta, Z. Akhtar, S. Sen, Machine learning in cybersecurity: a comprehensive survey, J. Def. Model. Simul. (2020), https://doi.org/10.1177/1548512920951275.

[12] L. Kumar, et al., The study of biometrics and cyber security, J. Gujarat Res. Soc. 21 (14s) (2019) 494–501. (Accessed 29 March 2021). [Online]. Available: http://www.gujaratresearchsociety.in/index.php/JGRS/article/view/1393.

[13] R. Malathi, R. Jeberson Retna Raj, An integrated approach of physical biometric authentication system, Procedia Comput. Sci. 85 (2016) 820–826, https://doi.org/10.1016/j.procs.2016.05.271.

[14] J. Kour, M. Hanmandlu, A.Q. Ansari, Biometrics in cyber security, Def. Sci. J. 66 (6) (2016) 600–604, https://doi.org/10.14429/dsj.66.10800.

[15] A.K. Jain, A. Ross, S. Pankanti, S. Member, Biometrics: a tool for information security, IEEE Trans. Inf. Forensics Secur. 1 (2) (2006), https://doi.org/10.1109/TIFS.2006.873653.

[16] A. Ross, R. Nadgir, A thin-plate spline calibration model for fingerprint sensor interoperability, IEEE Trans. Knowl. Data Eng. 20 (8) (2008) 1097–1110, https://doi.org/10.1109/TKDE.2007.190696.

[17] J. Novakovic, Speaker identification in smart environments with multilayer perceptron, in: 2011 19th Telecommunications Forum, TELFOR 2011—Proceedings of Papers, 2011, pp. 1418–1421, https://doi.org/10.1109/TELFOR.2011.6143821.

[18] H.N.M. Shah, M.Z. Ab Rashid, M.F. Abdollah, M.N. Kamarudin, C.K. Lin, Z. Kamis, Biometric voice recognition in security system, Indian J. Sci. Technol. 7 (2) (2014) 104–112, https://doi.org/10.17485/ijst/2014/v7i1.9.

[19] D. Bhattacharjee, A. Seal, S. Ganguly, M. Nasipuri, D.K. Basu, A comparative study of human thermal face recognition based on Haar wavelet transform and local binary pattern, Comput. Intell. Neurosci. 2012 (2012), https://doi.org/10.1155/2012/261089.

[20] S.H. Chae, D. Moon, K.R. Ko, J. Shin, S.B. Pan, Security enhancement for smartphone using biometrics in cyber-physical systems, Int. J. Distrib. Sens. Netw. 2014 (2014), https://doi.org/10.1155/2014/136538.

[21] E. Hurwitz, A.N. Hasan, C. Orji, Soft biometric thermal face recognition using FWT and LDA feature extraction method with RBM DBN and FFNN classifier algorithms, in: 2017 4th International Conference on Image Information Processing, ICIIP 2017, Mar. 2018, pp. 650–655, https://doi.org/10.1109/ICIIP.2017.8313796. vol. 2018-January.

[22] H. Bahsi, S. Nomm, F.B. La Torre, Dimensionality reduction for machine learning based IoT botnet detection, in: 2018 15th International Conference on Control, Automation, Robotics and Vision, ICARCV 2018, Dec. 2018, pp. 1857–1862, https://doi.org/10.1109/ICARCV.2018.8581205.

[23] P. Campisi, Security and Privacy in Biometrics, Springer, 2013.

[24] A.K. Jain, A. Ross, Bridging the gap: from biometrics to forensics, Philos. Trans. R. Soc. B Biol. Sci. 370 (1674) (2015), https://doi.org/10.1098/rstb.2014.0254. royalsocietypublishing.org.

[25] J. Bringer, H. Chabanne, G. Cohen, B. Kindarji, G. Zémor, Theoretical and practical boundaries of binary secure sketches, IEEE Trans. Inf. Forensics Secur. 3 (4) (2008) 673–683, https://doi.org/10.1109/TIFS.2008.2002937.

[26] D.P. Kingma, M. Welling, Auto-Encoding Variational Bayes, Dec. 2014, (Accessed 29 March 2021). [Online]. Available: https://arxiv.org/abs/1312.6114v10.

[27] B. Barton, S. Byciuk, C. Harris, D. Schumack, K. Webster, The Emerging Cyber Risks of Biometrics, 2005, search.proquest.com, (Accessed 1 April 2021). [Online]. Available: https://search.proquest.com/openview/d7bce659133b0156dd55b8030d73140f/1?pq-origsite=gscholar&cbl=47271.

[28] K. Gregor, A. Mnih, C. Blundell, I. Danihelka, D. Wierstra, Deep autoregressive networks, Proceedings of the 31st International Conference on Machine Learning (ICML), JMLR: W&CP, vol. 32, 2014. http://proceedings.mlr.press/v32/gregor14.html.

[29] S. Venkatraman, I. Delpachitra, Biometrics in banking security: a case study, Inf. Manag. Comput. Secur. 16 (4) (2008) 415–430, https://doi.org/10.1108/09685220810908813.

[30] R. Geetha, T. Thilagam, A review on the effectiveness of machine learning and deep learning algorithms for cyber security, Arch. Comput. Methods Eng. (2020), https://doi.org/10.1007/s11831-020-09478-2.

[31] G. Apruzzese, M. Colajanni, L. Ferretti, A. Guido, M. Marchetti, On the effectiveness of machine and deep learning for cyber security, in: International Conference on Cyber Conflict, CYCON, Jul. 2018, pp. 371–389, https://doi.org/10.23919/CYCON.2018.8405026. vol. 2018-May.

[32] S. Moraboena, G. Ketepalli, P. Ragam, A deep learning approach to network intrusion detection using deep autoencoder, Rev. d'Intelligence Artif. 34 (4) (2020) 457–463, https://doi.org/10.18280/ria.340410.

[33] B. Dong, X. Wang, Comparison deep learning method to traditional methods using for network intrusion detection, 2016 8th IEEE International Conference on Communication Software and Networks (ICCSN), 2016, pp. 581–585.

[34] W. Zong, Y. Chow, W. Susilo, Dimensionality Reduction and Visualization of Network Intrusion Detection Data, 2019, (Accessed 29 March 2021). [Online]. Available: https://ro.uow.edu.au/eispapers1https://ro.uow.edu.au/eispapers1/2992:https://ro.uow.edu.au/eispapers1/2992.

[35] V. Ford, A. Siraj, Applications of machine learning in cyber security, in: 27th International Conference on Computer Applications in Industry and Engineering, CAINE, 2014.

[36] A. Javaid, Q. Niyaz, W. Sun, M. Alam, A deep learning approach for network intrusion detection system, EAI Endorsed Transactions on Security and Safety, vol. 3, EAI Endorsed Transactions on Security and Safety, 2015, doi:10.4108/eai.3-12-2015.2262516.

[37] S. Mohammadi, H. Mirvaziri, M. Ghazizadeh-Ahsaee, H. Karimipour, Cyber intrusion detection by combined feature selection algorithm, J Inf. Secur. Appl. 44 (2019) 80–88.

[38] P. Kobojek, Application of recurrent neural networks for user verification based on keystroke dynamics, J. Telecommun. Inf. Technol. 3 (2016) 80–90.

[39] T. Morris, R. Das, T.H. Morris, Machine Learning and Cyber Security, ieeexplore.ieee.org, 2017, https://doi.org/10.1109/ICCECE.2017.8526232.

[40] C. Xiaorong, W. Yan, G. Xin, Network security risk assessment based on association rules, in: Proceedings of 2009 4th International Conference on Computer Science and Education, ICCSE 2009, 2009, pp. 1142–1145, https://doi.org/10.1109/ICCSE.2009.5228484.

[41] B. Gupta, Q. Sheng, Machine Learning for Computer and Cyber Security: Principle, Algorithms, and Practices, CRC Press, Taylor & Francis, Boca Raton, FL, 2019.

[42] M.V. Thomas, K. Chandrasekaran, Identity and access management in the cloud computing environments, in: Identity Theft, IGI Global, 2016, pp. 38–68.

[43] G. He, M. Yang, J. Luo, X. Gu, Inferring application type information from tor encrypted traffic, in: 2014 Second International Conference on Advanced Cloud and Big Data, Nov. 2014, pp. 220–227, https://doi.org/10.1109/CBD.2014.37.

[44] Z. Katzir, Y. Elovici, Quantifying the resilience of machine learning classifiers used for cyber security, Expert Syst. Appl. (2018). Elsevier, (Accessed 1 April 2021). [Online]. Available: https://www.sciencedirect.com/science/article/pii/S0957417417306590?casa_token=lN1zUw eaI8EAAAAA:c-NJXxNTizg7jPPyNIHslS9dCGUdxueAdzzP0_tBGLixbGwKU1lacdLQG5D o5K1vkJ-WyjrpW6Q.

[45] E. Hurwitz, C. Orji, Multi biometric thermal face recognition using FWT and LDA feature extraction methods with RBM DBN and FFNN classifier algorithms, Adv. Sci. Technol. Eng. Syst. 4 (6) (2019) 67–90, https://doi.org/10.25046/aj040609.

[46] A. Buczak, E. Guven, A survey of data mining and machine learning methods for cyber security intrusion detection, IEEE Commun. Surv. Tutorials (2015). ieeexplore.ieee.org, (Accessed 1 April 2021). [Online]. Available: https://ieeexplore.ieee.org/abstract/document/7307098/.

[47] Q. Niyaz, W. Sun, A.Y. Javaid, M. Alam, A deep learning approach for network intrusion detection system, EAI Endorsed Trans. Secur. Saf. (2015), https://doi.org/10.4108/eai.3-12-2015.2262516.

[48] I. Amit, J. Matherly, W. Hewlett, Z. Xu, Y. Meshi, Y. Weinberger, Machine Learning in Cyber-Security-Problems, Challenges and Data Sets, 2019, (Accessed 1 April 2021). [Online]. Available: https://www.virustotal.com/.

[49] S. Anwar, J. Mohamad Zain, M.F. Zolkipli, Z. Inayat, S. Khan, B. Anthony, V. Chang, From intrusion detection to an intrusion response system: fundamentals, requirements, and future directions, Algorithms 10 (2) (2017) 39.

[50] I.H. Sarker, A.S.M. Kayes, S. Badsha, H. Alqahtani, P. Watters, A. Ng, Cybersecurity data science: an overview from machine learning perspective, J. Big Data 7 (1) (2020) 41, https://doi.org/10.1186/s40537-020-00318-5.

[51] M. Aydos, O. Yavanoglu, A Review on Cyber Security Datasets for Machine Learning Algorithms Logo Detection and Classification View Project Data Privacy View Project A Review on Cyber Security Datasets for Machine Learning Algorithms, ieeexplore.ieee.org, 2017, https://doi.org/10.1109/BigData.2017.8258167.

[52] N. Shone, T.N. Ngoc, V.D. Phai, Q. Shi, A deep learning approach to network intrusion detection, IEEE Trans. Emerg. Top. Comput. Intell. 2 (1) (2018) 41–50, https://doi.org/10.1109/TETCI.2017.2772792.

[53] A.H. Lashkari, G.D. Gil, M. Saiful, I. Mamun, A.A. Ghorbani, Characterization of Tor Traffic Using Time Based Features, 2017, https://doi.org/10.5220/0006105602530262.

[54] L. Rila, Denial of access in biometrics-based authentication systems, in: Lecture Notes in Computer Science (Including Subseries Lecture Notes in Artificial Intelligence and Lecture Notes in Bioinformatics), vol. 2437, 2002, pp. 19–29, https://doi.org/10.1007/3-540-45831-x_2.

Chapter 11

A secure biometric authentication system for smart environment using reversible data hiding through encryption scheme

V.M. Manikandan
Computer Science and Engineering, SRM University-AP, Amaravati, Andhra Pradesh, India

1 Introduction

For the last few years, face recognition-based authentication systems are in various places to ensure the entry of authorized persons in the restricted places. Even nowadays, face recognition-based authentication in the Internet of things (IoT)-controlled smart homes are very common [1–3]. Face recognition involves the following steps:

1. Capture the image of a person using a digital camera
2. Detect the face regions from the person images
3. Compare the features of the detected face with the features in the database and identify the person.

Note that the features of the face images of authenticated people also should be stored securely and storing it on the client side will be difficult due to limited resources. These issues are solved by the prominent technology called cloud computing. There are lots of cloud service providers available now to provide a sufficient amount of storage and computational facility. So nowadays most of the people or companies are using cloud storage to keep the biometric data, such as face images [4]. In general, the image of the person during authentication will be captured using a camera, and those images will be transmitted to the cloud to do computationally complex operations, such as feature extraction and face recognition. The cloud service provider will carry out the face recognition task and the response will be given back to the access control mechanism at the client

Machine Learning for Biometrics. https://doi.org/10.1016/B978-0-323-85209-8.00002-X

side. Based on the response from the cloud service provider, the access control mechanism will allow access to the person or give an alert to the concerned person to indicate the presence of an unauthorized person in the restricted place.

There is a lot of research going on areas like face detection and face recognition. The main challenges in face recognition are the identification of faces from low lighting images, where some portion of faces may be occluded with some other objects, identification of faces with spectacles or cap, etc. [5]. Many researchers are working in this domain to improve face recognition accuracy in all such challenging situations.

Similar to the face recognition system, fingerprint recognition is a universally accepted biometric authentication scheme and is used in places to mark attendance in offices or to provide access to restricted places [6]. The fingerprints are unique for each person, and the recognition accuracy is very high as compared to face recognition. To use a fingerprint-based authentication system, a fingerprint scanner will be placed and the user will press the finger on the scanner to capture the fingerprint image. The features from the captured image will be matched with the features of the registered fingerprints. Again, for fingerprint authentication also, we may use a cloud-based approach in which all the registered fingerprints will be kept in cloud storage; later, the scanned fingerprint image will be transmitted to the cloud service provider for further feature extraction and recognition.

The combinations of fingerprint and face recognition can be used at the places where we need to provide a better level of security [7]. In such cases, the face image should be captured using a camera and the fingerprint should be captured using a fingerprint scanner and that information can be transmitted separately to the cloud service provider for the further recognition task. The major concern in cloud-based biometric authentication schemes is that from the client side, all the biometric information should be transmitted to the cloud through the Internet, and there is a possibility of taping such critical biometric data by some intruders and they may make use of it illegally to control the access environment. The image encryption process will help us to provide some level of security to provide confidentiality by converting the face images of fingerprint images into an unreadable form.

Data hiding is a widely studied area of research in the field of secure data transmission in the last three decades. In this scheme, a secret message will be concealed using a cover medium, and the cover medium can be any digital data, such as image, audio, and video.

In this chapter, we propose a new model for the secure transmission of face images and fingerprints by using a RDH through an encryption scheme [8–10]. The fingerprint data will be embedded into the face image of the respective person using RDH through the encryption scheme. The output of the scheme will be an encrypted image that will be transmitted through the Internet to the cloud service provider. This will ensure the secure transmission of biometric data between the user and the cloud service provider. The cloud service provider will decrypt the received image, recover the original image, and extract the embedded details, which is the fingerprint of the corresponding person and it will be used for further authentication purposes. The overview of the proposed framework is given in Fig. 1.

The novelty of the proposed scheme is listed in the following:

- The RDH scheme is introduced in the domain of biometric security.
- The proposed scheme embeds the compressed fingerprint details in the face images during encryption. This ensures secure communication of fingerprints and protects the confidentiality of the face images.
- We introduce the use of run-length encoding and Elias gamma encoding procedure for fingerprint compression.

The chapter contents are organized as follows: a detailed literature review is discussed in Section 2, the new scheme is detailed in Section 3, an illustrative description is given in Section 4, the experimental study and result analysis are detailed in Section 5, and the chapter is concluded in Section 6.

2 Literature review

RDH is an active research area in the field of information security. The RDH scheme allows us to hide some secret messages in digital content for secure transmission. On the receiver side, the original cover content can be recovered while extracting the hidden message. The existing RDH schemes are mainly used for the following two applications:

1. **Medical image transmission:** In medical image transmission, the RDH schemes are used to transmit the patient record along with the medical image [11–14].
2. **Cloud service provider:** The cloud service provider uses RDH schemes to hide some additional metadata information in the digital content, which is uploaded to the cloud by the users. Since the data that are uploaded by the

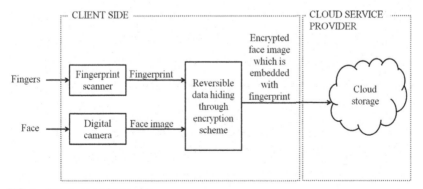

FIG. 1 The proposed framework.

users should return back as it is to the cloud users, the cloud service providers are not permitted to make any permanent changes in the uploaded data. In this situation, the cloud service providers can use RDH schemes [15, 16].

The existing RDH schemes can be broadly classified into three:

1. **RDH on natural images:** During data hiding, the data hider changes the original pixel values. The well-known RDH schemes on natural images are based on the concepts called histogram shifting, difference expansion. A few other schemes are also available [17–19].
2. **RDH on encrypted images:** In this scheme, the data hider will get an encrypted image, and the encrypted pixels will be modified by the data hider during the RDH process. Two main approaches for RDH on encrypted images are reserving room before encryption and reserving room after encryption [20–22].
3. **RDH through encryption:** In this scheme, the RDH will be carried while encrypting the image. The RDH process will be fine-tuned in such a way that data hiding will be possible during the encryption process [8, 9].

In our proposed scheme, we used the RDH through an encryption scheme in such a way that the face image captured using the camera will be considered as the original image and the compressed fingerprint data will be considered as data. By using RDH through an encryption scheme, the fingerprint data will be embedded into the face image. Finally, we will have an encrypted image that contains a hidden message.

The RDH through encryption schemes is introduced in 2018. The overview of the existing RDH schemes is given in Table 1.

TABLE 1 Overview of the existing RDH through encryption schemes.

Scheme	Basic approach used
Scheme [8]	• Three different encryption and/or decryption keys are used. • A single bit can be embedded in a block of size $B \times B$ pixels • Entropy is used as the key measure during image recovery
Scheme [9]	• Three different encryption and/or decryption keys are used. • A single bit can be embedded in a block of size $B \times B$ pixels • A trained support vector machine model (SVM) is used for data extraction and image recovery.
Scheme [10]	• Three different encryption and/or decryption keys are used. • Three bits can be embedded in a block of size $B \times B$ pixels • Ensured 0 bit error rate during image recovery. • A trained support vector machine model (SVM) is used for data extraction and image recovery.

3 Proposed scheme

The proposed scheme is detailed in this section. The proposed scheme will be useful for a biometric authentication system where we used the cloud service provider to store the details of the authenticated people. The proposed scheme used a two-level authentication scheme where face recognition and fingerprint recognition were used for authentication. At the time of registration and authentication, the face images of the users and the fingerprints should be transmitted to the cloud storage. To make a secure communication of biometric details, such as face images and fingerprints, we have used a RDH scheme through the encryption process. The proposed scheme uses a RDH through an encryption scheme, which is very similar to the scheme reported in Ref. [8], but used a new measure to distinguish the correctly decrypted block from the wrongly decrypted block. The key idea behind the proposed scheme is that by using a digital camera, the user's face image will be captured and the fingerprint will be captured using a fingerprint scanner. Further, the fingerprint data will be embedded in the face image before transferring to the cloud. For the embedding purpose, we have used RDH through the encryption process. The key steps in the proposed scheme are given in the following:

Step 1:	Capture the color face image using camera
Step 2:	Capture the fingerprint using fingerprint scanner
Step 3:	Convert the fingerprint image (gray scale) to the corresponding binary image
Step 4:	Apply run-length encoding on the binary fingerprint
Step 5:	Encode the run-length sequence using Elias gamma encoding procedure
Step 6:	With the help of RDH through encryption hide the compressed fingerprint details in the face image to get the encrypted image with hidden data
Step 7:	Transmit the encrypted face image that contains fingerprint details to the cloud service provider.

One of the limitations of RDHs schemes is less embedding rate. The fingerprint data are compressed to make sure that the RDH schemes will not face any kind of difficulty to embed the details in the face image. From the face image, all the three color planes, say R, G, and B, are extracted separately, and each plane is processed separately while embedding fingerprint data. Each color plane will be divided into nonoverlapping blocks, and in each block, we shall embed one-bit data from the compressed fingerprint details. The output of the data hiding phase will be ended with an encrypted image. The encrypted image can be transmitted securely to the cloud service provider for storage or authentication purpose. The cloud will process the received data and an authentication control message will be given back to the client side to activate some hardware module to allow the user to enter into the restricted domain. The sequence of operations at the sender side is given in Algorithm 1.

Algorithm 1: Proposed algorithm for hiding fingerprint data in the face image

Input	:	The face image F (in RGB format) and the fingerprint image P and the encryption keys K_1 and K_2
Output	:	The encrypted face image E which is embedded with the compressed version of P
1	:	Convert P into the corresponding binary image through thresholding and keep it in P itself.
2	:	Find the run length encoding sequence L from the binary fingerprint image P
3	:	Encode the run length sequence L using Elias gamma encoding scheme to get P^c
4	:	Find the all the three color planes R, G, and B from the given face image F. Let us assume the three color planes are denoted by F^R, F^G, F^B respectively.
5	:	Generate two pseudo-random integer matrices M^0 and M^1 based on the encryption keys K_1 and K_2
6	:	Divide the image color planes F^R, F^G, F^B into the non-overlapping blocks of size $B \times B$ pixels. Let us assume $F^K_{x,y}$ denotes the image block where $1 \leq x \leq \lfloor R/B \rfloor$ and $1 \leq y \leq \lfloor C/B \rfloor$ and $K \in \{R, G, B\}$. Each of the color planes will have N number of blocks, where $N=\lfloor R/B \rfloor \times \lfloor C/B \rfloor$. The total number of blocks in the face image will be $3N$.
7	:	$S=(F^R, F^G, F^B)$
8	:	$K=1$
9	:	While $L \neq \phi$ do
10	:	Remove the first color plane F^K from the list S and keep it in G
11	:	While $x \leq R\text{-}B$ do
12	:	While $y \leq C\text{-}B$ do
13	:	$b= P^c_K$ //Access the Kth bit from P^c
14	:	If $b==0$ then
15	:	Encrypt the image block $G_{x,y}$ using $M^0_{x,y}$ by pixel-wise XOR operation.
16	:	ElseIf $b==1$ then
17	:	Encrypt the image block $G_{x,y}$ using $M^1_{x,y}$ by pixel-wise XOR operation
18	:	EndIf
19	:	$y=y+1$
20	:	EndWhile
21	:	$x=x+1$
22	:	EndWhile
23	:	Keep $G_{x, y}$ at the corresponding position of F^K
24	:	$K=K+1$
25	:	EndWhile
26	:	Combine all the updated F^Ks to get the final encrypted image E
27	:	Output E

An illustrative example of the proposed scheme is given in Fig. 2. The input will be a color face image and fingerprint image, and the output will be the encrypted face image, which contains compressed fingerprint data.

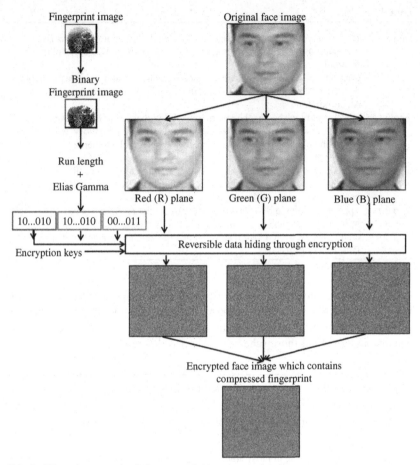

FIG. 2 Illustrative example of the proposed scheme.

In the proposed scheme, the user and the cloud service provider should be agreed on two common encryption and/or decryption keys, say K_1 and K_2. Once the cloud service provider received an encrypted image with hidden data (hidden data are basically compressed fingerprints), the following sequence of actions should be carried out:

Step 1:	Separate each of the color planes from the encrypted image
Step 2:	Consider one of the planes at a time and divide the plane into nonoverlapping blocks of size $B \times B$ pixels
Step 3:	Access the blocks in row-wise linear order and consider one image block at a time.

Continued

cont'd

Step 4:	Try to decrypt the selected image block using the pseudorandom matrices generated using the encryption keys K_1 and K_2 to obtain two different blocks B_1 and B_2
Step 5:	Compute the correlation between adjacent pixels in B_1 and B_2 using the algorithm defined in Algorithm 2. Let us assume the M_1 and M_2 are the measures obtained by Algorithm 2.
Step 6:	Whichever block having the minimum correlation value will be considered as the correctly recovered block. If the B_1 is the correctly recovered block, we will extract 0 from the block and if B_2 is the correctly recovered block then we will extract 1 from the block.
Step 7:	Recover all the blocks from all the three different color planes (Repeat Step 1 to Step 6) and extract all the hidden details. Let us assume the extracted bits are kept in M' and the recovered color image F.
Step 8:	Apply Elias gamma decoding procedure to get the run-length data.
Step 9:	Apply the run-length decoding procedure to get the actual fingerprint data P.
Step 10:	Output the recovered face image F and extracted the extracted fingerprint data P for further processing.

The extracted fingerprint and the recovered face images will be used for further face recognition and fingerprint recognition. The cloud service provider can use any efficient algorithms for face recognition or fingerprint recognition. The discussion about those schemes is beyond this research.

Algorithm 2: Finding the adjacency relationship between pixels

Input	:	An image block C having size B × B
Output	:	A measure of adjacency property of the pixels in C, say M
Step 1	:	Apply quantization on the image block C to get C^Q with the values from 0 to 64
Step 2	:	Find the histogram H from C^Q.
Step 3	:	Find the peak in the histogram H and return the height of the peak, say M.
Step 4	:	Return M

The key idea that we have used to distinguish the correctly recovered image block and the wrongly decrypted block is analyzing the block after quantization. The quantization process will bring the close pixel values into the same bucket. In a natural image (face image) block, the pixels in an image block will be very close, and hence, the peak value from the histogram will be high. But in wrongly recovered image blocks, the pixels will have a random distribution.

4 Illustrative examples

For a better understanding of the fingerprint compression using a combination of run-length encoding and Elias gamma encoding procedure, an illustrative example is discussed here.

Step 1:   Let us assume that the fingerprint F is a small image having size 16 × 16 bits size as given below:

1	1	1	1	1	1	1	1	1	1	1	1	1	1	1	0
1	1	1	1	1	1	1	1	1	1	1	1	1	1	1	0
1	1	1	1	1	1	1	1	1	1	1	1	1	1	1	0
1	1	1	1	1	1	1	1	1	1	1	1	1	1	1	0
1	1	1	1	1	1	1	1	1	1	1	1	1	1	1	0
1	1	0	1	1	0	0	0	1	0	0	0	0	0	1	0
1	1	0	1	0	0	0	0	0	0	0	0	0	0	1	0
1	1	0	1	0	0	0	0	0	0	0	0	0	0	1	0
1	1	0	0	0	0	0	0	0	0	0	0	0	0	1	0
1	1	1	1	0	0	0	0	0	0	0	0	0	0	1	0
1	1	1	0	0	0	0	0	0	0	0	0	0	0	1	0
1	1	1	0	0	0	0	0	0	0	0	0	0	0	1	0
1	1	1	0	0	0	0	0	0	0	0	0	0	0	1	0
1	1	1	0	0	0	0	0	0	0	0	0	0	0	1	0
1	1	1	1	0	0	0	0	0	0	0	0	1	1	1	0
0	0	0	0	0	0	0	0	0	0	0	0	0	0	0	0

Step 2:   Let us assume that the run-length encoding procedure going to consider the pixel values of F in column-wise linear order. Basically, the first bit value we have to keep as a reference then the number of consecutive 1's or 0's will be identified by the run-length encoding procedure. The run-length encoded sequence is given in the following:

| 1 | 15 | 1 | 15 | 1 | 15 | 1 | 15 | 1 | 15 | 1 | 2 | 1 | 2 | 3 | 1 | 5 | 1 | 1 | 2 | 1 | 1 | 10 | 1 | 1 | 2 | 1 | 1 | 10 | 1 | 1 |

| 2 | 12 | 1 | 1 | 4 | 10 | 1 | 1 | 3 | 11 | 1 | 1 | 3 | 11 | 1 | 1 | 3 | 11 | 1 | 1 | 1 | 3 | 11 | 1 | 1 | 1 | 4 | 8 | 3 | 17 |

Step 3:   The run-length sequence will be encoded using Elias gamma encoding procedure. To encode a number P that requires N bits, we will add (N−1) 0's as the prefix of the number. To represent an N-bit binary number, we need 2·N−1 number of bits.

| 1 | 0 | 0 | 0 | 1 | 1 | 1 | 1 | 1 | 0 | 0 | 0 | 1 | 1 | 1 | 1 | 1 | 0 | 0 | 0 | 1 | 1 | 1 | 1 | 1 | 0 | 0 | 0 | 1 | 1 |

| 1 | 1 | 1 | 0 | 0 | 0 | 1 | 1 | 1 | 1 | 1 | 0 | 1 | 0 | 1 | 0 | 1 | 0 | 0 | 1 | 1 | 1 | 0 | 0 | 1 | 0 | 1 | 1 | 1 | 0 |

| 1 | 0 | 1 | 1 | 0 | 0 | 0 | 1 | 0 | 1 | 0 | 1 | 1 | 0 | 1 | 0 | 1 | 1 | 0 | 0 | 0 | 1 | 0 | 1 | 0 | 1 | 1 | 0 | 1 | 0 |

| 0 | 0 | 0 | 1 | 1 | 0 | 0 | 1 | 1 | 0 | 0 | 1 | 0 | 0 | 0 | 0 | 0 | 1 | 0 | 1 | 0 | 1 | 1 | 0 | 1 | 1 | 0 | 0 | 0 | 1 |

| 0 | 1 | 1 | 1 | 1 | 1 | 0 | 1 | 1 | 0 | 0 | 0 | 1 | 0 | 1 | 1 | 1 | 1 | 1 | 0 | 1 | 1 | 0 | 0 | 0 | 1 | 0 | 1 | 1 | 1 | 1 | 0 |

| 1 | 1 | 0 | 0 | 0 | 1 | 0 | 1 | 1 | 1 | 1 | 1 | 0 | 0 | 1 | 0 | 0 | 0 | 0 | 0 | 1 | 0 | 0 | 0 | 0 | 1 | 1 | 0 | 0 | 0 | 0 |

| 1 | 0 | 0 | 0 | 0 | 1 |

In the previously mentioned example, the number of bits in the original fingerprint image is $16 \times 16 = 256$ bits. The number of bits in the final Elias gamma encoded sequence is 185, which results in a compression ratio of 1.38. We can think of using some other better binary image compression techniques for real-time applications.

5 Experimental study and result analysis

In this paper, we propose an application of RDH scheme through encryption for the secure transmission of biometric data from the users' site to the cloud service provider. The proposed algorithms were implemented using Matlab 2020b, and we have used the SOCOFing fingerprint dataset and UTKFace dataset [23]. The SOCOFing (Sokoto Coventry Fingerprint Dataset) is a biometric fingerprint database designed for academic research purposes. The UTKFace dataset is a large-scale face dataset with a long age span (range from 0 to 116 years old) [24]. Since this is a large image dataset, we have considered 100 random face images and 100 fingerprint images. The face images are too small, so it cannot be capable to hide the fingerprint details. So during the experimental study, we have resized the image to 1024×1024 pixels.

As part of the experimental study, we have analyzed the following parameters:

1. **Compressed ratio (CR):** The compression ratio is defined as follows:

$$CR = \frac{\text{Total number of bits in the original fingerprint image}}{\text{The number of bits in the compressed fingerprint image}}$$

2. **Security analysis:** The randomness in the encrypted image is evaluated using entropy and histogram analysis.
3. Analysis of a histogram-based measure for classifying original image block and wrongly decrypted block.

A. Analysis of the compression ratio

In the proposed scheme, we have used the run-length encoded sequence and Elias gamma encoding procedure to compress a binary fingerprint image. The size of the fingerprint images in the SOCOFing dataset is 103×96, which needs 9888 bits in the original binary representation. The run-length encoding procedure makes use of the redundancy in the adjacent bits. For the 100 randomly selected images, the compression ratio obtained after the compression is graphically shown in Fig. 3.

B. Security Analysis

As per the proposed scheme, we can use any random stream generator for encryption purposes. For the simulation purpose, we have used the RC4 random

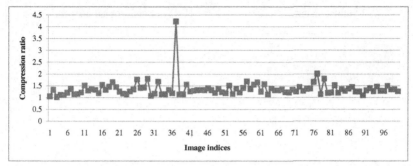

FIG. 3 Compression ratio obtained from 100 fingerprint images.

stream generator. The proposed scheme can use any secure random stream generator for encryption purposes. To analyze the security of the encryption process, we have used histogram analysis and entropy.

Four sample face images and the histograms of all those images are given in Fig. 4. To show that the final encrypted image that we have obtained after the RDH process is having enough randomness in pixel distribution, we have plotted the histograms of encrypted images, which are given in Fig. 5.

The entropy measure obtained from 50 randomly selected face images after the data hiding process is shown in Fig. 6. It can be seen that from all those images the entropy value after the encryption process is maximum (very close to 8) irrespective of the entropy from the original image. The $E1$ measure shows the entropy of the original face image, and the $E2$ indicates the entropy obtained after data hiding through the encryption process.

C. Analysis of new histogram-based measure

The key idea that we have used for data extraction and image recovery is a histogram-based measure. The peak value from the histogram is used to distinguish original image blocks from the wrongly recovered block. Note that at the cloud service provider's side, they know two different keys have been used by the users during the data hiding and image encryption process. Which stream cipher is used for encrypting a selected block is not known to the receiver. So they will create histograms of both the blocks that are obtained after attempting the encryption process and the histogram of the newly obtained blocks is analyzed. In a face image, there is a high probability that the pixels in a block are highly close in turn. To depict the reason to use the histogram-based measure to recover the image block, we have plotted the peak value observed from the correctly recovered image block (OM) and the wrongly recovered image block (WM).

From Fig. 7, it can be observed that always the measure is high from the correctly recovered block as compared to wrongly recovered blocks.

Original images	Histogram of original images

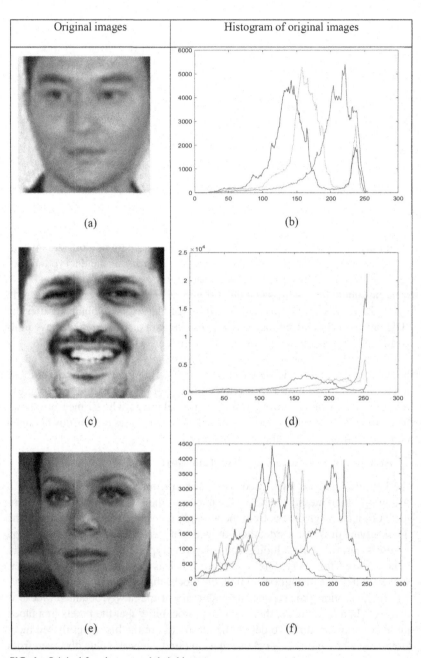

FIG. 4 Original face images and their histograms.

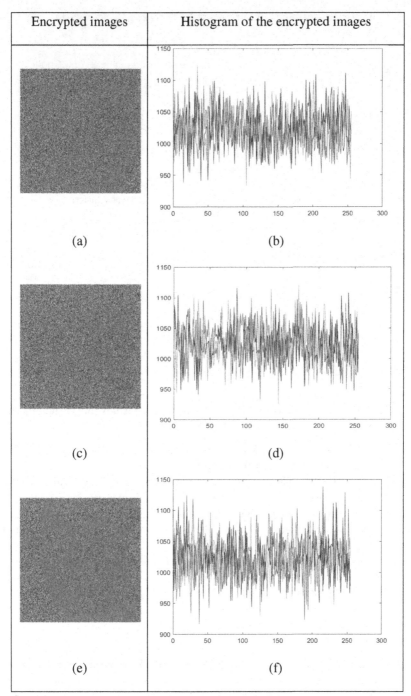

FIG. 5 Face images obtained after RDH through encryption process and the corresponding histograms.

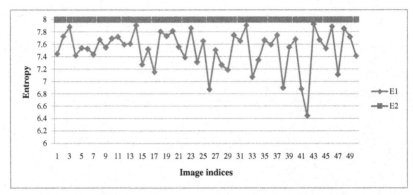

FIG. 6 Analysis of entropy measure from original image and encrypted image.

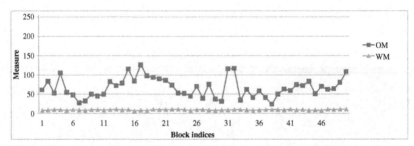

FIG. 7 Histogram-based measure obtained during image recovery.

The key observations during the experimental study are listed in the following:

- The use of run-length encoding with Elias gamma encoding process ensures very good compression in the fingerprint data.
- A new histogram measure is used in the proposed scheme to identify the correctly recovered block at the receiver side. This measure is working efficiently, and the experimental study claims that this measure is capable to distinguish the natural image block from the wrongly recovered decrypted block.
- The comparative study of the proposed scheme is omitted since the RDH through encryption scheme to embed fingerprint details in face images is first introduced in this chapter.

6 Conclusion

In this chapter, we have proposed a secure framework that can be used for a two-level biometric authentication process where the cloud service providers may be responsible for the verification task. Sending biometric data, such as face images or fingerprints, from the client side to a cloud service provider through a network, is not safe. So the proposed scheme utilizes a RDH scheme through an encryption process to hide the compressed fingerprint data in the face image. The key advantage is that the final image that will be transmitted to the client will be in the form of an encrypted image and the fingerprint details are already hidden in it. The run-length encoding scheme along with the Elias gamma encoding procedure is also used in the proposed scheme for compression of fingerprint data. The proposed scheme can be used in the areas where we need to use secure multiple biometric verifications.

References

[1] H. Ai, T. Li, A smart home system based on embedded technology and face recognition technology, Intell. Autom. Soft Comput. 23 (3) (2017) 405–418.

[2] T.S. Gunawan, et al., Development of face recognition on raspberry pi for security enhancement of smart home system, Indones. J. Electr. Eng. Inform. 5 (4) (2017) 317–325.

[3] V. Lytvyn, et al., A smart home system development, in: International Conference on Computer Science and Information Technology, Springer, Cham, 2019.

[4] S. Guo, T. Xiang, X. Li, Towards efficient privacy-preserving face recognition in the cloud, Signal Process. 164 (2019) 320–328.

[5] B. Lahasan, S.L. Lutfi, R. San-Segundo, A survey on techniques to handle face recognition challenges: occlusion, single sample per subject and expression, Artif. Intell. Rev. 52 (2) (2019) 949–979.

[6] A. Siswanto, N. Katuk, K.R. Ku-Mahamud, Biometric fingerprint architecture for home security system, in: Innovation and Analytics Conference & Exhibition (IACE), vol. 3, 2016.

[7] D.J. Berini, et al., Multi-biometric enrollment kiosk including biometric enrollment and verification, face recognition and fingerprint matching systems, U.S. Patent No. 9,256,719. 9 Feb. 2016.

[8] V.M. Manikandan, V. Masilamani, A novel entropy-based reversible data hiding during encryption, in: 2019 IEEE 1st International Conference on Energy, Systems and Information Processing (ICESIP), IEEE, 2019.

[9] V.M. Manikandan, V. Masilamani, Reversible data hiding scheme during encryption using machine learning, Procedia Comput. Sci. 133 (2018) 348–356.

[10] V.M. Manikandan, A.A. Bini, An improved reversible data hiding through encryption scheme with block prechecking, Procedia Comput. Sci. 171 (2020) 951–958.

[11] Y. Liu, X. Qu, G. Xin, A ROI-based reversible data hiding scheme in encrypted medical images, J. Vis. Commun. Image Represent. 39 (2016) 51–57.

[12] B. Ma, et al., A code division multiplexing and block classification-based real-time reversible data-hiding algorithm for medical images, J. Real-Time Image Proc. 16 (4) (2019) 857–869.

[13] B. Ma, et al., Code division multiplexing and machine learning based reversible data hiding scheme for medical image, Secur. Commun. Netw. 2019 (2019) 1–9.

[14] J. Li, et al., A partial encryption algorithm for medical images based on quick response code and reversible data hiding technology, BMC Med. Inform. Decis. Mak. 20 (14) (2020) 1–16.

[15] L. Xiong, X. Zhengquan, High-capacity and lossless reversible data hiding for encrypted multimedia data in cloud computing, J. Internet Technol. 19 (4) (2018) 1187–1193.

[16] A.N. Khan, et al., An efficient separable reversible data hiding using paillier cryptosystem for preserving privacy in cloud domain, Electronics 8 (6) (2019) 682.

[17] S. Yi, Y. Zhou, Z. Hua, Reversible data hiding in encrypted images using adaptive block-level prediction-error expansion, Signal Process. Image Commun. 64 (2018) 78–88.

[18] P.C. Mandal, I. Mukherjee, B.N. Chatterji, High capacity reversible and secured data hiding in images using interpolation and difference expansion technique, Multimed. Tools Appl. 80 (3) (2020) 1–22.

[19] Y. Jia, et al., Reversible data hiding based on reducing invalid shifting of pixels in histogram shifting, Signal Process. 163 (2019) 238–246.

[20] P. Puteaux, W. Puech, An efficient MSB prediction-based method for high-capacity reversible data hiding in encrypted images, IEEE Trans. Inf. Forensics Secur. 13 (7) (2018) 1670–1681.

[21] C. Qin, et al., Separable reversible data hiding in encrypted images via adaptive embedding strategy with block selection, Signal Process. 153 (2018) 109–122.

[22] L. Xiong, Z. Xu, Y.-Q. Shi, An integer wavelet transform based scheme for reversible data hiding in encrypted images, Multidim. Syst. Sign. Process. 29 (3) (2018) 1191–1202.

[23] Sokoto Coventry Fingerprint Dataset (SOCOFing). https://www.kaggle.com/ruizgara/socofing, (Accessed November 2020).

[24] UTKFace Dataset. https://www.kaggle.com/jangedoo/utkface-new, (Accessed November 2020).

Chapter 12

An efficient and untraceable authentication protocol for cloud-based healthcare system

Suryakanta Panda and Samrat Mondal
Department of Computer Science and Engineering, Indian Institute of Technology Patna, Bihta, India

1   Introduction

The implementation of information and communication technology in healthcare industry provides remote and self-monitoring medical services through internet. In particular, the exponential growth in wireless body area network (WBAN) and cloud computing enhance the remote medical service and also reduce the medical expenditure and time of patients. WBAN is a type of low power wireless personal area network around a human body, which consists of various wearable medical sensors and a personal mobile device [1]. The medical sensors collect various physiological information, such as heart and breathing rate, sugar level, blood pressure, and body temperature, of a patient. Those symptoms are communicated to the doctor through a mobile device. It provides round-the-clock monitoring of patient's physical condition and prompt diagnosis report from doctors by maximizing the utilization of medical resources [2, 3].

The increasing demands of homecare services for various chronic diseases increase the medical data very fastly [4]. To process such huge amounts of data for diagnosis report generation is a difficult task in traditional WBAN because of the limited storage and computing power devices. So, by associating cloud computing technology with the WBAN empowers the doctors to generate a timely diagnosis report and attend the emergency situations. Cloud computing provides data storage and accomplishes compute-intensive tasks efficiently

Machine Learning for Biometrics. https://doi.org/10.1016/B978-0-323-85209-8.00006-7

217

with minimum expenses [5]. Usually, the communication between the patient and cloud is performed through a public, insecure channel. Similarly, the doctor and cloud communicate through the public channel. As the patient's information is very critical and the communication channels are public, security and privacy are a major concern [6, 7].

Strong cryptographic operations to perform secure communication between the patient and doctor cannot be applied in this scenario because patient's WBAN devices are naturally limited by computational ability, communication bandwidth, storage, and battery power. Therefore, it requires a lightweight, efficient mutual authentication, and key agreement protocol to maintain the security during communication [8].

Although lightweight authentication and key agreement protocol ensure privacy of data during transmission, there is always a risk of data loss from patient's mobile device. The mobile device may be stolen by an adversary, and the adversary gets the physiological information of the patient, diagnosis report of the patient from that mobile device unless the mobile device is fully secured. Hence, it is necessary to protect the stored data in patient's mobile device, so that after stealing patient's mobile device, the adversary does not get any advantage.

Authentication is a promising cryptographic solution that provides secure access to confidential information stored in the mobile device. All the authentication techniques rely on at least one of the following methods.

- Something the user has: It is also called as token-based authentication. In this mechanism, each user (who needs to be authenticated) has some physical identification object, which identifies the user uniquely, for example, smart card.
- Something the user knows: It is also called as knowledge-based authentication. In this mechanism, a user has to remember a password or PIN for the authentication process.
- Something the user is: It is also called as biometric-based authentication. This includes the mechanism of fingerprint scan, iris scan, etc.

Password-based authentication is the most widespread user authentication technique due to its simplicity and ease of deployment. Unfortunately, passwords are vulnerable to some security threats because of the limited cognitive capacity of human memory [9]. Similarly, biometric- and token-based authentication systems have also certain limitations and are vulnerable to some security threats, that is, privacy concerns for static biometric templates and sharing of identity token. Biometric hashing is a two-factor authentication system that mitigates the problem of password-based authentication and biometric authentication system [10]. It adds an additional layer of security by using biometric features during authentication.

Thus, in telecare medical information system (TMIS), there is a need for lightweight authentication and key agreement protocol using biometric hash.

1.1 Contribution

In order to fulfill the security requirements in TMIS, we have proposed an improved lightweight authentication protocol for medical data exchange in cloud environment. The major research contributions of this work are as follows.

- The proposed protocol establishes mutual authentication between the communicating parties, that is, patient and doctor.
- Using biometric hashing, we have ensured the security of patient's mobile device and also the security of doctor's device.
- We examined the protocol using both formal analysis and informal analysis methods and found that our protocol achieves required security properties and resistance to various known attacks.
- Session key is established using only hash operation and XOR operation, so it requires less computational cost and lightweight.
- Performance analysis shows that the proposed protocol is efficient as compared to other existing protocols.

2 Related work

Researchers in the field of authentication and key agreement scheme have proposed many authentication protocols to provide integrity and confidentiality to the cloud-based medical data. In 2014, Chen et al. [11] proposed a cloud-based medical data exchange scheme protecting patient's privacy. However, Li et al. [12] found that the protocol [11] does not provide real-time monitoring service and unavailability of nonrepudiation proof in diagnosis report. Later, Chen et al. [13] proposed another protocol for medical data exchange on cloud environment. However, Chiou et al. [14] found that the protocol [13] fails to deliver message authentication, patient anonymity. Moreover, it does not allow patients to directly access the diagnosis report. To address these limitations in [13], Chiou et al. [14] proposed an improved protocol. However, Mohit et al. showed that the protocol [14] is vulnerable to patient anonymity and stolen mobile device attack. Then, they introduced an enhanced protocol [6] for the same environment. Later on, Li et al. [15] and Kumar et al. [16] separately reviewed Mohit et al.'s protocol. They found that Mohit et al.'s protocol is vulnerable to patient anonymity, patient unlinkability, diagnosis report revelation, and forgery attack. Then, both Li et al. and Kumar et al. separately proposed two improved versions of mutual authentication protocol with privacy preservation. Later, Kumar et al. [17] noticed that Li et al.'s protocol fails to provide message authentication and cannot generate a session key in healthcare center upload phase. Moreover, it is vulnerable to impersonation attack, patient anonymity, and patient linkability. Kumar et al.'s protocol [16] is vulnerable to medical report forgery attack, privileged insider attack, DoS attack, and stolen mobile device attack. Chandrakar et al. [18] proposed another cloud-based authentication protocol for healthcare monitoring system, which is not resistant to patient anonymity, doctor unlinkability, impersonation attack, and also fails to provide message authentication [19].

The above literature study suggests that an authentication and key agreement protocol in TMIS should provide mutual authentication, patient privacy, integrity, and confidentiality of medical data. To the best of our knowledge, none of the lightweight key agreement protocols in the existing literature fulfill all the required properties simultaneously.

- Chen et al.'s protocol [11] does not provide real-time monitoring and nonrepudiation proof.
- Chen et al.'s protocol [13] fails to deliver message authentication, patient anonymity.
- Chiou et al.'s protocol [14] is vulnerable to patient anonymity and stolen mobile device attack.
- Mohit et al.'s protocol [6] is vulnerable to patient anonymity, patient unlinkability, diagnosis report revelation, and forgery attack.
- Li et al.'s protocol [15] fails to provide message authentication, and vulnerable to impersonation attack, patient anonymity, and patient linkability.
- Kumar et al.'s protocol [16] is vulnerable to medical report forgery attack, privileged insider attack, DoS attack, and stolen mobile device attack.
- Chandrakar et al.'s protocol [18] fails to provide patient privacy and integrity.

3 System model and security goals

In this section, we briefly discuss about the network model, threat model, and security goals for the proposed authentication protocol.

3.1 Network model

Our network model for the cloud-based healthcare system is presented in Fig. 1. This model comprises five major entities: (1) the wearable sensor nodes, (2) a mobile device, (3) cloud server, (4) doctor, and (5) an authentication server. The physiological information of a patient is collected by the mobile device using wearable sensors and transmitted to the cloud server (CS). Then, the doctor takes the physiological information from the cloud server. All the patients and doctors need to register at the trusted authentication server (AS) for performing a secure communication between them.

3.2 Threat model

In this work, we follow the widely used Dolev-Yao threat model [20] in which the communication between two entities is through an insecure channel. So, the adversary may eavesdrop all the messages played between two parties.

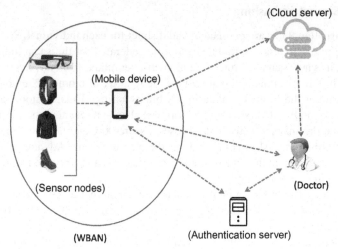

FIG. 1 Network model.

Moreover, the adversary can perform active attacks such as replay of old messages, alternation, deletion, and redirection of messages. The adversary can also physically capture patient's mobile device and any wearable sensing device. After that, the stored information can be extracted from the memory using power analysis attack [21]. In addition, the adversary can access the stored data in cloud server.

3.3 Security goals

- *Authentication*: Before accepting any message, all the participants should be able to verify the claimed identity of the sender. It prevents impersonation attack, man-in-the-middle attack in security protocols.
- *Report confidentiality*: Preserving the secrecy of patient's health information is crucial in TMIS. Other than the designated medical professionals, no insiders and outsiders should be able to get the secret report.
- *Integrity of report*: Any unauthorized modification of imperative medical data may deteriorate patient's life [22]. So, before accepting any message, all the participants should be able to verify the accuracy and trustworthiness of received data.
- *Patient anonymity*: Patient's real identity should be hidden, that is, after eavesdropping the transmitted message any adversary should not able to link a message with a particular patient or two messages are from a single patient.
- *Patient unlinkability*: The association or relationship between a patient and her doctor should be kept secret. Otherwise, it endangers patient's privacy and anonymity.

3.4 Biometric hashing

Biometric templates are permanent and distinct for each individual. So, once it is compromised, a new template cannot be generated for the same individual. Hence, it is necessary to protect the biometric templates from adversaries. Biometric hashing is a method that ensures the security of biometric templates by transforming the biometric data into a binary string. Thus, it stores a transformed or modified version of the biometric data and reveals less information about the original biometric data. It uses a secret key and noninvertible functions in order to transform or randomize the biometric data. Advantage of using the secret key is that the transformed biometric data can be revoked or modified by changing the secret key [23, 24].

The steps for obtaining biometric hash from a biometric data are as follows.

(i) Using a feature extraction procedure to obtain feature vector from the biometric data.

(ii) Generate a set of pseudo-random vectors using the secret key provided by the user.

(iii) Make the generated pseudo-random vectors orthonormal applying Gram-Schmidt procedure.

(iv) Compute inner product between the biometric feature vector and the orthonormal vectors.

(v) Compute biohash bit string using a predetermined threshold. If the resulted inner product is greater than the predetermined threshold, set the bit 1, otherwise, set the bit 0.

4 Proposed protocol

In this section, we propose a new security-enhanced protocol for medical data exchange using cloud computing. Table 1 explains all the notations used in this chapter. Our proposed protocol consists of four phases, as described here.

4.1 Registration phase

In this phase, all the participants get registered to the trusted AS. The registration phase can be splitted into doctor registration and patient registration.

4.1.1 Doctor registration

- Step 1: Doctor sends her unique identity ID_D and a registration request to AS in a secure manner.
- Step 2: After accepting the registration request from the doctor, AS computes $A_1 = h(ID_D\|\alpha)$, where α is a secret key of AS. Then, AS sends A_1 to the doctor using a secure channel and stores ID_D of the doctor.

TABLE 1 Explanations of used notations.

Notation	Description
HC	Healthcare center
CS	Cloud server
AS	Trusted authentication server
ID_H	Healthcare center's identity
ID_P	Patient's identity
SID_P	Patient's pseudo identity
ID_D	Doctor's identity
$\parallel$	Concatenation operation
$\{m\}_k$	Symmetric encryption of message m using key k
$h()$	One way hash function
$\oplus$	XOR operation
TS_i	Timestamp at instant i

- Step 3: After receiving A_1, the doctor extracts her biometric hash (R_D) and selects a password (PW_D). Then, computes $DP_1 = h(PW_D\|R_D)$, $DP_2 = A_1 \oplus DP_1$. Finally, the doctor stores $h(DP_1)$, DP_2 in its device.

4.1.2 Patient registration

- Step 1: Patient sends a unique pseudo-identity SID_P and doctor's identity ID_D along with a registration request to the AS through a secure channel.
- Step 2: After receiving the registration request from a patient, AS retrieves A_1 corresponding to ID_D and computes $A_2 = h(SID_P\|A_1)$, $A_3 = h(r\|A_1)$, where r is a random number. Finally, AS sends A_2, A_3, r to the patient through a secure channel.
- Step 3: After receiving A_2, A_3, r, the patient extracts her biometric hash (R_U) and selects a password (PW). Then, computes $P_1 = h(PW\|R_U)$, $P_2 = A_2 \oplus P_1$, $P_3 = A_3 \oplus P_1$. Finally, the patient stores $h(P_1)$, P_2, P_3, r in its mobile device.

4.2 Patient data upload phase (PUP)

This phase executes the following steps to upload encrypted sensor information in the cloud and communicates the key to the doctor for decryption after establishing a mutual authentication.

- Step 1: Initially, patient collects all the sensor information, say M_B. Then, it selects a random key kp. Calculates $E_B = \{M_B\}_{kp}$, $P_4 = h(M_B\|R_1\|ID_D\|SID_P)$, where R_1 is a random number. Then, uploads $M_0 = \{E_B, SID_P, P_4\}$ to the CS.

  After that, when the doctor is available online, the patient inputs her password and biometric hash to the mobile device. Then, the mobile device computes $h(PW\|R_U)$ and verifies it with P_1. If the verification holds, mobile device retrieves $A_3 = P_1 \oplus P_3$. Next, calculates $P_5 = A_3 \oplus R_1$, $P_6 = h(R_1) \oplus SID_P$, $P_7 = h(SID_P\|ID_D\|r\|R_1\|TS_0)$. Finally, sends $M_1 = \{P_5, P_6, P_7, r, TS_0\}$ to the doctor.

- Step 2: After receiving message M_1, the doctor verifies the timestamp TS_0. Then, inputs her password (PW_D) and biometric hash (R_D) to her device. Then, the device computes $h(PW_D\|R_D)$ and verifies it with the stored DP_1. If the verification holds, the device retrieves $A_1 = DP_1 \oplus DP_2$. Next, the doctor extracts $R_1 = P_5 \oplus h(r\|A_1)$, $SID_P = P_6 \oplus h(R_1)$ and verifies P_7. After successful verification, it generates two random numbers r' and R_2. Then, computes $D_1 = h(r'\|A_1)$, $D_2 = h(h(SID_P\|A_1)\|R_1) \oplus R_2$, $D_3 = h(R_2) \oplus D_1$, $D_4 = h(h(SID_P\|A_1)) \oplus r' \oplus R_2$, $D_5 = h(R_1\|R_2\|r'\|TS_1)$, $SK = h(R_1\|R_2)$. Finally, the doctor sends message $M_2 = \{D_2, D_3, D_4, D_5, TS_1\}$ to the patient.

- Step 3: Upon receiving message M_2, patient verifies TS_1 and extracts $R_2 = h(A_2\|R_1) \oplus D_2$, $D_1 = h(R_2) \oplus D_3$, $r' = h(A_2) \oplus R_2 \oplus D_4$. Then, computes and verifies D_5. If the verification holds, then it computes $SK = h(R_1\|R_2)$, $P'_3 = D_1 \oplus P_1$. Finally, replaces P_3 with P'_3 and r with r'.

- Step 4: After authenticating the doctor and establishing the session key, the patient encrypts the kp with the session key SK and sends it to the doctor. At the end, the patient computes $PK_i = A_2 \oplus kp$ and stores PK_i.

Fig. 2 illustrates all the steps of this phase.

4.3 Treatment phase (TP)

- Step 1: Doctor sends its identity ID_D, the patient's pseudo-identity SID_P along with a request to the CS.
- Step 2: After receiving the request from a doctor, CS sends the patient's data $M_3 = \{E_B, P_4, TS_2\}$ to the doctor.
- Step 3: Upon receiving M_3, doctor verifies timestamp TS_2 and decrypts E_B. Then, verifies P_4. If the verification holds, the doctor goes through the patient's report M_B and prepares the diagnosis report M_D. Then, encrypts M_D as $E_D = \{M_D\}_{kp}$ and computes $D_6 = h(M_D\|ID_D\|R_2\|SID_P)$. After that the doctor uploads E_D and D_6 to the CS.

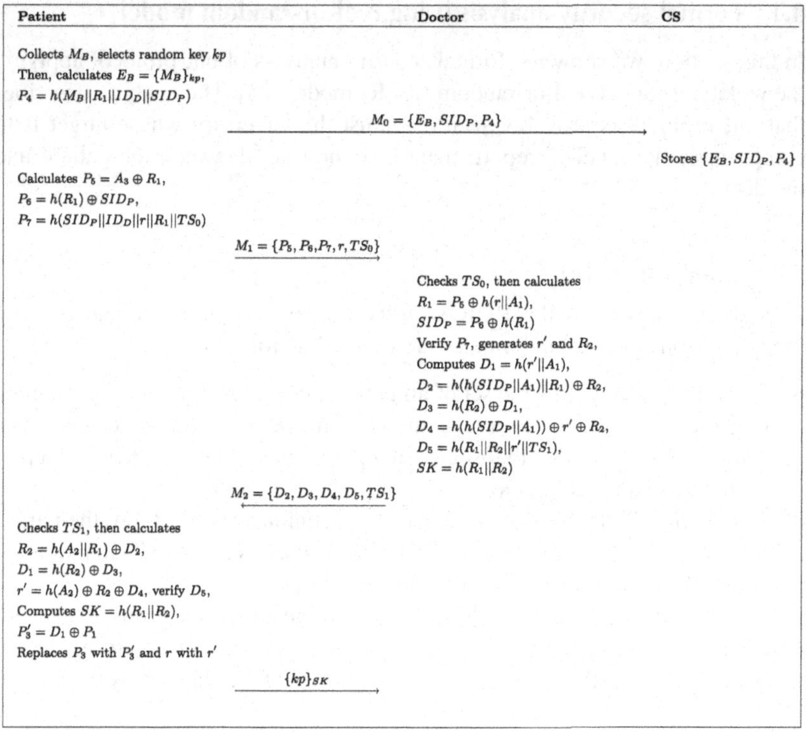

Patient	Doctor	CS
Collects M_B, selects random key kp Then, calculates $E_B = \{M_B\}_{kp}$, $P_4 = h(M_B\|R_1\|ID_D\|SID_P)$		
	$M_0 = \{E_B, SID_P, P_4\}$ ⟶	
		Stores $\{E_B, SID_P, P_4\}$
Calculates $P_5 = A_3 \oplus R_1$, $P_6 = h(R_1) \oplus SID_P$, $P_7 = h(SID_P\|ID_D\|r\|R_1\|TS_0)$		
	$M_1 = \{P_5, P_6, P_7, r, TS_0\}$ ⟶	
	Checks TS_0, then calculates $R_1 = P_5 \oplus h(r\|A_1)$, $SID_P = P_6 \oplus h(R_1)$ Verify P_7, generates r' and R_2, Computes $D_1 = h(r'\|A_1)$, $D_2 = h(h(SID_P\|A_1)\|R_1) \oplus R_2$, $D_3 = h(R_2) \oplus D_1$, $D_4 = h(h(SID_P\|A_1)) \oplus r' \oplus R_2$, $D_5 = h(R_1\|R_2\|r'\|TS_1)$, $SK = h(R_1\|R_2)$	
	⟵ $M_2 = \{D_2, D_3, D_4, D_5, TS_1\}$	
Checks TS_1, then calculates $R_2 = h(A_2\|R_1) \oplus D_2$, $D_1 = h(R_2) \oplus D_3$, $r' = h(A_2) \oplus R_2 \oplus D_4$, verify D_5, Computes $SK = h(R_1\|R_2)$, $P_3' = D_1 \oplus P_1$ Replaces P_3 with P_3' and r with r'		
	$\{kp\}_{SK}$ ⟶	

FIG. 2 Patient data upload phase.

4.4 Checkup phase (CP)

- Step 1: The patient sends the download request along with its pseudo-identity SID_P to CS to get the diagnosis report.
- Step 2: Upon receiving the request, CS sends E_D, D_6 to the patient.
- Step 3: Patient inputs her password and biometric hash to the mobile device. Then, the mobile device computes $h(PW\|R_U)$ and verifies it with P_1. If the verification holds, mobile device retrieves $A_2 = P_1 \oplus P_2$, $kp = PK_i \oplus A_2$. Then, the patient retrieves M_D from the received E_D using the key kp. Then, verifies D_6. If the verification holds, the patient trusts the received diagnosis report from the doctor M_D. Then, computes $P_8 = h(M_D\|PW\|SID_P)$. Finally, stores P_8 with the corresponding E_D in CS for future reference.

5 Security analysis

Using both formal security analysis and informal security analysis, in this section, we demonstrate that our proposed protocol is secure and prevents various known attacks.

5.1 Formal security analysis using real-or-random model

In this section, we show the formal security analysis of our protocol applying the widely accepted real-or-random (ROR) model [25]. The analysis describes that our protocol is provably secure against the adversary whose target is to compromise the medical report, that is, session key between the patient and the doctor.

5.1.1 Security model

This section describes the ROR security model. According to the security model, various queries and oracles are defined as follows:

- *Participants*: Let Π be the set of all participants, D be the set of all doctors, C is the set of all cloud servers, and H is the set of healthcare centers. The symbol Π^i denotes the ith instance of a participant Π. Any instance of a participant is called an oracle.
- *Partnering*: Partnering is expressed by the unique session ID of the participants involved in a communication. Two instances Π^i and Π^j are partnered if they have the same session ID in a session.
- *Adversary*: In this model, it is assumed that the adversary A runs in polynomial time. A has complete control on the network and can eavesdrop, block, alter, and replay the messages. The capabilities of A is defined by the queries discussed here:
  - Execute(Π^i, Π^j): In response to this query, the adversary A obtains all the messages communicated between two authorized participants Π^i and Π^j. It models the eavesdropping attack of A.
  - Send(Π^i, msg): Through this query, A can transmit a message msg to an authorized participate instance Π^i and also receives a corresponding reply from the participant. It models the replay attack, impersonation attack, and modification attack.
  - CorruptMD(P): Through this query, the adversary A extracts the information stored in the patient's mobile device. It models the mobile device lost attack.
  - Test(Π^i): This query represents the semantic security of the session key established by the participant Π^i. The response of Π^i in this test query depends on the result of an unbiased coin flip, c. A is unaware about flipped result, c. If $c = 1$, Π^i returns the actual session key to adversary A; else if $c = 0$, Π^i returns a random number in the same domain.
- Hash(x, k): Hash oracle represents the hash operation $h()$ and provides output $k = h(x)$ when queried with x. When someone queries for $h(x)$, it searches the table(x, k) and returns k if x appears in the table. Otherwise, it returns a uniformly random string k and inserts (x, k) to the table.
- Biohash(x, k'): Biohash oracle represents the biohash operation $h_{Bio}()$ and provides output $k' = h_{Bio}(x)$ for the input x. When someone queries for

$h_{Bio}(x)$, it returns k' if x matches with an existing value within a threshold. Otherwise, it returns a uniformly random string k' and inserts (x, k') into the table.

Semantic security of the session key: Providing the earlier-discussed queries, the adversary A is challenged to determine the value of flipped result c, that is, the session key is real or random. If A distinguishes the real key and random key successfully, then the protocol fails to deliver semantic security. Let *Succ* represents the event in which A wins, that is, correctly distinguishes the real key and random key. The advantage of A in cracking the semantic security of protocol P is $Adv_P^{ake} = |2 \cdot pr[Succ] - 1|$. The protocol P is secure in ROR model if Adv_P^{ake} is negligible.

Theorem 1. In random oracle model, an adversary A runs against our protocol P in polynomial time t. Let A executes q_h number of hash queries, q_s number of send queries, q_b number of biohash queries, and q_e number of execute queries to damage P. Then, the advantage of A in compromising the security of protocol P is as follows:

$$Adv_P^{ake}(A) \leq \frac{q_b^2}{H_1} + \frac{q_h^2}{H_2} + \frac{2q_s}{|D_1 \| D_2|}, \tag{1}$$

where $|H_1|$, $|H_2|$, $|D_1|$, and $|D_2|$ represents the range space of the biohash function, the range space of the hash function, the size of the uniformly distributed password dictionary, and the size of the uniformly distributed biometric template, respectively.

Proof. A sequence of games from G_0 to G_3 is defined for this proof. In each game G_i, adversary A tries to predict the correct value of c. Let $Succ_i$ denotes this event and $Pr[Succ_i]$ represents the corresponding probability.

- Game G_0: It models the actual attack of adversary A on our protocol P. Initially, the bit c is randomly selected. Hence, as per the definition we have

$$Adv_P^{ake} = 2 \cdot Pr[Succ_0] - 1. \tag{2}$$

- Game G_1: To improve the winning advantage, the adversary A instigates eavesdropping attack using the Execute(Π^i, Π^j) query. Then, in the Test(Π^i) oracle, A has to determine the value of c. Since SK is computed from R_1 and R_2, A tries to retrieve both R_1 and R_2 from M_1, M_2. We know that $R_1 = P_5 \oplus A_3$. So, to extract R_1, A needs the patient's password and biometric along with the mobile device. It is not possible to extract R_2 without R_1. Thus, the eavesdropping attack does not improve the winning advantage, and we have

$$Pr[Succ_1] = Pr[Succ_0]. \tag{3}$$

• Game G_2: In this game, the adversary A tries to mislead a participant instance to accept a counterfeit message with the help of Send(), Hash oracle, and Biohash oracle. It considers all the collisions that may arise in P. The adversary will not be able to find any collision because each message contains some random factors like timestamp, random number. So, according to the birthday paradox, we get

$$|Pr[Succ_2] - Pr[Succ_1]| \leq \frac{q_b^2}{2|H_1|} + \frac{q_b^2}{2|H_2|}. \tag{4}$$

• Game G_3: This game models the risks associated with the patient's mobile device loss. By querying the corruptMD() oracle A retrieves the stored credentials such as P_1, P_2, P_3. Then, A tries to guess both the password and biometric hash. Since, the password dictionary and biometric template are of size $|D_1|$ and $|D_2|$, respectively, we have

$$|Pr[Succ_3] - Pr[Succ_2]| \leq \frac{q_s}{|D_1||D_2|}. \tag{5}$$

After accomplishing all the games, A did not get any advantage in guessing c. Hence, we have

$$Pr[Succ_3] = \frac{1}{2}. \tag{6}$$

Thus, by combining Eqs. (2)–(6), we get

$$Adv_P^{ake}(A) \leq \frac{q_b^2}{H_1} + \frac{q_h^2}{H_2} + \frac{2q_s}{|D_1 \| D_2|}. \tag{7}$$

∎

So, the adversary does not get a nonnegligible advantage and our protocol achieves semantic security.

5.2 Informal security analysis

In this section, we informally explore that our proposed protocol can resist various known attacks.

5.2.1 Provides patient privacy

Patient's sensor report M_B and diagnosis report M_D are encrypted with a secret key kp and stored in CS. The key kp is only shared between patient and doctor, so no third parties, including the privileged insiders of CS, can decrypt patient's confidential reports. Moreover, the patient's pseudo-identity SID_P is not a fixed one and can be changed from doctor to doctor. So, the adversary cannot get the real identity of a patient from SID_P, and thus, the social life of a patient is secured.

5.2.2 Resistance to health report forgery attack

In the treatment phase, the doctor checks integrity of patient's sensor report M_B by computing and verifying P_4. To forge P_4, the adversary needs R_1, which is secretly shared only between the doctor and patient. So, the adversary cannot create a fake sensor report M'_B without R_1. Similarly, in the checkup phase, the patient checks integrity of diagnosis report M_D by computing and verifying D_6. To forge D_6, adversary needs R_2, which is secretly shared only between the doctor and patient. So, the adversary cannot create a fake diagnosis report without R_2. Thus, the proposed protocol resists health report forgery attack.

5.2.3 Resistance to man-in-the-middle attack

In every phase of our protocol, the receiver checks the authenticity of the message before accepting it. In the authenticity check, one secret variable is used and that is associated with the identity of the sender. For example, in the patient data upload phase, R_1 is associated with the pseudo-identity of patient, and R_2 is associated with the identity of doctor. Due to irreversible properties of hash function, it is not possible by the adversary to detach the existing secret variable and create a new one. So, our protocol resists man-in-the-middle attack and impersonation attack.

5.2.4 Resistance to replay attack

In our protocol, we have used random numbers and timestamps to generate distinct communication messages in each session. The receiver of a message can verify the timestamp during the integrity check. Due to the secret value used in irreversible hash operation, the adversary cannot forge timestamp used in P_7 and D_5. Thus, our protocol resists replay attack.

5.2.5 Resistance to stolen mobile device attack

The credentials of a patient that are stored in the patient's mobile phone are encrypted with password and biometric. Also, in the checkup phase, the patient receives encrypted diagnosis report. To decrypt the encrypted diagnosis report, patient requires kp, which is protected by the patient's password and biometric information. So, the stealing of mobile device does not give any advantage to the adversary.

5.2.6 Provision of nonrepudiation

Upon receiving message M_2, if the verification of D_5 is successful, the doctor cannot deny her involvement. Because, only the designated doctor can retrieve R_1 from message M_1. Similarly, if the session key SK is established, the patient cannot deny her involvement. Because, only the patient can retrieve R_2 from M_2. In the treatment phase, involvement of the patient can be ensured from the verification of P_4. Similarly, in the checkout phase, the involvement of the doctor can be ensured by verifying D_6. Thus, our protocol provides the property of nonrepudiation and convinces one party about the involvement of another party.

5.3 Simulation of the protocol

The session key agreement procedure and authentication between patient and doctor in our protocol is simulated using AVISPA, a protocol simulator tool [26, 27]. AVISPA is a powerful formal verification tool widely used for exploring the network security protocols. It validates the security protocols automatically and defines whether the protocol is safe or unsafe. The simulation result of our protocol in AVISPA is shown in Fig. 3, which shows that the protocol is safe. So, following the simulation result, our protocol is completely secure.

```
SUMMARY
  SAFE

DETAILS
  BOUNDED_NUMBER_OF_SESSIONS
  TYPED_MODEL

PROTOCOL
  /home/span/span/testsuite/results/new.if

GOAL
  As Specified

BACKEND
  CL-AtSe

STATISTICS

  Analysed  : 1 states
  Reachable : 1 states
  Translation: 0.02 seconds
  Computation: 0.46 seconds
```

FIG. 3 Result of AVISPA tool.

6 Performance analysis

This section evaluates the performance of our proposed protocol with other existing protocols designed for cloud assisted medical data exchange. Computation cost of all phases are taken into consideration for analyzing the protocols. Computation cost is expressed in terms of execution time. Table 2 summarizes the execution times of different cryptographic operations following Chiou et al.'s experimental results [14].

We have summarized the computation cost of our protocol and other related protocols in Table 3 following the measures given in Table 2. We can notice that the proposed protocol uses computationally efficient cryptographic operations only, that is, symmetric encryption/decryption and hash function. So, the proposed protocol takes very less execution time compared to others.

Finally, we list the comparison of security properties in Table 4. It shows that our protocol provides all the essential functionalities to counter all the discussed known attacks of existing protocols.

7 Conclusion

In this chapter, we have proposed a new security enhanced key agreement protocol for medical data exchange through cloud environment. Our proposed protocol delivers better security and privacy by upgrading the previous work. Simulation of the proposed protocol for formal security analysis using AVISPA tool shows that the protocol is safe. Informal security analysis demonstrates that the protocol achieves the required security properties and resists various known attacks. The security and performance analysis show that our protocol not only

TABLE 2 Execution times of different cryptographic operations.

Notation	Description
T_H	Time required for computing a one-way hash ($T_H \approx 0.0005$ s)
T_{BP}	Time required for computing a bilinear pairing ($T_{BP} \approx 0.0621$ s)
T_S	Time required for performing a symmetric encryption/decryption ($T_S \approx 0.0087$ s)
T_{AS}	Time required for performing an asymmetric encryption/decryption ($T_{AS} \approx 0.3057$ s)
T_M	Time required for computing a scalar point multiplication in an elliptic curve ($T_M \approx 0.0503$ s)
T_{SGV}	Time required for generating and verifying a signature ($T_{SGV} \approx 0.3317$ s)

TABLE 3 Comparison of computation cost.

	Chen et al. [11]	Chiou et al. [14]	Mohit et al. [6]	Kumar et al. [16]	Chandrakar et al. [18]	Our protocol
HUP	$1T_{SGV} + 1T_M + 2T_{BP} + 4T_S + 3T_{AS} + 2T_H$	$1T_{SGV} + 3T_{BP} + 2T_S + 7T_H$	$1T_{SGV} + 3T_S + 11T_H$	$1T_{SGV} + 3T_S + 10T_H$	$1T_{SGV} + 4T_S + 10T_H$	–
PUP	$1T_M + 2T_{BP} + 4T_S + 3T_{AS} + 2T_H$	$1T_{SGV} + 4T_{BP} + 2T_S + 12T_H$	$2T_{SGV} + 2T_S + 10T_H$	$2T_{SGV} + 6T_S + 11T_H$	$2T_{SGV} + 7T_S + 9T_H$	$2T_S + 15T_H$
TP	$2T_{SGV} + 1T_M + 2T_{BP} + 7T_S + 4T_{AS} + 2T_H$	$2T_{SGV} + 4T_M + 4T_{BP} + 4T_S + 6T_H$	$2T_{SGV} + 2T_S + 9T_H$	$2T_{SGV} + 6T_S + 10T_H$	$5T_{SGV} + 5T_S + 22T_H$	$2T_S + 2T_H$
CP	–	$1T_{SGV} + 2T_{BP} + 2T_S + 8T_H$	$1T_{SGV} + 2T_S + 5T_H$	$1T_{SGV} + 6T_S + 10T_H$	$2T_{SGV} + 2T_S + 8T_H$	$1T_S + 2T_H$
Total cost	$3_{SGV} + 3T_M + 6T_{BP} + 15T_S + 10T_{AS} + 6T_H$	$5T_{SGV} + 13T_{BP} + 4T_M + 33T_H + 10T_S$	$6T_{SGV} + 9T_S + 35T_H$	$6T_{SGV} + 21T_S + 41T_H$	$10T_{SGV} + 18T_S + 59T_H$	$5T_S + 19T_H$
Total time	4.7091 s	2.7705 s	2.086 s	2.1934 s	3.5031 s	0.053 s

TABLE 4 Comparison of security features.

Security features	Chen et al. [11]	Chiou et al. [14]	Mohit et al. [6]	Kumar et al. [16]	Chandrakar et al. [18]	Our protocol
Provides patient anonymity	No	No	No	Yes	No	Yes
Provides nonrepudiation	No	Yes	Yes	Yes	Yes	Yes
Resistance to inspection report forgery attack	Yes	Yes	No	No	Yes	Yes
Resistance to report revelation attack	Yes	No	No	No	Yes	Yes
Resistance to impersonation attack	No	Yes	Yes	Yes	Yes	Yes
Resistance to mobile device loss	No	No	No	No	No	Yes
Supports telemedicine	No	Yes	Yes	Yes	Yes	Yes

ensures the security properties but also improves the computational efficiency. In future, we would like to enhance our proposed protocol so that a patient can share her sensitive physiological information with multiple doctors without reencrypting the same data repeatedly.

References

[1] P.T. Sharavanan, D. Sridharan, R. Kumar, A privacy preservation secure cross layer protocol design for IoT based wireless body area networks using ECDSA framework, J. Med. Syst. 42 (10) (2018) 196.

[2] L. Zhang, Y. Zhang, S. Tang, H. Luo, Privacy protection for e-health systems by means of dynamic authentication and three-factor key agreement, IEEE Trans. Ind. Electron. 65 (3) (2018) 2795–2805.

[3] M. Kompara, S.K.H. Islam, M. Hölbl, A robust and efficient mutual authentication and key agreement scheme with untraceability for WBANs, Comput. Netw. 148 (2019) 196–213.

[4] J. Shen, Z. Gui, S. Ji, J. Shen, H. Tan, Y. Tang, Cloud-aided lightweight certificateless authentication protocol with anonymity for wireless body area networks, J. Netw. Comput. Appl. 106 (2018) 117–123.

[5] G. Sharma, S. Kalra, A lightweight multi-factor secure smart card based remote user authentication scheme for cloud-IoT applications, J. Inf. Secur. Appl. 42 (2018) 95–106.

[6] P. Mohit, R. Amin, A. Karati, G.P. Biswas, M.K. Khan, A standard mutual authentication protocol for cloud computing based health care system, J. Med. Syst. 41 (4) (2017) 50.

[7] R. Amin, S.K.H. Islam, G.P. Biswas, M.K. Khan, N. Kumar, A robust and anonymous patient monitoring system using wireless medical sensor networks, Futur. Gener. Comput. Syst. 80 (2018) 483–495.

[8] A.G. Reddy, E.-J. Yoon, A.K. Das, K.-Y. Yoo, Lightweight authentication with key-agreement protocol for mobile network environment using smart cards, IET Inf. Secur. 10 (5) (2016) 272–282.

[9] S. Panda, M. Kumari, S. Mondal, SGP: a safe graphical password system resisting shoulder-surfing attack on smartphones, in: International Conference on Information Systems Security, Springer, 2018, pp. 129–145.

[10] R.M. Bolle, J.H. Connell, N.K. Ratha, Biometric perils and patches, Pattern Recogn. 35 (12) (2002) 2727–2738.

[11] C.-L. Chen, T.-T. Yang, T.-F. Shih, A secure medical data exchange protocol based on cloud environment, J. Med. Syst. 38 (9) (2014) 112.

[12] C.-T. Li, C.-C. Lee, C.-C. Wang, T.-H. Yang, S.-J. Chen, Design flaws in a secure medical data exchange protocol based on cloud environments, in: International Conference on Algorithms and Architectures for Parallel Processing, Springer, 2015, pp. 435–444.

[13] C.-L. Chen, T.-T. Yang, M.-L. Chiang, T.-F. Shih, A privacy authentication scheme based on cloud for medical environment, J. Med. Syst. 38 (11) (2014) 143.

[14] S.-Y. Chiou, Z. Ying, J. Liu, Improvement of a privacy authentication scheme based on cloud for medical environment, J. Med. Syst. 40 (4) (2016) 101.

[15] C.-T. Li, D.-H. Shih, C.-C. Wang, Cloud-assisted mutual authentication and privacy preservation protocol for telecare medical information systems, Comput. Methods Prog. Biomed. 157 (2018) 191–203.

[16] V. Kumar, S. Jangirala, M. Ahmad, An efficient mutual authentication framework for healthcare system in cloud computing, J. Med. Syst. 42 (8) (2018) 142.

[17] V. Kumar, M. Ahmad, A. Kumari, A secure elliptic curve cryptography based mutual authentication protocol for cloud-assisted TMIS, Telemat. Inform. 38 (2019) 100–117.

[18] P. Chandrakar, S. Sinha, R. Ali, Cloud-based authenticated protocol for healthcare monitoring system, J. Ambient Intell. Humaniz. Comput. 11 (2020) 3431–3447.

[19] A. Kumari, V. Kumar, M.Y. Abbasi, EAAF: ECC-based anonymous authentication framework for cloud-medical system, Int. J. Comput. Appl. (2020) 1–10.

[20] D. Dolev, A. Yao, On the security of public key protocols, IEEE Trans. Inf. Theory 29 (2) (1983) 198–208.

[21] P. Kocher, J. Jaffe, B. Jun, Differential power analysis, in: Annual International Cryptology Conference, Springer, 1999, pp. 388–397.

[22] X. Yan, W. Li, P. Li, J. Wang, X. Hao, P. Gong, A secure biometrics-based authentication scheme for telecare medicine information systems, J. Med. Syst. 37 (5) (2013) 1–6.

[23] B. Topcu, C. Karabat, M. Azadmanesh, H. Erdogan, Practical security and privacy attacks against biometric hashing using sparse recovery, EURASIP J. Adv. Signal Process. 2016 (1) (2016) 100.

[24] D.C.L. Ngo, A.B.J. Teoh, A. Goh, Biometric hash: high-confidence face recognition, IEEE Trans. Circuits Syst. Video Technol. 16 (6) (2006) 771–775.

[25] M. Abdalla, P.-A. Fouque, D. Pointcheval, Password-based authenticated key exchange in the three-party setting, in: International Workshop on Public Key Cryptography, Springer, 2005, pp. 65–84.
[26] AVISPA: Automated Validation of Internet Security Protocols and Applications, http://www.avispa-project.org/ (Accessed September 2019).
[27] A. Armando, D. Basin, Y. Boichut, Y. Chevalier, L. Compagna, J. Cuéllar, P.H. Drielsma, P.-C. Héam, O. Kouchnarenko, J. Mantovani, et al., The AVISPA tool for the automated validation of internet security protocols and applications, in: International Conference on Computer Aided Verification, Springer, 2005, pp. 281–285.

Index

Note: Page numbers followed by *f* indicate figures, and *t* indicate tables.

Printed in the United States
by Baker & Taylor Publisher Services